PARSI

To my dearest mother and father,
for their constant love and support.

Humata, hukhata, huvareshta
Good thoughts, good words, good deeds

-- Zoroastrian proverb

Khana peena ne khodai apnar
Eat and drink and god will give

-- Parsi proverb

FAROKH TALATI

PARSI

FOOD PHOTOGRAPHY BY

SAM A. HARRIS

INDIA PHOTOGRAPHY BY

OLIVER CHANARIN

BLOOMSBURY ABSOLUTE

LONDON · OXFORD · NEW YORK · NEW DELHI · SYDNEY

standing –

Meher & Pheroze Talati
request the pleasure of the company of
SOONIE & GODREJ SS
at the Navjote ceremony of their son

Farokh

on Saturday, 27th June 1992
Roj Adar, Mah Bahman, 1361 Y.Z.
at 5.30 pm
at the 'Zoroastrian House'
88 Compayne Gardens, London NW6 3RU
and to dinner thereafter

R.S.V.P.
Tel: 0705-251298

With Compliments of:
Soonie & Godrej Talati
Koomi & Fali Sethna

Nawajbai
sitting on
Dhunbai –

Bachan is Soo

'JAMVA CHALO JI'
FOREWORD

'A good Parsi cook rebels against the constraints of a defined method'

–– Bapsi Nariman, *A Gourmet's Handbook of Parsi Cuisine*

By Homi K. Bhabha and Leah Bhabha

'You'll never guess who was running the show,' Homi called his daughter Leah from a London hotel over FaceTime in September 2019. 'A Parsi guy born in London!' The 'show' was a celebratory gathering he'd hosted for family and friends at St. John Bread and Wine. Since Leah couldn't attend, Homi regaled her with details of a caramel-coloured suckling pig, Yorkshire puddings, free-flowing French reds, and a hometown boy at the helm. This was how we first encountered Farokh Talati – a fitting introduction for a food-obsessed father and daughter.

'Jamva Chalo Ji,' a simple phrase in Parsi-Gujarati, which translates literally as 'Come, let's eat!' invites guests to make their way to dinner. What sounds like a straightforward request is, in fact, the ritual call of a small Indian-Zoroastrian community to invite its people to dine in a spirit of generosity and hospitality. These three words 'Jamva Chalo Ji' signal to the throngs of guests at *lagaans* (weddings) and *Navjotes* (Zoroastrian initiation ceremonies) that the celebratory meal is about to begin. The epicurean Parsis require very little cajoling to come to the table. Imagine the scene: You enter the venue to find that a previously unexceptional space has been transformed into a garden of delights. Gateways are decorated with spectacular garlands, roses and lilies adorn tables, and from the ceiling descend chandeliers composed of marigolds, fairy lights and crystal balls. On a central stage, Parsi priests in long, white muslin robes and fitted caps pray in front of a great silver urn – the afarghan – that holds a raging blaze of aromatic sandalwood, the supreme symbol of the Zoroastrian faith. Couples are joined; children are blessed. The tableau is timeless, as if a Sasanian frieze has suddenly come to life in 21st century Mumbai.

The Parsi story, like that of so many minorities, is one of diaspora and assimilation. In the 7th century CE, Zoroastrians fled religious persecution in Iran and settled in Gujarat, on India's west coast. An enduring piece of lore that is oft repeated: When the Parsis arrived in India, the local leader Jadi Rana displayed a vessel full of milk to the newcomers, a visual illustration of an area already densely populated with no room for more. The head Parsi priest poured a spoonful of sugar into the milk, symbolising the way in which his community would sweeten the society without destabilising or overpowering it. Jadi Rana acquiesced.

As a non-proselytising faith, Zoroastrianism has kept its believers outside the realms of the religious conflict and communal violence frequently ignited by the issue of conversion. India's Parsis maintain a fine balance between the integrity of their minority milieu and the need to belong to the larger societal mosaic. Though they don't press for autonomy or resort to the power play of identity politics, their sizable and sustained contribution to the growth of a modern civic consciousness has established them as progressive pioneers in the

Right: First Dastoor
Meherjirana Library

Left: Vatcha Agiary
Right: Dasturji Khurshed, High Priest,
Iranshah Atash Behram, Udvada

development of urban India. The community played a major role in making social innovations appear both 'local' and historically inevitable by demonstrating that the institutions required by an evolving society – newspapers, schools and colleges, legal and medical services, forms of government – could be established in tune with Indian traditions. We have largely aligned ourselves more closely with municipal rather than national politics and worked towards piecemeal reform rather than social revolution (although a number of Parsi leaders were involved in the struggle for Indian independence).

Though we are a fast-dwindling group with fewer than 200,000 members worldwide and, according to some estimates, only around 50,000 remaining in India, Parsis work hard to preserve their distinctive culture and beliefs. Navjotes and lagaans have a significance that goes beyond family celebrations; they are occasions on which the community affirms a shared identity that may not exist for many generations to come. When Homi's father Kharsedji complained about the large number of events he had to attend during one winter wedding season, Homi suggested that he might politely turn down an invitation. 'I can't,' he replied. 'I must show my face.' We need to 'show our face' to acknowledge our presence and to signal to ourselves and our neighbours that we recognise the importance of belonging and the responsibility of representation.

As the Parsis have woven themselves into India's civic tapestry, so too have they drawn from the threads of cuisines that surround them and culinary traditions further away. In her 1984 book, *A Gourmet's Handbook of Parsi Cuisine*, Bapsi Nariman astutely observes: 'Parsi cooking is a manifestation of the Parsi personality – highly individualistic. In it there is always room for a little experimentation, a little innovation – a good Parsi cook rebels against the constraints of a defined method.' For example, the combination of lentils and rice, known throughout South Asia as 'khichdi' gets reimagined in Parsi cuisine as the treasured and typical dish, khichdi saas. The starch and legume recipe is paired with a fish saas (sauce) whose uniquely silky texture is achieved by incorporating elements of the French roux (butter and flour).

Let's return to the party. The religious ceremony has ended, the celebrants have been appropriately fêted with showers of rice and rose petals, and the festivities commence. White-coated waiters circulate with hors d'oeuvres: curried spicy mutton meatballs on toothpicks, pastry rolls filled with masala shrimp, chicken liver pâté spread thickly on tiny toasts, creamy chicken vol-au-vents, and potato-pea samosas. One is never far from a stiff pour of Chivas Regal or a chilled glass of nariyal pani (fresh coconut water). Spring rolls seasoned with both Chinese five spice and Indian panch phoron (a five-spiced blend of cumin, fenugreek, brown mustard seeds, fennel and nigella seeds) appear alongside bruschette brushed with tomato and Kashmiri chilli-spiked coriander chutney. But just as the Bombay Parsi bourgeoisie are indulging their cosmopolitan palates, a wizened voice rises above the glitter and gossip. 'Jamva Chalo Ji.'

Suddenly there is chaos in paradise. Dinner is served, the high point of an evening for a group known for its gourmandise. Guests rush towards rows of trestle tables set with banana leaves to grab side-by-side seats for family and friends. The meal will likely start with topli na paneer

Right: Tea time

(homemade basket-ripened cheese) and spiced akuri eggs flecked with green chillies, red onion and tomato. Next up: healthy portions of patra ni macchi (fish baked in green chutney), mutton pulao, masala dal, and jardaloo ma marghi (chicken stewed with apricots) garnished with addictively crunchy potato sticks known as sali. For a sweet finish, you'll be served lagaan nu custard, a creamy rose-scented pudding topped with nuts. If you still have an appetite (as most Parsis will), you won't say no to a scoop or two of kulfi and a glass of fuchsia falooda (rose and raspberry milkshake with vermicelli noodles). The meal concluded, the only thing left to do is deconstruct every course with your kin and compare each bite to those at previous weddings and Navjotes.

In *Parsi*, Farokh Talati celebrates both festive dishes and everyday home cooking. He manages to remain faithful to the classics of this edible oeuvre – patrel (stuffed and fried taro leaves), dhansak (meat and lentil stew), and aleti paleti (spiced chicken liver) – while breathing new life into them with streamlined techniques and methods honed from his years as a professional chef. In addition to incorporating more readily available ingredients as substitutions – a boon for home cooks abroad – he offers helpful and insightful contexts (ie: what dishes and condiments are typically paired and why). But beyond the technical merits of his recipes, Farokh imbues this impressive work with a deep sense of pride and the Parsi creed 'good thoughts, good words, good deeds' permeates throughout. Because what could be a better deed than sharing a cuisine that belongs to the few with the many? Although we are small in numbers, we grow in stature as we extend our hospitality to all who will celebrate with us and are only too happy to introduce our culture through its food. So, to you, we say '*Jamva Chalo Ji*,' let's eat.

Left: Prayer book

Right: Student at Dadar Athornan Institute

INTRODUCTION

Not all Zoroastrians are Parsis, but all Parsis are Zoroastrians. Around
the seventh century, during the Arab conquest of Persia, a small group
of Zoroastrians fled persecution by sailing from what is now known as
Iran and found themselves on the shores of India. After some movement
around the islands of Gujarat they were granted asylum and settled in
the coastal town of Sanjan, which was ruled over at the time by Jadi Rana.

   Throughout the centuries, the Parsi community has interwoven
itself into the community, adapting their language, approach towards
religion and ways of cooking and eating, borrowing the best aspects
and including them as part of their own identity, a sort of symbiotic
relationship.

   The community that originally settled in Sanjan became known as the
Parsis because of their Persian heritage, and throughout the centuries
they spread across India, finding homes in different towns and cities.
When the British came to India, many Parsis took to learning English
and moved away from small farming villages to city centres where they
provided services and routes of trade with neighbouring countries. Here
began the relationship with British, Portuguese and French merchants
and the rise of the prominent Parsi industrialists and philanthropists.

MY FAMILY

My grandad settled the family in Gandhidham in the 1960s. He worked for the Kandla Port Trust as the chief architect. The town of Kandla was still in its infancy and the port had developed a large plot of land into a colony for port employees to reside, known as Gopal Puri. Bungalows would be assigned to the workers depending on their hierarchy within the port: A bungalows were assigned to the top management, B to the senior staff and C and D to the rest. As the architect who designed the bungalows in the colony, my grandad was offered a B-rated bungalow, but he turned it down in favour of a C bungalow.

C17 was a modest bungalow with small rooms, a well-sized garden with lemon, banana and papaya trees and best of all, due to its location within the colony, it had uninterrupted views of the yet-to-be developed open plains of Kandla all the way to the next town of Anjar, 40km away.

It was here at C17 that my mother fondly remembers my grandad on his only mode of transport, his bicycle, taking her to the market for their monthly pantry top-up. Having to go to each individual vendor to buy their eggs, bread and milk. At the final stop on the trip there would be vendors selling hot foods. My mother remembers the gent with a huge tava (flat iron skillet) frying off aloo tiki, small patties of potato and spices coated in semolina, another with a sagdi, a very crude clay barbecue, on which he would cook huge rotli that would puff up entirely as it blistered on the grill, 'smelling heavenly'. The last man would be serving patli dal, a thin soupy dal. All of these foods were parcelled up and taken home to be eaten by the family with delight, a sort of take away of its time.

It was in this bungalow that my grandad would come home with fresh whole fish, either a surmai or rawas, and teach my mum how to scale, gut and cut up the fish to make a coconut and coriander curry. Sometimes my grandma would chop a drumstick down from the tree which she would wash, string, chop and tie and throw into the curry for bonus flavour. The leaves of the tree would also be added to the curry for the sabzi (vegetable) element of the dish.

My grandparents did not have it easy in those days, bringing up a family of seven in a small bungalow on a modest salary. My mum recalls the convoluted procedure of just lighting their now vintage single burner Primus stove. My grandma would take a glass bottle to the pantry and fill it with kerosene which would then have to be poured into the stove, and, after a few pumps to get the kerosene all the way through, the stove could be lit. All this just to boil the kettle to make a simple cup of tea.

Mum came to the UK in April of 1980 at the age of 28, leaving the blistering 34°C heat of Mumbai for the 4°C biting chill of a 'dark and miserable' London. One of my dad's first jobs was at the Wall's factory in Southall; he would bring home food from the staff shop – sausages, gammon, steak and kidney pies and ice cream – and all were enjoyed with fresh enthusiasm. But the novelty soon wore off and the desire to cook and eat homemade food settled in.

Alperton, an area within Wembley had, and still has to this day, one of the largest Indian communities within London. Here you could buy the vegetables, herbs, meats and dry goods to cook delicious and familiar foods with relatively similar results as that back home in India. My mum could always cook – her parents were very proficient in the kitchen, passing on those skills and over time and with the help of some cookbooks and her mother-in-law, my mum started cooking Parsi food at home in London. Dal and rice, meat and vegetable stews all came

Left: Iranshah Atash
Behram, Udvada

Left: Toran
Right: Cooking on
wood fired stoves

back into the diet and so did the exploration of Parsi cuisine at home using the ingredients available to her at that time from the markets.

GROWING UP AND FIRST TRIPS TO INDIA

At the age of around seven, Zoroastrian children go through an initiation ceremony called a Navjote (Parsi) or Sedreh-Pushi (Iran) where a set of prayers are performed alongside a priest. During this ceremony the child is given a thin vest to wear called a sudreh and a long-woven cord made of lamb's wool called a kushti which, during the prayers, is wrapped around the waist three times as a representation of certain Zoroastrian morals including 'good thoughts, good words, good deeds'.

After this ceremony it is expected that the sudreh and kushti must be worn at all times here on after, being untied and re-tied five times a day while reciting certain prayers.

I remember my excitement for my Navjote. I was running around school telling all my classmates and teachers that my Navjote was coming up, my mum most likely having to explain what on earth I was talking about. My Navjote was performed alongside my cousins who were of similar age and family members from all over the globe came to the small Zoroastrian Centre established in a large town house in West Hampstead, affectionately nicknamed 'the Zoo House'. I wish I had taken more notice of the Parsi food on offer that day; instead I was too busy running around with my cousins having the time of my life.

Growing up, it was clear to me that the food we ate in our home was different. I would go to friends' houses and chips and burgers was the standard fare laid out on the dinner table. I would return home to be greeted by spicy lentils, steamed rice and stewed vegetables. Imagine my poor mother's despair in trying to convince me to eat such food while my friends were tucking into their burgers and chips!

My first trip to India was at the age of six. Meeting my mother's side of the family for the first time, we were adorned with garlands threaded with roses, honeysuckle and jasmine, and intricate chalk patterns tapped out on the marble floors of the doorways welcomed us into family homes. Upon entering, small squares of rock sugar were placed into our mouths as a way of wishing us good luck and prosperity on our trip. I can still remember the smell of burning sandalwood from the fire temple where we would go to pray every day, the fish swimming in the well in the temple, and taking home the blessed fruits to share with our family.

I visited India a few more times as I got older, and, although I was still not into food or cooking at that point, could not help being drawn in by the smells, flavours and colours. The ceremony surrounding food was enchanting and the anticipation and excitement for the next meal became a huge part of the day. The markets of fresh fruit and vegetables dazzled in vibrant colour; vendors selling unidentifiable hot fried snacks from cauldrons of boiling oil would summon you over to try before you buy; young coconuts being cut open on the side of the street for thirsty passers-by to nourish themselves with the sweet water. Sweets in all shapes and enticing colours laid out on huge trays in shop windows were enough to capture my young heart, and my loving uncles and aunties were more than happy to oblige my sweet tooth (on reflection a young child is a great excuse for an adult to buy lots of sweets!).

One thing that struck me, more than the odd cow ambling the streets with indifference, was that everywhere you looked people were eating

Right: Chalk patterns adorning the Parsi home

or drinking. In every side street and at every corner, shop front and stall, people would gather to eat as if it were a national pastime. For many it was a way to catch up with friends and family, for some a moment of self-reflection with a plate of deep-fried bhaja. And with the food being so fresh and so tasty, it seems like a logical pastime to have.

The mystery of the unknown can be both exciting and scary. As a Parsi growing up in the UK, I did not know how to cook any of the dishes I had tried on my many trips to India, or even what the ingredients involved to create these amazing flavours were. There were no aunties or uncles to ask at that time, as those family members who cooked the true Parsi food were in India and what was attempted here at home in the UK was a version with many key ingredients subbed out, often to the detriment of the original dish. What were these mysterious ingredients?

An excitement grew inside of me, an urge to discover, like a long-lost language or learning one's own mother tongue; food was now my conduit to connecting to my Parsi heritage. In one of my defining trips to India I stayed for three months, pestering every aunty and uncle to show me their cookbooks, teach me their tricks and let me cook together with them. I ate Parsi food for breakfast, lunch and dinner and when I wasn't cooking or eating, I was fervently writing down every last detail of what I had seen, eaten and heard that day.

WHY THIS BOOK

There is much written and documented about the Parsi community in India, so to me, here in this introduction, it is more important to write about what it means to me to be a Parsi, what brought me to the point of writing down these recipes and why writing this book is so important.

To be a Parsi is like being a member of a very special club, one that values humour and joviality, and holds food as an essential component of their culture. A respect for nature and one another is the order of the day. Zoroastrianism is based around a simple proverb, 'good thoughts, good words and good deeds'; a beautifully straightforward credo to live by. A simple ideology to follow and one that all Zoroastrians strive to adhere to in their daily life.

Researching, learning and cooking these recipes has demystified Parsi cooking for me, and it has highlighted the journey the first Zoroastrians took from Persia, then their journey through India and the cultures they met along the way, which can all be traced via their food.

It is a repertoire so varied yet familiar; it is no-nonsense food. To me, a Parsi cookbook should read like a timeline, with certain dishes representing a point in time when the Parsis first came into contact with the Portuguese, or the British, or the French, or the Gujaratis or the Hindus.

So from the Parsi's first arrival in India, let's fast-forward nearly a century-and-a-half to me sitting outside the much-loved French patisserie Maison Bertaux in Soho. There was loud music coming from an unknown room down an unknown set of stairs in the shop. I asked Michelle, the owner, if she had put in some speakers to play music; she seemed bemused with the idea and told me that there was a three-piece jazz band practising downstairs! Unsure whether this was Michelle's charming quirkiness or an actual fact, she led me down the stairs into a dimly lit room with walls painted deep red, and there in the far end were three musicians playing their hearts out.

Michelle told me she wanted to do something special in this space and I immediately suggested she let me do a night of Parsi food down here for some friends and locals. And so, the Soho Parsi Curry Night was born and went strong until early 2020. I would cook the food three floors up with the help of friends and then ferry it down the narrow winding stairs, down to the dining room we had set up in the basement. It was a joy to bring Parsi food to the mainstream and watch such a diverse spectrum of people enjoying the food with such positive feedback. Word got out and I would start to see more and more Parsis come to the night and with that came words of encouragement about how the food tasted like aunty or mum would make, and some of the Parsis who had settled from India exclaimed how they had not tasted such food for so long and spoke about the happy memories it brought back.

This was a thought that would constantly come back to me over the years of hosting the Parsi dinner; that here, in this tiny basement of a 150-year-old patisserie in London's Soho district are a handful of people tasting food that they would only otherwise find four-and-a-half thousand miles away in small pockets of India. This cemented what had been mulling over in my mind for a while, that Parsi food has wide appeal.

With the determination in mind that one day I would have a Parsi restaurant, I started to write all these recipes down in detail, adding notes as I cooked them for the supper club: use an extra teaspoon of this masala, don't add vinegar until the end, cook lentils for longer for better texture... and so on. I wanted these recipes documented in detail so that when I opened the restaurant, I would hit the ground running.

But one thing that never left my mind while I was writing these recipes down was that with such a dwindling population in the Parsi community and a generation of Parsis growing up in India in a world of fast food,

Left: A young
Zoroastrian priest

convenience over home cooking and food trends coming from the West, who will be left to remember these dishes, who will know how to make sambhar masala? Who will know the intricacies of dal ni pori? How will the flavours of dhansak my mother used to eat as a child stay true today and in the next 20 years?

It slowly dawned on me that these recipes, if put together with enough knowledge, understanding and skill, could be a way to preserve one of the most important aspects of being a Parsi: bloody good food! As I hold my tattered copy of *Vividh Vani*, a book of Parsi recipes printed over 100 years ago to try and decipher recipes, this too could be a book that can be picked up in many years to come and represent a slice of our culture and heritage, so as not to be lost through the ages.

This book of Parsi recipes has been formed through cooking these authentic dishes as I have learned to cook them, with recipes passed down through my family, or overheard conversations between aunties reminiscing about taste of a bygone era of their childhood, all of which helped form ideas and flavours in my head to recreate in the kitchen. It is fact that if you put two or more Parsis together in a room, within five minutes the conversation will be on food!

As important as it is to adhere to authenticity, it is also vital to be able to express yourself, allowing one's ideas and creativity to bubble forth; after all, that is what Parsi cooking has always been about, taking the best bits from here and there to create something wonderful. Do bear this in mind as you read and cook your way through this book. Do not be put off because your onion isn't the right colour or size, or because you are a few grams short of coriander leaves, or because you are missing a spice or two. Use that old tin of chickpeas that has been taunting you from the back of the cupboard instead of chicken, improvise with vegetables you have in your fridge, feel liberated enough to cook with what you have and according to your tastes.

To me, a cookbook should sweep the leaves away to reveal the path to a certain outcome, but how you choose to walk that path should be down to you. This comes with confidence and sometimes stubbornness. Like most things in life, the more you do them, the better you get at them. I remember my first attempt at making dhansak masala... and the tenth attempt too, trying to get the flavours just right. I remember my dal ni pori being politely rejected by the family as it just wasn't quite right. What I'm trying to say is, you have to crack a few eggs to make a Parsi omelette, and that burning rice is just one of the stops on the road to the perfect pulao. Don't be put off by the hurdles in home cooking, otherwise you may never know just how delicious your own cooking truly can be.

Remember, there is no right or wrong, only deliciousness.

As chefs, one of the most important ways to check if something is cooked is to try it. Sometimes there is no clearer indication than how it feels between the teeth. This is a standard way to check lentils, rice, beans and other grains, for example. As you're cooking, train yourself to taste, taste, taste; this is one the first things we are taught as chefs and a fundamental rule in any kitchen. The difference between good food and great food lies within a pinch of salt.

Enjoy experimenting!

Farokh Talati, 2022

Right: Café Colony, Dadar

Left: Marine Drive
Right: Kolah's Mumbai
Vinegar Factory, Navsari

A Note on Choosing Sizes

Throughout this book, I refer to small, medium and large ingredients. See above for a visual representation of what I mean.

A Note on Caramelising Onions

We are going from golden to light brown. This step can take up to 30 minutes.

If your onions do start to catch, add a splash of water, scrape the pan and continue caramelising.

HOW TO CRACK A COCONUT

Coconuts play an important role in Parsi cooking and are symbolic of prosperity and life in Zoroastrian culture and religion. At most food markets in India, there are stalls dedicated to cracking, peeling and grating coconuts, which makes life easier. If you're based somewhere without this luxury, it is a useful and rewarding skill to learn how to crack a coconut.

Before we can crack our coconut, we must first have a coconut to crack! There are tell-tale signs for good and bad coconuts and once you have them memorised, you will be able to tell a perfect coconut from a dud in seconds.

First, look for lots of fresh fibres on the coconut – the older the coconut, the drier the fibres; look for ones that are lush and almost damp. Second, pick up the coconut and feel the weight – there should be a reassuring heft to the coconut. If it feels light for its size, it is probably old and dried out. Check the surface of the coconut for any cracks that may have let air in and spoiled the flesh. This is no good. Finally, place that coconut up to your ear and give it a good shake – there should be a generous amount of sloshing of coconut water going on inside that shell. The more water, the less time it's been hanging around drying out.

To begin cracking, remove as much of the dried husk from the shell as possible, as this only gets in the way and dampens the blows. Go outside and find a hard piece of concrete, a brick, or a similar surface. Have next to you a bowl to collect the coconut water and a sturdy, pointed knife to prise the shell open.

Crouch down and, with a firm grip on your coconut, start giving it sharp blows on the ground around its equator. In this moment, I like to picture myself as one of the apes in the opening sequence of *2001: A Space Odyssey* as I strike the blows.

After every strike, turn the coconut a few centimetres around and strike a different area along its equator – you are not looking to smash the coconut to smithereens, only to strike with enough force to crack the shell open a little and allow you to slip the knife in. Soon enough the sharp cracking sound will turn to a dull thud. This means the force field has been breached!

Find the spot with the crack and give it a few short, sharp taps to open that crack up. Stick your knife gently into the gap and, holding the coconut over the bowl, twist the knife to open the shell and empty out the coconut water. Once you've drained all the coconut water, a few more blows around the coconut should be sufficient to break it in half. You can now use a butter knife to carefully prise the flesh way from the shell.

Taste the water before you use it – sometimes it can turn sour inside the shell, although this is not always a reflection of how the flesh will taste. If you can resist drinking all the water in one go, you can use the rest for cooking.

SPICES
AND
MASALAS

HOW TO CHOOSE, GRIND AND STORE SPICES

I don't want to come across as if I know a lot about spices; I know a little about a little and I know what works for me. I couldn't tell you the Latin name for cinnamon or which mountain in the Maldives grows the best peppercorns. Any wisdom I impart here is what I have observed and learned from cooking with spices at work and at home. I sometimes feel like an explorer when I search through my own spice cupboard, stumbling upon undiscovered powders in un-labelled jam jars that have never before seen the light of day. Spices can be notoriously difficult to keep track of; everyone has that spice they doubled up on because they forgot they had it or while shopping couldn't remember if they had this, that or the other.

Here are a few of my tips when it comes to buying and storing spices.

Buy your spices whole; this means not ground to a powder. Whole spices will keep their flavour and aroma for far longer than ground.

Without getting too technical, it is the specific compounds in the different spices that give them their unique characteristics; these compounds are volatile which means they readily evaporate, which is why spices become dull over time. This is the reason I recommend buying whole spices, which can last for a long time as opposed to ground spices which last only months before losing their pep (ground spices have so much more surface area for those vital compounds to evaporate away from). To slow this process down even more, use airtight containers to store your spices in (another great endorsement for keeping those old glass jam jars) and always keep them out of direct sunlight; tucked away inside a cupboard is best. I know spices in small glass jars look great in a rack on the kitchen counter but they are losing vital aromas and make for a very expensive yet flavourless display.

I never used to pay much thought to pepper, it was just always there like a trusty sidekick, ready to bring a bit of life to a salad or pasta dish. Only when I began reading more about how it came to be on dinner tables around the world did I realise how much respect it deserves. There were many ships that sailed, battles fought and lives lost over this small dried berry. That's why I feel you must give it the requisite respect, buy whole peppercorns and only grind the spice as you need it. Investing in a quality pepper mill is the least you can do to honour the history of this spice that was once traded for gold.

Another obvious tip for keeping your spices fresh is to use them often, experiment and be creative; spices are better off in your mouth than they are hanging around in your cupboard.

Buy your spices in larger packets, the kind typically found in Asian supermarkets. Spices sold at regular supermarkets in glass jars sure look good on the spice shelf but are generally 10 times the price of the bigger packets per gram and are never enough for what you need when making masalas. If stored correctly your spices will last for at least a year or more, so do not worry about the quantity being too much.

Use your whole spices until they are gone; there are no instances where your whole spices have been hanging around that long that you need to throw them away. Over time they may have lost some of their sprightliness, but that happens to the best of us. Spices are robust and if well looked after will still impart their flavour through your food.

PREPARING SPICES

Back when my mum was growing up in India, there would be someone who would grind the spices on a daily basis on a patta, a giant granite stone the size of a small coffee table. Using a large granite rolling pin, moving it back and forth over the spices, they would make the masala or paste for the day's meal. Older generations will swear that masalas ground on a patta taste better, although I feel much of that perception is down to nostalgia. Fast-forward a generation and we have spice and coffee grinders and not much time on our hands; these gadgets allow us to grind the exact amount of spices we want, when we want, in moments. This is a game changer when it comes to being dynamic and creative within the kitchen.

I am a huge advocate for having a small grinder at home. They are useful not only for spices but for grinding nuts, seeds, ginger, garlic, herbs and many other ingredients to a powder or paste with minimal effort.

A small pestle and mortar is important in the kitchen too, for light crushing of much smaller quantities that a grinder would struggle with. There is a great feeling when using a pestle and mortar, like reconnecting with the way our ancestors used to prepare foods.

Dhansak Masala   Sambhar Masala   Cashew and Coconut Masala

MASALA

Good food must start with a good base – get this right and you are well on the path to deliciousness. Like the use of stocks in European cooking, a risotto Milanese, braised oxtail or French onion soup, all must start with a good-quality stock. The same is to be said for the use of spices in Parsi cooking and a good quality masala will set you on the right path.

I have slowly grown to dislike the term curry powder – what is a curry, let alone a powder to make curry? Does curry powder generalise a whole subcontinent's food culture into a small generic packet? Has lazy marketing turned a nation's cuisine into something without identity, turning dishes created through tradition and love into plates of passable mediocrity, the essence having been removed over time? Are the ghosts of these dishes floating around us, searching for their bodies? Here once lay dhansak, RIP.

Can I make a pork vindaloo and a chicken tikka masala with exactly the same 'curry powder' yet stay true to the original dish? I doubt it.

Don't get me wrong, I am not saying that we should be coming home from work and getting the spice grinder out every time we want to make something exciting and different. At the end of the day if what you want is something quick and tasty then find a brand of curry powder that you like and use it as freely as your heart desires. But what I propose to you in the following pages are a few masalas (spice mixes) with an identity, made with intent and to be used with purpose.

Dhania Jeera Powder   Garam Masala   Chai Masala

HOW TO GET THE MOST OUT OF YOUR SAFFRON

My first and foremost piece of advice is to seek out the small, clear, rectangular tubs of saffron, which are less likely to be hugely inflated in price compared with some named brands. The latter are not at all worth the exaggerated costs and are often simply repackaged versions of the same saffron anyway. I quite like the saffron from Spain – I find it to be consistent in its high quality.

Having said that, it can take over 300 Crocus sativus flowers to produce a mere 1g of saffron – the stigmae of each flower having to be delicately handpicked. So do not expect to find saffron at a bargain price. If you do find saffron cheaper than the norm, be warned – cheap tends to be cheap for a reason.

A TOUCH OF SCIENCE

Picrocrocin and safranal are the compounds responsible for saffron's unique aromas and fragrance, and you can extract them using the solvent ethanol. In other words, if you put your saffron in some alcohol you can draw out the flavours and use that infused alcohol to flavour many things. Cheap vodka is my alcohol of choice because it is mostly devoid of any kind of flavour of its own, which would interfere with the saffron.

For every 2g of saffron, use 100ml flavourless alcohol mixed with 100ml distilled water. Pour the mixture into a sealable bottle.

Crush the saffron to a powder, taking care not to lose any. Place the crushed saffron onto a folded piece of paper and use this to slide the powder into the bottle of liquid. If you like the strands running through your dish, for example when using the essence to cook rice, you can leave the saffron whole. You will still get the same results. Place the cap on the bottle and leave the saffron liquid to infuse for 3 days.

Now it's down to you how and where you use the tincture. I use it to flavour desserts, rice dishes, marinades and more. Not only does it go further but in certain instances it moves itself through the dish more thoroughly.

This technique works well with vanilla pods as well.

A man who is stingy with saffron is capable of seducing his own grandmother.

-- Norman Douglas

A NOTE ON SPECIFIC SPICES

Some of the best **saffron** comes from Iran. I very rarely use saffron when cooking just for myself, it's too opulent. Saffron should be shared with others, an announcement of celebration; like a fine wine or champagne, its flavours are always best savoured with others.

I have learned the hard way that **turmeric** stains are for life. Be careful with how you use it, unless you want a constant reminder of the day you made fish curry. I empty my turmeric packet into a glass jar and leave a teaspoon inside to minimise the to-ing and fro-ing from the jar.

I almost always use **cassia** in my savoury cooking, as opposed to **cinnamon**. They are both the bark of a tree with familiar aromatic properties, but I find cassia to be more robust and rounded in flavour, which is ideal for Parsi cooking. Cinnamon has a subtle sweetness to it, it is more innocent, an aroma far more suited to sweet dishes, as well as European styles of cooking. Cassia can sometimes be labelled as Chinese cinnamon and looks like big pieces of rough bark.

Dhansak masala (see page 48) and **sambhar masala (see page 46)** are brothers in arms; they can often be found hanging around dhansak recipes together and when they come together, they become the life of the party, each bringing with them their own distinctive characters.

Dhansak masala is like the older sibling, more refined, more experienced in life and quietly confident; scratch beneath the surface and you will find layers of sophistication. Sambhar masala is the younger brasher sibling, rough around the edges with a fiery hot temper; get too close to this guy and you will get burned! But when these two come together, their characters complement, playing off each other like a well-rehearsed double act – together they bring harmonious balance and swathes of deep character to your dishes.

GINGER–GARLIC AND CHILLI PASTES

 These two pastes are the foundation stones of Parsi cooking. They're easy to scale up as you need; for the ginger–garlic paste, just make sure you keep the weight of peeled garlic and ginger equal to one another.

GINGER–GARLIC PASTE

In a food processor, blitz the garlic cloves and ginger root together with the vegetable oil and salt to a fine paste. If you like things spicy, add the green chillies into the mixture, too. If you don't have a food processor, you can use a fine grater: grate the garlic, ginger and finely chop the chillies (if using) into a bowl, squeezing in any juice left over in the ginger fibres, too, then mix in the salt and vegetable oil.

Transfer the paste to a clean, airtight jar and store it in the fridge for up to 2 months. Or (a neat trick my mum taught me), transfer the paste into an ice-cube tray and freeze it in portions – then just pop a portioned block out of the freezer as you need. It will defrost in less than a minute in a hot pan.

CHILLI PASTE

Blitz the chillies in a food processor with the salt, vegetable oil and apple cider vinegar. Transfer the paste to a clean, airtight jar and store in the fridge for up to 6 months.

A word of warning: a cough-inducing, eye-stinging mist will envelop your kitchen for a while – it's worthwhile having a few windows open while making this paste.

Leave the seeds in your chillies. If your intention is to make your food less hot, do not take all the seeds out of your chillies; just use fewer.

FILLS 1 SMALL–REGULAR JAM JAR

GINGER–GARLIC PASTE
100g peeled garlic cloves
100g peeled root ginger
50ml vegetable oil
1 teaspoon fine salt
5 small green chillies (optional)

CHILLI PASTE
500g super-fresh small green chillies
2 teaspoons fine salt
200ml vegetable oil
1 tablespoon apple cider vinegar

PEESALO MASALO
MASALA PASTE

MAKES 1 JAR

1 large onion (about 500g
    peeled weight)
about 30 garlic cloves
    (about 300g peeled
    weight)
200g fresh ginger, peeled
400ml vegetable oil
2 teaspoons salt
1 tablespoon garam
    masala (see page 46)

FOR A SPICY PASTE
4 tablespoons sambhar
    masala (see page 46)

FOR A MILD PASTE
4 tablespoons dhansak
    masala (see page 48)

**FOR SOMETHING IN-
BETWEEN**
2 tablespoons sambhar
    masala
2 tablespoons dhansak
    masala

When I was a kid, I used to love going to my grandma's house for her chicken and coconut curry. The flavours were unbelievable, the spices were perfectly balanced and the heat from the chilli was divine. I will never forget that curry. When I was old enough to be in the kitchen while my gran was cooking, she showed me the secret – it was a store-bought jar of masala paste! I learned two things that day: first, there is nothing wrong with a store-bought jar of paste, especially if it tastes delicious; and second, a good masala paste is an invaluable tool for a quick, simple and delicious meal. It's easy to make your own masala paste from the spice mixes in this book. Make it in one big batch and store it in a jar for 3 months in the fridge.

In a food processor, one after the other, blitz the onion, then the garlic and then the ginger to a paste. Keep them separate.

Pour the vegetable oil into a sturdy-bottomed pot and place it over a medium heat. Add the onion paste and the salt, and cook, stirring continuously, for about 15 minutes, until the onions begin to turn brown. Add the garlic and cook for 10 minutes, until the onions turn a deeper shade of brown and the garlic begins to follow suit. Add the ginger, and cook for 10 minutes, lowering the heat, until the entire mixture is dark brown. Be vigilant and stir and scrape constantly to stop the mixture sticking and burning at the bottom of the pan.

Adding the three ingredients in separate stages is important because they each have a different moisture content. If you added them at the same time, the ginger would burn before the onion had the chance to caramelise – which is what gives the mixture its appealing, sweet aroma (burning paste smells harsh and unappealing).

Once the paste has darkened, lower the heat to its lowest setting and stir through the garam masala and your choice of other masala(s), depending on whether you are looking for a spicy, mild or in-between end result.

The paste will thicken and want to stick to the bottom of your pan, so keep stirring and scraping for about 8 minutes, until the spices have become hot and fragrant and the oil begins to seep from the paste. Once your masala paste has cooked out in this way, allow it to cool and place it in a clean, sterilised jar. Store it in the fridge until needed, or for up to 3 months.

GARAM MASALA

FILLS ½ JAM JAR

6g cardamom pods
10g cloves
30g ground cinnamon
1 whole star anise
4g black peppercorns
2 dried bay leaves
4g mace blades
½ nutmeg, grated

 A pinch of garam masala can have some surprisingly pleasing results – don't hold back from adding a bit of spice into your life! Garam means hot, implying the spices will bring warmth to the dish – rather than spiciness as you would expect from chillies. I use the blend to bring a balanced heat that warms the body and invigorates the soul.

Tip all the spices into spice grinder or food processor and blitz to a fine powder. Store in a clean, airtight jar in the cupboard for up to 12 months.

SAMBHAR MASALA
SPICY CHILLI AND GARLIC MASALA

FILLS 1 JAM JAR

20g cumin seeds
20g yellow mustard seeds
40g salt
25g fenugreek seeds
3g black peppercorns
3g cloves
1 whole star anise
100g dried Kashmiri
    chillies
30g garlic cloves, roughly
    chopped
30g ground turmeric
2g hing (asafoetida; about
    ¼ teaspoon)
100ml vegetable oil

 Where dhansak masala brings complexity and balance, sambhar masala brings the heat – it is just as quintessential to Parsi cooking, but it is neither quiet nor subtle. The chilli and garlic make this a deliciously versatile masala, with extra heat from the black pepper and mustard seeds and an intriguing piquancy from the fenugreek and hing.

This will become your go-to spice mix, ideal for more than just Parsi curries. Mixed with oil, it makes a great marinade for roast meats, fish and vegetables; or mixed with sea salt flakes, it makes a spicy seasoning for all sorts of snacks – from toasted cashew nuts, popcorn and far far (see page 105).

Blitz the cumin seeds, mustard seeds, salt, fenugreek seeds, peppercorns, cloves and star anise in a spice grinder or food processor to a fine powder. (You may have to do this in several stages depending on the size of your grinder.) Empty the powder into a bowl.

Next, blitz the chillies (in stages if needs be) and empty the powder into the bowl with the rest of the spices.

Blitz the remaining ingredients together for 1 minute, making sure the garlic has blended in and is almost unnoticeable. Tip the mixture of finely ground spices into the food processor and blitz until everything has mixed together and become one. Store in a clean, airtight jar, packing the masala down tightly to keep any air out. It will keep in a cupboard for 12 months.

NARIAL NE KAJU MASALO
CASHEW AND COCONUT MASALA

One of my uncles in Mumbai taught me this spice mix. He was a sailor in the Merchant Navy and is an exceptional cook. His tips on freezing certain nuts and spices show a level of care and understanding gained only from many years of experience.

Toasting the cashew nuts, coconut, spices and seeds breathes life into the masala, dragging it out of the mundane. I think of that moment in The Wizard of Oz *when Dorothy steps out of her black-and-white house into a glorious world of colour – everything becomes vibrant and full of life. If cashew nuts are not your thing, you can use almonds or even peanuts – they will give a different flavour, but equally delicious.*

FILLS 1 LARGE JAM JAR

60g shelled cashews
60g unsweetened desiccated coconut
2½ tablespoons white sesame seeds
2½ tablespoons white poppy seeds
5 tablespoons coriander seeds
5 cloves
2 tablespoons cumin seeds
5 cardamom pods
2 pieces of cassia bark or cinnamon sticks (about 5g in total)
20g dried Kashmiri chillies
1½ tablespoons ground turmeric
100g channa dal

Preheat the oven to 200°C/180°C fan. Place the cashew nuts on a baking tray and roast them for 10 minutes, giving them a mix after 5 minutes to ensure they colour evenly, until they turn golden all over. Remove from the oven and set aside on a cool tray (to prevent them toasting further).

Meanwhile, tip the coconut, sesame seeds and poppy seeds together on another baking tray and roast them for about 15 minutes. This tray will need more of your attention – stir and mix things around every 3 minutes, or until light brown and fragrant and the mixture resembles golden sand. Remove from the oven.

Combine the cashew nuts with the coconut and seed mixture and transfer everything to a freezer-proof container. Leave to cool, then freeze for 30 minutes. (This seems like an odd step, but the chill from the freezer solidifies the natural fats and oils in the nuts and seeds so they grind better, becoming more of a powder instead of turning into a paste.)

Heat a sturdy-bottomed pot or skillet over a low–medium heat. When hot, add the coriander seeds and cloves and toast, stirring continuously, for 2–3 minutes, until they are the colour of a dark, tanned leather. Add the cumin seeds and toast for a further 3 minutes, or until the cumin becomes fragrant and lets off a light smoke. Once the spices have toasted, tip them out immediately on to a plate or tray to cool – do not let them sit in the pan as they will continue to toast and may burn.

Remove the roasted nuts and seeds from the freezer (after 30 minutes), and tip them with the toasted spices into a spice grinder or food processor. Add the cardamom, cinnamon, chillies, turmeric and channa dal and blitz until you have as fine a powder as your grinder or processor will allow. (You may have to grind in batches if you have a smaller grinder.) Once ground, pack the powder into a clean, airtight jam jar.

In the hot Indian climate, the fats in the nuts and coconut can quickly turn rancid, affecting the quality and flavour of the masala. My uncle keeps his masalas in the freezer, but in the UK, the temperate climate of the home fridge is sufficient. The masala will store like this for 6 months.

DHANSAK MASALA

FILLS 1 JAM JAR

100g coriander seeds
50g cumin seeds
8g dried bay leaf
20g black peppercorns
20g dried Kashmiri chillies
5g black cumin seeds
5g green cardamom pods
8g black cardamom pods
3g caraway seeds
8g cinnamon or
   cassia bark
8g cloves
4g ground fenugreek
1 blade of mace
1 nutmeg, grated
8g poppy seeds
a pinch of saffron
2 whole star anise
25g ground turmeric
5g mustard seeds
1 whole dried black lime
   (a Persian speciality)

 Dhansak is a classic Parsi dish of lentils, vegetables and often mutton, and it calls for this special blend of spices. I find this masala extremely versatile, so I use it as my all-purpose spice mixture whenever I am cooking – it beats anything you may find on the supermarket shelf. For that reason, I implore you to take the time to make this masala as it will allow you to unlock the true flavours of many of the recipes in the book and taste them in their full glory.

There are a lot of spices here and some of them you may never have come across, but hear me out: they are all very easy to get hold of – you'll find every single one in Asian grocery stores. Once you've found them, the hard part is over – after that, it's just grinding.

Using a spice grinder or food processor, blitz all the ingredients to as fine a powder as your grinder or processor will allow (you may have to do this in batches, depending on your grinder's capacity). Pass the ground spices through a sieve on to a tray and re-grind anything left in the sieve to get the finest powder you possibly can. Store your dhansak masala in a clean, airtight jar for up to 12 months.

DHANIA JEERA
CUMIN–CORIANDER POWDER

FILLS 1 JAM JAR

2 teaspoons black
   peppercorns
500g coriander seeds
   (dhania)
250g cumin seeds (jeera)

 Sometimes the mood calls for something a little more restrained. This is where dhania jeera powder steps in. Cumin and coriander are two very important spices in Parsi cooking. This recipe has black pepper in it as well, as I find it brings a warmth to the cooking.

Place a large, heavy-based frying pan over a medium heat. Add the black peppercorns and coriander seeds and toast, moving them back and forth continuously, for 2 minutes, until a gentle fragrance emanates from the pan. Add the cumin seeds and toast for a further 30–60 seconds, until the cumin begins to darken.

Immediately tip the contents of the pan on to a tray or plate and leave to cool. Once cool, transfer the mixture to a spice grinder or food processor and grind it to a fine powder. Store in a clean, airtight jam jar in a cupboard for up to 12 months.

CHAI MASALA
WARMING TEA SPICES

A tea-time treat in any Parsi household is to drink spiced tea accompanied by bun maska or khari biscuit (see pages 327 and 329) – it's a cooling brew in hot summer months and a warming one during cold winters. Alternatively, a pinch of the mixture in your daily porridge will give you the pep you need for the day ahead. When I make this mixture during winter, I add an extra teaspoon of black peppercorns and an extra teaspoon of ground ginger to the quantities below, to create a much more warming blend.

Blitz all the spices to a fine powder in a spice grinder or food processor, then pass the mixture through a fine sieve into a bowl. Re-grind anything left in the sieve and add this to the bowl. The blend will keep in an airtight jar in a cupboard for up to 12 months.

To use, make your cup or pot of tea as normal and add ¼ teaspoon of tea masala per person or per cup. For the authentic Parsi café experience, add excessive amounts of sugar! (You can drink it as it is, if you prefer.)

FILLS 1 JAM JAR

1 nutmeg, grated
50g ground ginger
20g cardamom pods
12g ground cinnamon
1 whole star anise
12 cloves
4g mace
1 teaspoon black
    peppercorns

PICKLES,
PRESERVES
AND DIPS

Top row: Herby Mayonnaise, Mango Pickle Mayonnaise, Coconut Yoghurt Dip, Tamarind Ketchup
Bottom row: Turmeric Pickle, Beetroot and Mustard Seed Chutney, Wedding Pickle, Quince Rose Paste

KHAJOOR NE AMLI PRESERVE
DATE AND TAMARIND PRESERVE

FILLS 1 JAM JAR

200g deseeded dried
    dates
200g deseeded tamarind
50g caster sugar
a pinch of salt
1 teaspoon rose water

This is a versatile preserve with many sweet uses. I spread it on the bottom of tart cases before filling them with egg custard to add a fruity richness, or smear it over raw puff pastry and bake it for a deliciously rustic jammy tart, or simply spread it over hot buttered toast for an indulgent snack. How and where you use it is entirely down to how creative you want to get.

Place all the ingredients in a medium saucepan with 100ml of water over a low–medium heat. Simmer until everything is soft. With a whisk or a fork, mash everything to a paste; or for something a bit more refined, blitz to a smooth paste in a food processor. Place the mixture in a clean, sterilised jam jar and store at room temperature for up to 3 months.

HERBY MAYONNAISE

FILLS 1 LARGE JAM JAR

1 egg and 1 egg yolk
juice of 1 lemon
1 tablespoon Dijon
    mustard
2 teaspoons fine salt
a few grinds of black
    pepper
2 large garlic cloves
2 small bird's eye chillies
1 small bunch of coriander,
    leaves picked
½ large bunch of mint,
    leaves picked
½ small bunch of tarragon
    leaves
½ small bunch of dill
    leaves
600ml good-quality
    olive oil

You don't need the exact quantities of these herbs to make this mayonnaise – nor even these precise herbs themselves. Feel free to express yourself with herbs that you enjoy. You are guaranteed a delicious outcome.

Stalks of soft green herbs are packed with flavour and nutrients; chop them fine or blend them and use in your cooking.

Place all the ingredients, except the oil, in a food processor and blitz for 30 seconds, until you have a green purée. With the motor running, ever so gradually add the olive oil – just the slowest of trickles – through the feed tube. (If you're unfamiliar with making mayonnaise, it can split very easily at this stage, so take your time.) Things will start to thicken up as the oil makes its way through the herbs and eggs, until, by the last drop of oil, you will have herby mayonnaise.

It is a perfect accompaniment to chicken farcha (see page 204) or crispy brains (see page 243). Store in an airtight container in the fridge for up to 1 week.

If on the rare occasion your mayonnaise splits (where the oil separates and the mayo looks greasy), all is not lost. Empty the contents of the food processor into a bowl and give the processor a good rinse. Add 1 extra egg yolk and 1 tablespoon of water to the food processor and, with the blades spinning, spoon the mixture back in, bit by bit, through hole in the lid, and without adding another spoonful until the last one is thoroughly mixed in.

MANGO PICKLE MAYONNAISE

This mayonnaise was born out of desperation while I was catering for a friend's birthday party. Feeling like the chicken farcha I had made needed something delicious to be dipped into, and having already exhausted my coconut chutney recipe on another dish, I emptied a jar of spicy mango pickle and an egg into the blender and hoped for the best. Looking at the thick, pungent paste, I felt it needed to be tempered out a little, so I began emulsifying some oil into it – and hey presto! Mango pickle mayo was born. Spicy, tangy, salty and packed full of flavour, this is a versatile dip or spread that will really blow your socks off.

To avoid any confusion and botched batches, I must specify this recipe uses pickle not chutney. Pickles are salty, pungent and well spiced, while chutneys are very sweet and sticky.

FILLS 1 LARGE JAM JAR

200g of your favourite mango pickle (or any other spicy pickle you enjoy)
1 large egg
450ml vegetable oil

In a food processor or blender, blitz the mango pickle and the egg into a purée; things may splat up the sides of the bowl at first, so every now and then stop the mixer and use a spatula to push everything back down.

Keep the blades spinning and slowly and steadily start drizzling in the vegetable oil through the hole in the lid, aiming straight for the whirring blades, until you have a perfect, thick mayonnaise. Slow and steady drizzling is key – keep an eye that the oil does not pool in the mixer; your drizzle should match the rate at which the oil emulsifies into the mixture.

Once all the oil has been emulsified and you have a thick and even mayonnaise, stop the mixer and use a spatula to bring everything together. Store in an airtight container in the fridge for up to 1 week, and use without discretion.

KHATU MITHU TINDORA
SWEET AND SOUR PICKLED TINDORA

FILLS 1 JAM JAR

200g tindora
1 tablespoon salt

FOR THE PICKLING
  LIQUID
200ml white wine vinegar
100g caster sugar
1 whole star anise
5 cloves
5 black peppercorns
½ teaspoon yellow
  mustard seeds
⅛ teaspoon ground
  turmeric

 Like a tiny gherkin, tindora makes for the perfect, crunchy pickled vegetable to accompany your salty snacks. I love serving pickled tindora with chicken farcha (see page 204) – its sweet-sourness cuts through the salty spiciness of the fried chicken perfectly.

This is a simple, yet delicious recipe for pickling liquid, and you can be very creative with it. Think of all the other vegetables you can cut, salt and pickle – cucumbers, firm green tomatoes, breakfast radishes, mooli, sliced onions, okra, cauliflower, carrots, beetroot... The list is endless!

Wash the tindora and sparingly trim off and discard the black ends. Then cut the tindora in half along the length.

Stir the salt into 250ml of cold water until dissolved. Place the halved tindora in a bowl and cover with the salted water. Leave to brine for 6 hours.

About an hour before the end of the brining time, make the pickling liquid. Place the vinegar, sugar and spices in a saucepan and gently warm up the liquid, stirring until the sugar has dissolved. Remove from the heat and allow the pickling liquid to cool completely while the tindora finishes brining.

Pour off the salty water from the tindora and rinse them under cold water.

Place the tindora in a clean, sterilised jam jar and pour the pickling liquid over the top, totally submerging them. Leave for at least 2 days before enjoying.

MITHA NA PANI MA LILI HARAD
TURMERIC PICKLE

Many members of my family subscribe to the healing powers of turmeric. Drink it, eat it, gargle with it, dab it on a cut – you name it, turmeric will cure it. I cannot substantiate any of these claims, I can concur only with turmeric's versatility in the kitchen. My uncle Adil passed on this recipe to me.

This is a simple preparation and a great way to eat the fresh root. Turmeric itself is bitter, but salt and lemon juice bring balance and harmony, creating a piquant, flavourful punch. You just need a few days of patience to wait for the root to absorb the salt and acidity.

As an accompaniment on the plate, it delivers a welcome distraction from spiciness, diverting attention away from the heat. A scant spoonful through a salad will elevate it and pique a diner's interest with every bite.

FILLS 1 JAM JAR

500g fresh turmeric root
2 heaped tablespoons sea
　salt flakes
juice of 2 large lemons

Peel the turmeric with a small knife or, better still, scrape the skin away with the front tip of a small teaspoon – be careful with any juices as they will stain permanently (I don't recommend wearing your Sunday Best while you're performing this task). Use gloves if you wish, but I quite like the look of stained orange hands, to me it is a sign of a fruitful adventure in the kitchen and a great way to bring up in conversation the amazing pickled turmeric you just made!

Using your sharpest kitchen knife, slice the turmeric into discs 1mm thin – they will resemble thin slivers of carrot.

Place the turmeric in a large metal or glass bowl (the juices will stain plastic), along with the sea salt, and give everything a good mix until the salt has all but dissolved.

Pack the turmeric into a sterilised jam jar and pour over the lemon juice. If the liquid does not cover the turmeric, top up with fresh cold water from the tap. Refrigerate for 2 days before eating – with everything and nothing.

Health is wealth.
-- My mother

METHIA NU ACHAR
MANGO AND FENUGREEK PICKLE

FILLS ABOUT 2 JAM JARS

1 large green, unripe
    mango
1 small lime
1 small carrot, peeled
4 teaspoons salt
1 teaspoon ground
    turmeric
6 dried Kashmiri chillies or
    4 teaspoons chilli flakes
3 teaspoons fenugreek
    seeds
1 teaspoon black mustard
    seeds
1 teaspoon hing
    (asafoetida)
200ml mustard oil
    (vegetable oil will do,
    but won't give as much
    flavour), plus extra
    if needed

 A pickle such as this one is eaten with everyday meals. It brings a salty vibrancy to simple dishes such as lentils and rice, or when it's laid inside buttered rotli as a spicy snack. You will always find me with a dollop on the side of my plate whenever I am eating Parsi food. For the best results with this pickle, go for maximum green coverage on your mango and an all-around firm feel, especially at the base. If, after tasting the results, you feel you like things a little more or less spicy, adjust the chilli content accordingly the next time you make it.

Slice the mango flesh away from the stone, keeping the skin on, then dice the flesh into 5mm cubes. Cut the lime into 8 wedges, then each wedge into 3 chunks. Cut the carrot into 2mm matchsticks.

In a large bowl, toss the mango, lime and carrot together with the salt and turmeric, making sure everything is well coated. Let this sit for 2 hours to absorb the salt.

Preheat the oven to 60°C. Drain off all the water from the mixture in the bowl and lay the mixture in a layer on a baking tray. Place in the oven for 3 hours, leaving the oven door slightly ajar to let the moisture out, and giving everything a good turn every 30 minutes, until completely and evenly dried.

In a spice grinder, blitz the chillies, fenugreek seeds, mustard seeds and hing for 20 seconds to form a powder.

In a large bowl toss the dried mango, carrot and lime mixture with the ground spices, until everything is fully coated.

Heat the oil in a saucepan over a medium heat until the surface of the oil begins to shimmer and it gives off a pungent aroma. Take the oil off the heat and allow it to cool for 15 minutes (you want it to be hot but not burning). Evenly and slowly, pour the hot oil all over the mixture in the bowl. Gently stir together, until the oil has fully coated the mixture. The heat from the oil will start to draw out all the flavours and aromas from the spices.

Spoon the mixture into clean, sterilised jars, but do not pack it in tightly as you want space for the oil to mingle around the jar. Top the jars up with extra oil to ensure everything in the jar is submerged. Seal with the lids. Store in a cool, dark cupboard for 2 weeks, to allow time for the salt, spices and oils to permeate through the mango and its roommates. Once you have opened the jar, keep the pickle in the fridge and eat it within a month.

LAGAAN NU ACHAR
WEDDING PICKLE

 The name for this recipe translates literally as 'wedding pickle' – although to me this is less of a pickle and more of what I would call a chutney. It is also everything you could want in an accompaniment.

Lagaan nu achar was my introduction to the dynamic flavours of Parsi food, having all the qualities that make it uniquely delicious: hot, sweet, sour and savoury, all in one mouthful. For me, the specialness of lagaan nu achar is down to the use of brewed cane sugar (or 'Parsi vinegar', as it is affectionately called). Produced by small family-run operations in the city of Navsari in Gujarat, this vinegar, with its distinct dark colour, heady sweet molasses favour and unrivalled depth of character, is ubiquitous in Parsi cooking. However, it's not easy to find elsewhere in the world. The nearest I have come to it is date vinegar, which is popular in Middle Eastern cooking. I have also found that a good-quality apple cider vinegar brings similar characteristics, although it lacks the dark molasses flavour. If you're lucky enough to have cane sugar vinegar to hand, this is what you should use.

FILLS ABOUT 2 LARGE JAM JARS

30g dried deseeded dates, sliced into thin slivers
75g golden raisins
50g dried apricots, sliced into thin slivers
500g caster sugar
500g carrots, coarsely grated
60g jaggery, chopped
200ml apple cider vinegar
15g fresh ginger, peeled and sliced into thin slivers
5 large garlic cloves, very finely sliced (wafer thin)
2 teaspoons hot chilli powder
1½ teaspoons garam masala (see page 46)
1 tablespoon salt

Place all the dried fruits in a bowl and cover with boiling water. Leave the fruit to sit in the water for 30 minutes, then drain, discarding the water.

Put the sugar, carrots, jaggery, vinegar, ginger and garlic in a sturdy-bottomed pot and place over a high heat. Bring to the boil, then lower the heat and gently simmer for 25 minutes, until the carrots have softened. Add the soaked, dried fruits, simmer for a further 10 minutes, then stir in the chilli, garam masala and salt.

Pour the hot chutney into clean, sterilised jam jars and seal straight away. Unopened, the chutney will keep in a cool, dark cupboard for well over a year; once opened, keep in the fridge for a few months.

I like to eat lagaan nu achar with:
Fish grilled on the BBQ
Roasted meats like pork, lamb, chicken and quail
Patra ni macchi (classic flavours) (see page 192)
Kedgeree (see page 189)
In a cheese sandwich

PANI NU ACHAR
SALTED MANGO PICKLE

 Here is another recipe from the capable hands of Dinaz Aunty. Her memories of her uncle making this pickle when she was little were mainly of her and her sister pinching and eating pieces of salty mango as they lay in the hot sun to dry. For those at a geographical disadvantage (or with a lack of patience, like me), you can use your oven's lowest setting (40–60°C) with the door slightly ajar for the air-drying process – just keep an eye out for sneaky hands searching for salty snacks! For the best results with this pickle, go for maximum green coverage on the skin of your mangoes and an all-around firm feel, especially at the base.

FILLS ABOUT 1 LARGE JAM JAR

2 small unripe green
   mangoes
1 small carrot, peeled
2 limes, 1 quartered and
   thinly sliced with the
   skin on, the other juiced
100g salt
1 teaspoon ground
   turmeric
250ml water, boiled then
   left to cool completely

Slice the mango flesh away from the stone, keeping the skin on, then dice the flesh into cubes no bigger than 1cm (but don't worry about uniformity – it's not necessary). Slice the carrot in half along the length (you may not need to do this if your carrots are thin) and cut it into strips no more than 2mm thick.

Place the mango, carrot and lime slices in a large bowl and toss through 75g of the salt. Cover and leave this to sit for 3 hours, giving the contents of the bowl a mix every hour.

Heat your oven to its lowest setting. Drain off all the water from the mixture in the bowl, rinse and lay the mixture in a layer on a baking tray. Place in the oven for 2 hours, leaving the oven door slightly ajar to let the moisture out, and turning the pieces every 20 minutes, until completely and evenly dried.

Tip the dried mango, carrots and lime into a clean, sterilised jar and add the remaining 25g of salt, along with the lime juice and turmeric.

Pour the cooled boiled water into the jar to totally submerge the contents by at least 1cm. Screw on the lid and allow the pickle to sit for 4 days in the fridge, every day giving the jar a good shake. The longer you leave the pickle to sit in the brine, the more it will develop its soft, salty character. It will last up to 2 weeks in the fridge.

Make provisions for want in times of plenty.

-- Anon

QUINCE AND ROSE PASTE

MAKES 1 JAM JAR

1 large quince (at least
    300g in weight)
at least 500g caster sugar
40g jaggery, chopped
juice of ½ lemon
1 tablespoon rose water
1 teaspoon kerwa water
    (not essential, but lovely
    if you have it)

There's always an air of excitement when the first quinces of the year are delivered through the doors of the kitchen. Quince fever ensues and everything from jams and jellies to trifles and sorbets make their way on to the menu. Sometimes the quinces are left to blet, a controlled process where the fruit overripens, turning dark and soft. This 'rotting' brings a deep and sweet character to the fruit that can take desserts to the next level.

I must admit I was quite intimidated when first faced with this oddly shaped yellow orb. Now, though, when I buy my quinces, I like to hold on to them for a few days to admire the shape and colour and take in the scent. There is something very calming about a quince.

Making quince paste was one of the first things I was tasked to do with the fruit, which was a blessing as it is very simple to make, yet unbelievably rewarding. Spread it over hot, buttered toast, put a blob atop rice pudding (see page 288) or ravo (see page 283) and even create a smear on the bottom of your lagaan nu custar (see page 277). However, possibly its finest moment comes when served alongside a simple piece of roasted meat. The savouriness of a slice of roast mutton dragged through a dollop of sweet, aromatic quince paste is a sensation your taste buds will thank you for and ask for over and over. To make this paste, choose a quince with a bright, floral fragrance and a deep yellow blush.

Cut your quince into eighths with the skin still on. Chop each eighth into thin slices, including the core (the skin and core of quince contain pectin, which will give your paste its unctuous set).

Place the chopped quince in a small saucepan and add water so that it covers the fruit by a 1cm depth. Place the pan over a medium heat and bring the liquid to the boil, then lower the heat and gently boil for 20 minutes, until the pieces of quince are soft and mushy when pressed. Every now and then give the quince a stir while it's boiling and lower the heat as the water starts to evaporate.

Allow the quince and water to cool for 5 minutes, then tip the whole lot into a food processor and blend until smooth – the more thoroughly you blend, the more purée you will eventually yield. Push the quince purée through a sieve, making sure to get every last drop into a bowl to get rid of the debris and then weigh the purée.

Weigh out the same weight of sugar, less 40g, as you have purée (the 40g is to accommodate the jaggery).

Place the purée, jaggery and sugar into a sturdy-bottomed pot over a medium heat and bring the mixture to the boil. Lower the heat, stirring continuously as the mixture bubbles away. If the purée is boiling too aggressively and spluttering all over your kitchen like a volcano, lower the heat but do not stop stirring – if it catches (which it will do with ease) in the slightest, you will have a burnt taste through your paste. (If this does start to happen, though, just switch the paste to a new pan.)

Check the temperature of the paste with a cooking thermometer – when it reaches 106°C, turn off the heat and stir in the lemon juice. Allow the quince to cool for 10 minutes, stirring every minute to stop a skin forming. Once the quince has cooled slightly, stir in the rose water and kerwa water and, while still warm, pour the paste straight into a clean, sterilised jam jar. Immediately top with the lid.

Unopened, you can keep the paste in a cool, dark cupboard for over a year; once opened, eat it within a few months.

BEETROOT AND MUSTARD SEED CHUTNEY

MAKES A LITTLE OVER 1 JAM JAR

225g raw beetroot, coarsely grated
150g shallots, diced small or coarsely chopped in a food processor
175g caster sugar
100g golden raisins
½ tablespoon black mustard seeds
150ml malt vinegar
1 teaspoon cornflour
5 garlic cloves, very finely sliced (wafer thin)
2 teaspoons salt
½ teaspoon ground turmeric
¼ teaspoon chilli powder (mild or hot, as you like)
½ teaspoon garam masala (see page 46)

 This chutney is a lovely accompaniment to many Parsi snacks but is equally at home slathered inside a cheese sandwich.

Place the beetroot, shallots, sugar, raisins, mustard seeds, vinegar and 100ml of water in a sturdy-bottomed pot over a medium–low heat. Bring to the simmer and cook, simmering, for 15 minutes, stirring every few minutes, until the beetroot has completely softened, the sugar has dissolved and the volume has reduced by about one third. The mixture should bubble continuously, but not vigorously, throughout.

Mix the cornflour with 2 tablespoons of cold water in a cup until you have a slurry, then stir this into the mixture in the pot.

Add the garlic, salt, turmeric, chilli powder and garam masala and stir everything through. Carry on simmering for 3 more minutes, until the mixture has thickened to a moist, sticky chutney.

Transfer the hot chutney to a clean, sterilised jam jar and immediately seal it with the lid. Unopened, the chutney will keep for 6 months in a cool, dark cupboard; once opened, keep it in the fridge and eat it within a few weeks.

TAMARIND KETCHUP

MAKES ABOUT 1 LITRE (TO FILL 3 JAM JARS)

500g Bramley apples, peeled, cored and chopped
60g deseeded tamarind
60g dried deseeded dates
1 large ripe tomato, diced
½ medium onion, sliced
150ml malt vinegar
2cm fresh ginger, peeled and chopped
½ teaspoon garam masala (see page 46)
2 teaspoons salt
200g caster sugar
50g jaggery, chopped
50ml apple juice

 For chips, chops and butties. Use packs of pitted tamarind for this recipe – not paste, which may have added ingredients.

Place all the ingredients in a sturdy-bottomed pot and place it over a high heat. Bring the mixture to the boil and then immediately reduce the heat to medium. Simmer for 25 minutes, stirring every now and then to make sure nothing is catching on the bottom, until the vinegar and apple juice reduce and you have a pot of thick, glossy, stewed ingredients. (Increase the frequency of your stirs during the last 10 minutes of cooking.)

Allow the mixture to cool slightly, then transfer it to a food processor and blitz it to a smooth purée. Pass the purée through a fine sieve into a bowl, discarding any bits that catch in the sieve.

Spoon the ketchup into clean, sterilised jam jars and refrigerate for up to 3 months.

KOPRA NU CHUTNEY
COCONUT AND CORIANDER CHUTNEY

This chutney is the main component of patra ni macchi (see page 192), but with some creativity it's easy to transform into a dip, a sandwich spread or a delicious accompaniment to a meal. When I was a kid, my mum used to give me this chutney sandwiched between two slices of buttered bread, sometimes with a bit of cheese inside. Delicious! With a few spoonfuls of yoghurt or crème fraîche stirred through, it becomes a creamy coconut dip for tortilla chips and other snacks.

Coconut chutney is one of the first things I remember my mum making that was different to the everyday foods I had enjoyed as a kid. It bursts with bold flavours – tangy green mango, spicy chillies, delicious coconut and deep, herby coriander. I was always tasked with cracking and peeling the coconut, and at that age I thought being able to smash open a coconut was the best job ever! It also was the greatest temptation – my dad and I never found it easy to resist eating the coconut before it had made its way into the blender. More often than not, my mum's recipe was always off by a few chunks.

You'll find green sour mangoes in the fruit and vegetable section of Asian grocery stores. They are varieties that have been picked early and are usually no bigger than a duck egg. Look for a small, firm green mango, as the riper ones have a bright orange flesh that is sweet and delicious, but won't give you the sour qualities you need for this recipe.

You'll need a food processor, ideally – although those dedicated enough can achieve similar results with a fine cheese grater and a sharp knife and some patience.

MAKES ABOUT 500G

1 coconut, cracked open, coconut water reserved, peeled

1 green sour mango, peeled and flesh sliced away from the stone

5 garlic cloves

2.5cm fresh ginger, peeled and chopped

2 teaspoons cumin seeds, toasted

5 small green chillies

about 80g mint, leaves picked and roughly chopped

about 150g coriander, leaves and stalks roughly chopped

juice of 1 lemon

3 tablespoons apple cider vinegar, or Parsi vinegar if you have it

1 teaspoon grated jaggery or dark brown soft sugar

2 teaspoons salt

Chop the coconut and mango into chunks small enough for your food processor and add them to the processor bowl. Add the coconut water (if it's usable), along with the garlic, ginger, cumin and chillies and blitz to a coarse paste.

Add the mint leaves, coriander, lemon juice, vinegar, jaggery or sugar and salt. Blitz again, stopping and scraping the sides of the bowl from time to time, until you have an evenly ground, coarse green paste – the texture should be similar to a thick pesto. It's okay to add few tablespoons of water to get the texture right, if you need to.

Your chutney is ready to eat – now explore recipes throughout the book for many exciting possibilities on how to use it.

Left: Salt flats, Kutch
Right: Boomla (Bombay duck)
drying in the sun, Bhadreshwar

DAIRY

GHEE
HOW TO MAKE GHEE

FILLS 1 JAM JAR

250g unsalted butter

Making ghee the traditional way is quite an involved process. You need to slowly simmer whole milk, then cool it with live yoghurt. Once it has curdled, you churn it into butter and boil it down. The boiling lightly cooks the milk solids and gives them a nutty, caramelised note. The resulting fat is then strained off as ghee, leaving the solids behind.

Happily, we have the luxury of being able to skip a few of those steps by using shop-bought butter.

Place the butter in a small saucepan over a low heat. Let the butter melt down until it's completely liquid, increase the heat slightly so that it gently bubbles away. After about 10 minutes of bubbling, you will notice that a white foam is forming on the top of the butter. Lower the heat and, without stirring at this point, allow the butter to keep bubbling away. After another 10 or so minutes, you will notice the white foam begin to dissipate and the milk solids (which look like very small crumbs) will have sunk to the bottom of the pan and begun to turn golden brown.

Very lightly whisk the bottom of the pan where the milk solids have settled so they do not burn – you want them to evenly brown within the fat, giving a wonderful aroma that always reminds me of digestive biscuits. If at any point you are thinking to yourself, 'Am I making brown butter?', yes, you are. Once the solids are golden brown and smelling biscuity, remove the pan from the heat. Allow to sit for 15 minutes.

Carefully strain the hot ghee through a muslin cloth into a sterilised jam jar, catching all the browned milk solids in the cloth (set the filled cloth aside). Secure the lid on the jar and allow the ghee to cool to room temperature. Once cooled, it will keep for 3 months.

Jevoo ghee tevoo gullyoo.
    – Gujarati saying

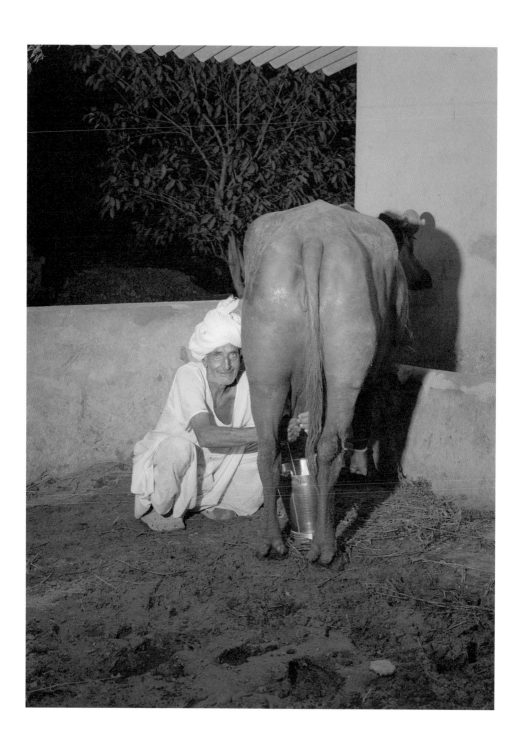

Left: A moment to one's self
Right: Pirabhai Mewabhai
Desai milking his buffalo

DHAI
HOW TO MAKE YOGHURT

MAKES 800ML

800ml whole milk
20g caster sugar (to make
    sweet yoghurt only)
1 tablespoon live natural
    yoghurt

 Dhai (yoghurt) is an important food in Parsi culture – we use it during Zoroastrian ceremonies as a representation and mark of respect towards animal life.

When I was growing up, making yoghurt was a weekly event. My mum would use a little of last week's yoghurt to help set the new batch in our airing cupboard, where the warmth of the hot water tank was the perfect temperature to set the yoghurt overnight. The warmth of a cooling oven would be perfect, too.

From the outset, it seemed strange to me that you need yoghurt to make yoghurt. The key is one particular type of bacterium that causes the warm milk to set. For this reason, it is absolutely vital to use live yoghurt, which is packed full of little bacteria helpers – anything else will just not work.

Pour the milk into a large, sturdy-bottomed pot and place it over a medium heat. Bring the milk to the boil, then reduce the heat to low so that the milk bubbles away at a gentle simmer. Use a spatula to gently stir the milk to avoid scalding on the bottom of the pan. If you are making sweet yoghurt, add the sugar. Simmer the milk for 20 minutes, stirring continuously. Then remove the milk from the heat and allow it to cool to 35°C on a cooking thermometer. At this point, stir in the live yoghurt, mixing it thoroughly into the milk.

Pour the mixture into a glass or ceramic dish with a lid. Place the lid on top and leave it in a warm place (such as an airing cupboard, by a radiator or a sunny window, or in a warming oven) for 8 hours, or until set. (My preferred method is to heat about 5–7cm of water to 45°C in a casserole pan. I pour the milk mixture into a container that fits inside the pan, then place it inside the pan and put the lid on. Every now and then I check the temperature of the water with a thermometer and if it drops below 35°C, I place it on the hob and give it a very gentle boost of heat.)

Once the yoghurt has set, transfer it to the fridge to store. It will keep for 3–4 days.

To thicken your yoghurt, place a piece of muslin over a deep bowl, securing the muslin over the bowl using an elastic band or piece of string tied around the rim. Push the cloth down slightly into the bowl to create a sort of muslin hammock. Pour the yoghurt into the muslin and refrigerate for 12 hours. The whey from the yoghurt will drip through the muslin and collect in the bowl, leaving behind a thicker result. You can use the whey to make chaas (see page 346) or to cook with.

A lovely way to finish off sweetened yoghurt is to grate nutmeg over the top and serve it with raisins, chopped almonds and a drizzle of honey.

PANEER
HOW TO MAKE PANEER

Typically in India, buffalo milk is used to make paneer – it has a higher fat content than cow's milk and a richer flavour. If you can get your hands on whole buffalo milk, then do use it, but you can still get great results using regular cow's milk. Extra-creamy Jersey milk, which has a higher fat content, will give you a slightly higher yield.

I use lemon juice to split the curds from the whey, as it leaves a slight lemony taste, but you can instead use vinegar, if you prefer. Distilled malt vinegar is a good choice, as it does not leave any aftertaste.

MAKES ABOUT 350G

2 litres whole milk
juice of 1 lemon
or 2 tablespoons distilled vinegar, plus extra if needed
sea salt flakes

Pour the milk into a heavy-based pot and place it over a medium heat. Bring the milk to a gentle boil, stirring continuously to ensure the milk does not scald on the bottom of the pot. Remove the milk from the heat, add the lemon juice or vinegar and stir through. You will see the curds begin to separate from the whey as the milk curdles – if this doesn't happen after 1 minute, add 1 tablespoon more of lemon juice or vinegar. Leave the milk to sit for 1 minute to fully separate.

There are two ways to strain the curds from the whey:

First, you can line a sieve with muslin cloth (large enough eventually to fold back over the curds in the sieve) and place it over a bowl. Carefully pour the curds into the muslin and sprinkle a few sea salt flakes over the top. Fold over the muslin and stack a few saucers on top to press down.

My aunty's favoured technique, on the other hand, was to wrap the curds in muslin and tie the bundle to her overhanging kitchen tap so the excess whey would drip into the sink – brilliantly efficient!

In either case, I always keep the whey (put a bowl in the sink to catch it, if you use Aunty's method) and use it in place of stock or water in cooking, particularly dals and curries. The whey has a great acidity and is full of protein.

The final texture of your paneer will depend on how long you hang it for and how firmly (and if) you press it. For a loose paneer, strain the curds without pressing. If you like a soft, spreadable paneer, hang for just a few hours (my aunt's kitchen-sink technique is ideal for this). If you prefer something that you can crumble (through recipes such as the pea, fennel and paneer salad; see page 128), then a gentle pressing with some saucers topped with unopened food tins is what you need (I prefer the sieve technique for this). If you prefer something even firmer, then

Continued overleaf...

double your saucer-and-tin stack and press the paneer overnight in the fridge. The result in this case will be a paneer you can dice and cook while still retaining its integrity.

Once you have pressed them, you can turn the curds out into an airtight container, seal them and keep them in the fridge for up to 3 days.

Finally, feel free to jazz up your paneer with a few simple ingredients – add these after you have strained off the curds. For example, you could add crushed cumin seed, finely chopped chilli, finely ground coriander seeds, chopped coriander leaves, chopped mint leaves or chopped fenugreek leaves – among many others.

Left: Curds hanging
in a muslin sack

Cheese is milk's leap towards immortality.
–– Clifton Fadiman

TOPLI NU PANEER
CURDS SET IN BASKETS

MAKES 10

1 litre whole milk
2 drops of liquid rennet
(see rennet pack for
setting instructions)
sea salt flakes and freshly
cracked black pepper

*My very first bite of topli nu paneer made me realise that,
although Parsi food can be unique, it still shares many
techniques with other cultures from across the globe.*

*Having gone to the city of Pune in the midst of summer to visit
relatives, we took shelter indoors to escape the oppressive heat.
Lunchtime had come around and my uncle and mother were
discussing what to eat. My uncle mentioned that the Parsi lady
downstairs made the best topli nu paneer. My mother's ears
pricked up. My uncle came back minutes later with a large glass
jar filled with soft, white orbs submerged in a cloudy liquid.
These delicate homemade cheeses had been formed in small
wicker baskets – and each one was patterned with the imprint of
the wicker weave. It's this pattern than gives the paneers their
name – topli is the Gujarati word for basket. My uncle scooped
the orbs out of their salty whey and placed one on each of our
plates. I was unsure what to expect, but the first mouthful
revealed a curd so soft and giving it almost disappeared in my
mouth, leaving behind a salty, fresh taste. It reminded me of a
creamy Italian burrata.*

*You do not need wicker baskets to make this paneer, but it is a
nice touch. I use small ricotta moulds, which you'll find at most
cheese-making suppliers. And, ideally, you'll need a cooking
thermometer (although I've given an alternative in the method,
if you don't have one).*

Pour the milk into a sturdy-bottomed pot and place it over a gentle heat,
warming it up until it reaches 35°C on the cooking thermometer. (If you
don't have a thermometer, dip your finger into the milk – you're aiming
for body temperature, but no warmer.) Carefully add the rennet and stir
in well.

For the rennet to set the milk, the mixture needs to stay at around 35°C
for about 1 hour – check the temperature every 10 minutes and if it drops
below, give the milk a gentle tickle on the stove on a low heat to bring it
back up. Avoid stirring as this will break up the set. The milk is starting to
set when a gentle wobble back and forth shows a soft, jelly-like texture.
At this point, the curds are ready to be scooped out and placed in their
moulds for the whey to drain off.

Using a large spoon, cleanly scoop up big chunks of curd. You don't want
to break up the curds, so be gentle. Drop the curds into the moulds,
filling them all the way up to the top. Sprinkle each with sea salt.

Place the moulds on a tray to catch the whey and keep the tray in the
fridge. Return to the tray after 1 hour and carefully drain off the whey into
a tub. Keep this in the fridge – you will need it later for storing the paneer.

Repeat this process over the next 2 hours, until there is no more whey to drain off.

Leave the curds in the fridge overnight to fully set before gently turning them out to reveal their imprinted patterns. Transfer the paneer to the tub, submerging them in the whey, and refrigerate for up to 3 days.

Serve seasoned with sea salt and freshly cracked black pepper and piles of coarsely chopped mint, generously dressed with lemon and cumin dressing (see page 136).

MAWA

The Great Rann of Kutch, in the state of Gujarat, is one of the largest salt deserts in the world – vast plains of brilliant white crystals as far as the eye can see. The Rann makes for a great day trip when I go and visit my cousins. On the drive there we pass herds of water buffalo, wallowing in mud baths, taking shade from the baking heat. At around the halfway mark, we pass a small village called Khavda, famous for its incredible mawa.

Every morning in the village of Khavda, the people collect the local buffalo milk from the farmers, then slowly cook it down in huge open pans, stirring continuously until the milk becomes a thick, golden paste – mawa. Nestled between the roadside chai walas and snack shops of Khavda, you'll find folk tending to small pots of freshly made golden mawa, sweetened with sugar to make a rich paste – just one small bowl is plenty enough to give an energy boost for the remaining drive on to the salt plains.

You most likely won't have access to fresh buffalo milk, or for that matter the hours in your day to stand over a pan of milk. Thankfully, you will easily be able to buy evaporated milk, which has already had roughly 50 per cent of its water removed. A very helpful headstart indeed.

Before we move on to how to make mawa at home (see overleaf), I would like to talk about two inevitabilities. First, you will at some point scald and burn your milk at the bottom of the pan, no matter how diligently you stir. For this reason, I always have two pans on hand to make my mawa – every time the bottom of one catches, I pour the mawa through a sieve into the clean one and carry on cooking. I wash the first pan and repeat the transfer a few times until the mawa is ready.

Second, making mawa even with evaporated milk is time-consuming – it will need a good hour or so of undivided attention. But, like many things that take time, the results far outweigh the commitment.

Right: Making mawa, Kutch

MAKING MAWA
AT HOME

To make the mawa cake (see page 338), leave the mawa to cool and store it in a container until you need it. I like to make a big batch at a time (because it's so time-consuming), cool it, cut into 100g squares and freeze it, so that I can pull it out, defrost it and use it as needed.

If you want to turn your mawa straight into a sweet treat (just as it is), add 2 tablespoons of caster sugar to the pot while the mawa is still hot and stir it through until fully mixed in. Allow the mawa to cool slightly before eating it by the spoonful.

MAKES ABOUT 200G

2 400g tins of
   evaporated milk

Spoon the evaporated milk into a sturdy-bottomed pot (a pan with a thin, tinny base is no good here). Place the pot over a medium heat and, stirring continuously, bring the milk to a gentle simmer. Simmer vigorously for 5 minutes, then reduce the heat and keep stirring. It may feel like not much is happening and you are just stirring a pan of hot milk, but as the milk steams away and gently reduces, it will become thick like double cream and begin turning caramel brown. Even using evaporated milk, it will take at least 30 minutes of simmering and stirring to get to this stage.

After 30–45 minutes, reduce the heat to its lowest setting and carry on cooking and stirring for another 30 minutes. By this time your milk will have reduced to a brown fudge-like paste with the consistency of thick porridge. When you drag your spoon across the bottom of the pan, the mawa should part like the Red Sea, then slowly creep back together. You are very close at this stage – give it another 10 minutes or so of cooking and the mawa will begin to ball up like a firm dough. Congratulations, you have made mawa!

The science which feeds men is worth at least as much as one which teaches how to kill them.

-- Brillat-Savarin

BREAKFAST

AKURI
ADIL UNCLE'S PARSI SCRAMBLED EGGS

SERVES 4

2 tablespoons butter
or ghee
1 medium red onion,
finely diced
1 teaspoon ginger–garlic
paste (see page 43)
1 very ripe medium
tomato, diced small
½ teaspoon of ground
turmeric
2 teaspoons of cumin–
coriander powder
(see page 48)
1 teaspoon salt
6 large eggs, beaten
1 small bunch coriander,
roughly chopped
3 small green chillies,
finely chopped (add
more for a even more
fiery akuri)

 Akuri is a Parsi's way of showing the egg how much we love them.

On a recent trip to India, my uncle Adil decided he would cook us his famous akuri on our last night staying with him and the family. After a busy day in the office, he returned home with all the ingredients, donned his makeshift chef's hat and began making us this classic Parsi breakfast… for dinner. That night we sat out in the garden in the somewhat cool 28°C heat of Gandhidham and scoffed down helpings of the most delicious, spicy scrambled eggs with servings of soft buttered rolls. It was a suitably fitting end to a very memorable trip.

Melt the butter or ghee in a heavy-bottomed frying pan on a medium–high heat. Add the onion and stir for 3 minutes until they become translucent then add the ginger–garlic paste and lower the heat slightly, frying for a further 2 minutes until mellow notes of caramelisation hit the nose.

Stir in the chopped tomato, turmeric, cumin–coriander powder and salt, and once the tomato begins to bubble and stew (this will take 3 minutes or so) add in the beaten egg.

Use a spatula to drag the liquid egg through the pan, back and forth, back and forth and in a short period of time the egg will form into delicate pieces entangled with the tomato and spice. I say drag because this action produces chunkier pieces of egg; if you are more inclined to smaller pieces of scrambled egg then a moderately paced stir is what you are after.

Once the eggs have achieved your desired texture (some like it runnier than others; I myself prefer a well-cooked akuri, allowing the tomato to add the necessary moisture) throw in the coriander and chopped chilli, folding them through the pan.

Serve your akuri immediately, making sure you have plenty of buttered soft white rolls, gently warmed through in the oven, and endless cups of hot milky tea to take you through the morning… or night.

EGGS FOR BREAKFAST

 There is a series of Parsi dishes that all end in the words per eedu, which means 'with eggs' or 'with eggs on top'. These dishes are usually intended for breakfast or lunch, as they provide good sustenance for the day's chores. Tamatar per eedu is the classic of these dishes – a spicy tomato stew with all the familiar flavours of ginger, garlic, masala and coriander. Over the following pages, I use this recipe as a base to create a few more Parsi classics.

The best thing about the dishes that follow is that, if you are organised, each one can take less than 15 minutes to make. Every one is a one-pan wonder and who doesn't love that? (Think of all that time saved washing up!)

SERVES 2

3 tablespoons vegetable oil
½ small red onion, finely chopped
2 small green chillies, chopped
1 teaspoon ginger–garlic paste (see page 43)
2 tomatoes, finely chopped
1 teaspoon dhansak masala (see page 48)
½ teaspoon sea salt and freshly cracked black pepper
4 large eggs
a small handful of coriander, leaves picked and chopped, to serve

TAMATAR PER EEDU
EGGS BAKED ON SPICY TOMATOES

Preheat the oven to 200°C/180°C fan.

Heat the oil in an ovenproof frying pan over a medium heat. When hot, add the onion, chillies, and ginger-garlic paste and cook for 2 minutes, then add the tomatoes, dhansak masala, salt and half a cup of water. Bring the mixture to the simmer and simmer for 5 minutes, or until the tomatoes have cooked down and softened. If the tomatoes have not cooked down by the time the water has evaporated, add a splash more water to help them along.

Crack the eggs, one at a time, directly onto the tomatoes, spacing them out so that you can serve one per person at the table. Place the frying pan in the oven to bake the eggs for 5 minutes, until cooked. I prefer a runny yolk, but the choice is yours.

To serve, finish with a few cracks of black pepper, a pinch of sea salt upon each egg and a scattering of chopped coriander leaves.

SERVES 2

1 recipe quantity of the tamatar per eedu
about 8–10 okra fingers
½ teaspoon fine salt

BHEEDA PER EEDU
EGGS BAKED WITH OKRA

Wash the okra and trim off the tops, then cut into pieces 1cm thick.

Follow the tamatar per eedu recipe, adding the okra in with the onions, chillies and ginger–garlic paste so that they fry alongside. Simmer the okra with the tomatoes and the extra salt for 4 minutes before cracking the eggs on top and continuing as in the tamatar per eedu method.

SALI PER EEDU
EGGS BAKED WITH FRIED POTATO STRAWS

Follow the tamatar per eedu recipe to the point where the tomatoes have simmered and collapsed, then add the sali and stir it through the tomatoes until they soften and settle flat in the pan. Crack in the eggs and continue as in the recipe for tamatar per eedu.

SERVES 2

1 recipe quantity of the tamatar per eedu
about 200g of sali (see page 113)

CHAWAL PER EEDU
EGGS BAKED ON YESTERDAY'S RICE

Follow the tamatar per eedu recipe to the point where the tomatoes have simmered and collapsed, then stir in the rice and salt and allow the rice to absorb the heat of the stew for a moment. Crack in the eggs and continue as in the original tamatar per eedu.

SERVES 2

1 recipe quantity of the tamatar per eedu
about 200g cooked basmati rice
¼ teaspoon fine salt

KANDA PAPETA PER EEDU
EGGS BAKED ON FRIED POTATOES AND ONIONS

Preheat the oven to 200°C/180°C fan.

Heat the oil in a large ovenproof frying pan over a medium heat. When hot, add the potatoes and stir them in the pan for 10 minutes, until they are evenly golden and cooked through. Using a slotted spoon, remove the potatoes from the pan, keeping as much of the oil behind as possible, and set aside.

Add the onion to the pan and cook over a medium heat for 5 minutes, or until golden. Add the ginger–garlic paste, crushed cumin seeds, and chillies, and cook for a further 1 minute.

Return the fried potatoes to the pan, along with the dhansak masala, salt and coriander, tumbling the potatoes through with the onions and coriander until everything is evenly distributed. Add 3 tablespoons of water to moisten things up.

Settle the potatoes flat in the pan and, one at a time, crack in the eggs, spacing them well apart. Place the frying pan in the oven to bake the eggs for 5 minutes, until cooked.

To serve, finish with a few grindings of black pepper, a further pinch of salt, and a scattering of chopped coriander leaves

SERVES 2

100ml vegetable oil
500g potatoes, peeled and cut into 1cm cubes (or salad potatoes, skin on and cut into cubes)
1 medium onion, thinly sliced
1 teaspoon ginger–garlic paste (see page 43)
1 teaspoon cumin seeds, lightly crushed in a pestle and mortar
3 small green chillies, finely chopped
1 teaspoon dhansak masala (see page 48)
1 teaspoon fine salt, plus extra to serve
a small handful of coriander, leaves picked and chopped, plus extra to serve
4 eggs
freshly cracked black pepper

A hen is only an egg's way of making another egg.
-- Samuel Butler

See overleaf for images.

EDA NU PORO
PARSI OMELETTE

**SERVES 1 HUNGRY
SOUL**

2 tablespoons ghee or
vegetable oil

½ small red onion,
finely diced

2 teaspoons ginger–garlic
paste (see page 43)

1 small green chilli,
thinly sliced

a pinch of salt

1 teaspoon dhansak
masala (see page 48)

½ teaspoon garam masala
(see page 46)

¼ teaspoon ground
turmeric

3 large eggs, beaten with
a pinch of salt

2 tablespoons grated
cheese (whatever you
may have lurking in the
back of your fridge)

a small handful of
coriander, leaves picked
and chopped, plus extra
to serve

 Continuing the love affair with the egg, here is a typical Parsi café-style omelette, based on my favourite breakfast in Mumbai at Café Colony in the Parsi colony at Dadar. A well-seasoned, cast-iron or non-stick frying pan is essential for making the perfect omelette, so it comes away from the pan in one piece.

Heat the ghee or oil in a heavy-based frying pan over a medium heat. When hot, add the onion, along with the ginger–garlic paste, chilli and salt. Allow to sizzle for 2–3 minutes, until the onion begins to brown. Add both the masalas and the turmeric and stir together for another 30 seconds to allow the spices to release their flavour.

Pour in the eggs and quickly mix all the ingredients together in the pan. Gently stir the eggs with a spatula, bringing the egg mixture from the bottom of the pan to the top, and allowing the runny egg from the top to seep to the bottom. Once that egg has lightly set, agitate again. Continue this process for a further 1 minute, until you have a semi-set, custard-like wobble on the top of the mixture, then sprinkle the cheese and the coriander over the top.

Now it's time to flip your omelette – you must let the omelette know you are in control and that you mean business. Have a plate ready to the side. Firmly hold the frying-pan handle and give the pan some firm nudges, jiggles and taps to loosen the omelette from the bottom. Then, using a spatula, fold the omelette over on itself, encasing the cheese and coriander (I bring 3 o'clock over to 9 o'clock so that the pan handle is not in the way when I turn the omelette). Bring the pan to the plate and invert the pan over the plate, turning out the omelette in one quick and confident motion.

To serve, squeeze a healthy wedge of lemon over the top and add a sprinkle more coriander and a few slices of raw red onion. Serve hot buttered rotli (see page 114) or toast on the side.

No wonder, child we prize the hen
whose egg is mightier than the pen.
                                    -- Oliver Herford

MASALA OATS

Masala oats is my go-to staff breakfast during the manic weekends at work. After a frantic morning shift of slinging out hot breakfasts to the crowds of East London, we find a welcome pause to sit down to a sustaining bowl of hot, spicy, savoury oats – our own energising breakfast to ready the team for the forthcoming lunchtime onslaught.

Melt the ghee or butter in a sturdy-bottomed pot over a low heat. When hot, add the onion, celery and carrot and cook for about 10 minutes, until the onions are translucent and the vegetables have softened, but none have taken on any colour.

Add the tomato, chillies, garam masala and salt. Season with a few healthy grinds of black pepper and stir everything together. Increase the heat to medium and cook for 3 minutes, until the tomatoes begin to break down.

Add the oats, turmeric, hing and stock or water. Bring the mixture back to a simmer, stirring continuously, for about 2–4 minutes, until the oats cook and thicken – you want the consistency of a well-formed but loose porridge, as this is the essence of what you're creating.

Place the hot masala oats in serving bowls and top each with a spoonful of tangy onions (see page 161) and a sprinkling of chopped parsley.

SERVES 4

100g ghee or unsalted butter
1 small red onion, finely diced
1 celery stick, finely diced
1 carrot, peeled and finely diced
1 large tomato, finely chopped
2 small green chillies, finely chopped
1 tablespoon garam masala (see page 46)
1 teaspoon salt
100g rolled oats or porridge oats
¼ teaspoon ground turmeric
a pinch of hing (asafoetida)
500ml chicken stock or water
4 tablespoons tangy onions (see page 161)
a small handful of well-chopped curly-leaf parsley
freshly cracked black pepper

S N A C K S

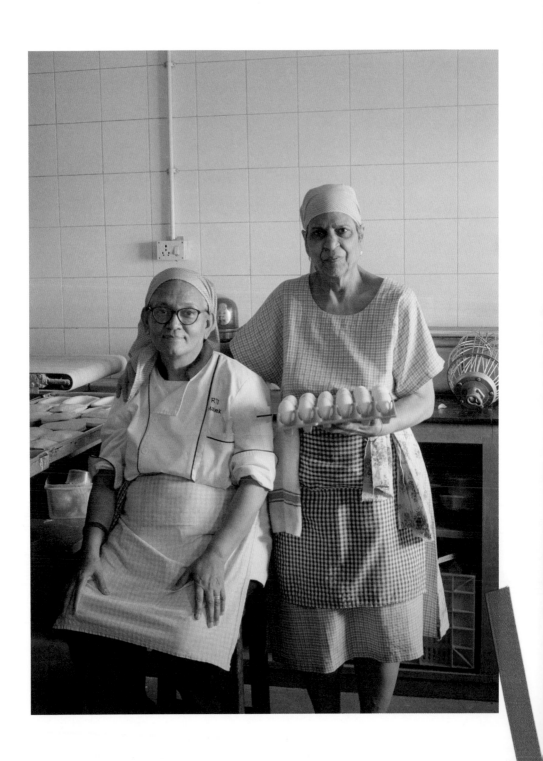

From left to right: Maneck
Aunty and Nergish Aunty

SIR RATAN TATA INSTITUTE
PRODUCTION SLIP

No. **2860**   Date 3/Aprz 22

FAROKH TALATI   Stall I

Quantity	Particulars	Rate Rs. P.	Amount Rs. P.
100	(S) Dal ni Pori		135 Each
100	Sev + Dahi		180 Each
100	BHAKRA		110 Each
50	Sas ni Macchi		400 Each
100	Chicken Farcha		155 Each
50	Dhan Dar Prawn PATIO		350 Each
100	Lagan nu Custard.		50 Each
50	Sariya (Pkt)		40 Each
50	lagan nu achaar		175 Each
100	Rotli's		6/- Each
100	Raspberry Soda.		20/- Each
5 kg	2 Tire Wedding Cake Dutch TRUFFLE		

Receiver's Signature _____   Signature _____

PATREL
STUFFED AND FRIED TARO LEAVES

MAKES ABOUT 12

290ml vegetable oil,
 divided:
  30ml (2 tablespoons)
   for Part One
  200ml for frying the
   patrel slices
  60ml (4 tablespoons)
   for Part Four
6 large taro leaves or
 6 large outer leaves of
 1 large savoy cabbage
 (if using cabbage leaves,
 blanch in boiling water
 for 1 minute to soften
 slightly)
juice of 1 lemon
salt

PART ONE – THE SPICES
3 dried Kashmiri chillies
3 small green chillies
1 tablespoon ginger–garlic
 paste (see page 43) (or
 3 garlic cloves and 1cm
 fresh ginger)
½ teaspoon cumin seeds
¼ teaspoon ground
 turmeric
1½ teaspoons salt

**PART TWO – THE SWEET
 AND THE SOUR**
1 small, overripe banana
 (the mushier the better)
30g jaggery (use caster
 sugar, if necessary)
1 tablespoon tamarind
 paste
juice of 1 lemon

**PART THREE – THE
 THICKENER**
90g chickpea flour
1 heaped tablespoon
 plain flour
1 heaped tablespoon
 cornflour

A spicy, deep-fried snack of taro leaves, spread with a spicy chickpea paste, rolled, steamed and fried, patrel is one of those dishes that Parsis adopted from the Gujarati community. Making patrel is a labour of love, so I save them for get-togethers where the delight of family and friends makes the hard work worth it.

Large, dark green and about the size of a dinner plate, fresh taro leaves are usually available in Asian vegetable stores, either in rolls or packs. More readily available savoy cabbage leaves make a good alternative – the flavour of the crispy, fried cabbage is deliciously moreish. If using cabbage (I do recommend you give it a try), find a cabbage with big outer leaves.

Patrel is a joy to eat with something to dip it in: try herby mayonnaise, mango pickle mayo, tamarind ketchup (see pages 54, 55 and 64) or your favourite chilli sauce.

Blitz all the ingredients for Part One together in a food processor for 30 seconds or until the garlic, ginger and chilli have all broken down to a coarse paste.

Place a large frying pan over a low heat and add 2 tablespoons of the vegetable oil. When hot, add the paste and fry for 3 minutes, until fragrant. Remove from the heat and return the paste to the processor.

Add all the Part Two ingredients to the processor with 120ml of water and blitz for 30 seconds, until the banana has become paste-like.

Mix all the flours in Part Three together. One spoonful at a time, add the flour mixture to the paste in the processor, blitzing between each addition, until you have added all the flour and the paste is somewhat thick and smooth.

Using a knife, trim the centre stalk away from each taro leaf (if you're using cabbage leaves, cut a V-shaped notch in the bottom of the centre stalk). Give the taro leaves a gentle rinse in cold water and leave to drip dry for 5 minutes (you do not need to wash the cabbage leaves).

Place a whole leaf front side down on a clean work surface or chopping board. Place ½ tablespoon of the paste on the leaf and, using your fingers or the back of a spoon, spread it all the way across the surface of the leaf. Spread the paste thinly enough that you can see the green of the leaf through it (think jam on toast). If you're using cabbage leaves, start with the biggest leaf, then alternate between small ones and big ones. (Depending on the size of your smaller leaves, you may need to rip a few to cover the full surface of the leaf before in the next step.)

Place another leaf face down on top of the first leaf and repeat the process. Do this until you have a stack of 6 taro or cabbage leaves with paste in between (the final leaf has just a smear of paste on top). If using cabbage, I find that you can make two stacks of six leaves, as cabbage leaves are much smaller than taro.

Fold in the sides of the taro-leaf stack by 2cm, then roll from the ends of the leaves to the tops, until you have a cigar shape. Using butcher's string, tie the roll at each end to hold it together. (If using cabbage, tightly roll the stack into a cigar and tie it together in the centre with string.)

Using a bamboo steamer (or saucepan with a steamer insert), steam the rolls for 20 minutes, until soft and giving when pressed. Allow the cooked rolls to cool, then place them on a tray and refrigerate for 2 hours to firm up. While they are still hot, they will flatten under their own weight – once they are firm, you can reshape them with a gentle press to make them cylindrical again. Another technique to help them keep their shape and tightness is, once they have slightly cooled, to wrap them tightly in cling film like a sausage.

Once chilled and reshaped, remove the cling film (if you used it) and the string. Cut each roll into 1cm-thick slices.

Pour the 200ml of vegetable oil into a large frying pan or wok and heat it to 170°C (or until a cube of day-old bread sizzles and turns golden within 60 seconds). A few pieces at a time, fry the patrel for 4 minutes, turning them over in the oil half way through the cooking time, until golden brown. Keep an eye on them, especially the cabbage ones, as they can go from golden brown to burnt in not much time. Set aside on kitchen paper to get rid of excess frying oil while you fry the next batch.

Make the garnish. Heat the 60ml of vegetable oil in a frying pan over a medium heat. (If you're eating your patrel straight after frying them, you can use 60ml of the same frying oil, although I suggest straining it and giving the pan a wipe first.) Add the shallot and garlic and fry for about 2–3 minutes, until they turn golden, almost crispy. Turn the heat down to its lowest setting and add the sesame seeds and curry leaves. Allow the curry leaves a moment to crackle and splutter, then turn the heat off.

Arrange the fried patrel on a platter and give a light sprinkle of salt over the top, sprinkle generously with lemon juice and finally spoon the crispy garnish over each piece. Once steamed, the patrel will keep in the fridge for a week; once fried, eat within a day or so.

PART FOUR – THE GARNISH
1 shallot, halved and very finely sliced
2 garlic cloves, very finely sliced
1½ teaspoons sesame seeds (either black or white are fine, or use a mix if you wish)
12 fresh curry leaves (give or take)

See overleaf for images.

For those who venture through this recipe and come out the other end to read this, I extend a silent nod – a mutual understanding of the knowledge we now have to create such delicious snackery.

FAR FAR / SARIA
A COLOURFUL, CRISPY SNACK

Walking through the aisles of an Asian supermarket, your eyes scan the shelves and are drawn to packets of mysterious foods with unfamiliar names. Powders, spices, seeds and other ingredients all with obscure shapes and colours. The curious shopper takes a moment to ponder buying and experimenting: have you discovered a game-changing ingredient or a hidden flavour for guests to talk about at the next dinner party? But then culinary cowardice creeps in. You have no idea how to even begin cooking with it and you concede that this will be one of those packets you find unopened in the back of the cupboard when you next spring clean. The packet goes back on the shelf. Far far is one of these hidden gems.

Available in many different shapes and colours, and traditionally made from potato or tapioca flour, these little crispy snacks are a staple of Parsi weddings, usually served alongside the main meal and a very helpful vehicle for scooping up the dal or chicken gravy for those who like to eat without cutlery. A big bowl on the table at the start of a dinner party is just the thing to get tongues wagging and appetites going. Far far are flavourless so you can have as much expression as you like with the seasoning; salt and pepper goes a long way but my personal favourite is to sprinkle chaat masala over them for a salty, tangy, slightly sulphurous mouthwatering taste.

MAKES ENOUGH TO FILL 1 LARGE BOWL

500ml vegetable oil, for frying
250g packet of far far
salt and freshly cracked black pepper or chaat masala

Heat the oil in a sturdy-bottomed pot over a medium heat until the temperature reaches 180°C on a cooking thermometer. Alternatively, to test the oil temperature, I drop a piece of far far into the oil as it is heating up – when the oil is hot enough, the far far will puff up, almost tripling in size.

When the oil is ready throw in a small handful of your far far. Remember: these will expand vastly, so do not be tempted to cook too many at one time, as they'll just overflow from the pot (or not cook properly).

Within a few seconds the far far will expand and puff – use a slotted spoon to move them around the oil for 30–40 seconds so they all puff evenly, then use your spoon to scoop them out, allowing any excess oil to drip back into the pot as you do so. Set aside the cooked far far to drain on kitchen paper, while you cook the remainder.

Place the far far in a bowl large enough to toss them around as you sprinkle in the seasoning. For a simple seasoning, a sprinkle of salt and black pepper will do; for the more authentic flavour of Indian street snacks, season them with a light sprinkle of store-bought chaat masala.

PAPETA NE TARKARI NA PATTICE
POTATO AND VEGETABLE CUTLETS

MAKES 6

600g potatoes, peeled
    and cut into equal-sized
    chunks (about 4cm)
2 tablespoons ghee or
    vegetable oil
4 small green chillies,
    finely chopped
1 teaspoon ginger–garlic
    paste (see page 43)
1 small onion, finely diced
1 teaspoon garam masala
    (see page 46)
60g green beans, chopped
    into very small pieces
60g frozen peas (or fresh
    peas, if you have them)
1 carrot, peeled and
    finely diced
a small handful of
    coriander, leaves picked
    and chopped
1½ teaspoons salt
½ teaspoon freshly
    cracked black pepper
6 tablespoons patyo sauce
    (see page 197, or any
    tomato sauce you have
    available)

FOR COATING AND
    FRYING
500ml vegetable oil, for
    frying
250g semolina (I prefer
    coarse semolina for
    texture)
3 eggs, beaten

 Taking a side step away from Parsi's fondness for meat, these vegetable pattice are a firm party favourite, full of spice, texture and flavour. Do not feel bound to having to use peas, green beans or carrot. Similar vegetables in different seasons can provide an exciting change. Maybe small diced sweet potato instead of carrot? Do you have some sweetcorn lurking in the back of the freezer? If green beans are not in season why not play around with some capsicums for a different crunch and addition of colour. Have fun improvising.

Bring a pan of well-salted water to the boil, then add the potatoes and boil for about 10–12 minutes, until tender to the point of a knife. Drain the potatoes in a colander, then spread them out on a baking tray and leave them to steam dry for 5 minutes (the less moisture there is in the potato, the easier it will be to work with). Then tip the potato back into the pan and mash until smooth.

Heat the 2 tablespoons of ghee or vegetable oil in a frying pan over a medium heat. Add the chillies, ginger–garlic paste and onion and fry for 8 minutes, until the onion has browned. Turn off the heat and stir in the garam masala.

Bring another pan of salted water to the boil and add the beans, peas and carrot. Boil for 1 minute, then drain and cool.

Tip the mashed potato into a large bowl with the chilli and onion mixture, cooked vegetables, chopped coriander and salt and pepper. Mix to combine, then divide the mixture into 6 equal-sized balls.

Place a thumb into each ball and make a cup shape big enough to place a tablespoonful of the patyo sauce inside. Form the sides of the cup over and around the sauce, closing and sealing the sauce inside. Ever so gently flatten the ball to form a burger shape, taking care not to squish out the filling.

Heat the 500ml of vegetable oil in a wok or frying pan to 180°C. If you do not have a thermometer you can drop a small piece of bread into the oil when it begins to fry and turn golden brown, the oil is ready.

While the oil is heating up, tip the semolina on to a plate and dip each cutlet into it, ensuring an even coating all over. Then dip the cutlets into the beaten egg, again ensuring the egg fully coats each one.

Fry the cutlets two at a time for 4 minutes per batch, turning half way through the cooking time, until they are golden brown on the outside and piping hot inside.

Serve with yoghurt stirred through with a little coconut and coriander chutney or mango pickle mayonnaise.

See overleaf, images 1–5.

EEDA CHUTNEY NA PATTICE
POTATO, EGG AND CHUTNEY CUTLETS

 This is my favourite in the cutlet saga: boiled egg coated in tangy coconut and coriander chutney, surrounded by spicy mashed potato.

MAKES 6

Bring a pan of well-salted water to the boil, then add the potatoes and boil for about 10–12 minutes, until tender to the point of a knife. Drain them in a colander, then spread them out on a baking tray and leave them to steam dry for 5 minutes (the less moisture there is in the potato, the easier it will be to work with). Then tip the potato back into the pan and mash until smooth.

Heat the 2 tablespoons of ghee or vegetable oil in a frying pan over a low-to-medium heat. Add the chillies, ginger–garlic paste and onion and fry for 8 minutes, until the onion has browned. Remove from the heat and stir in the garam masala to absorb the last of the heat.

Tip the mashed potato into a large bowl with the chilli and onion mixture and the salt and pepper. Mix to evenly combine, then divide the mixture into 6 equal-sized balls.

Place 1 potato ball on to a piece of cling film measuring about 20cm square. Use your fingers to spread the potato out into a disc about 10cm in diameter and about 5mm thick. Spread 1 tablespoon of coconut chutney over the centre of the potato disc and top with half an egg. Bring the corners of the cling film together to close the potato around the egg – the cling film will allow you to mould and press the potato casing without getting your hands messy.

Lightly press the potato ball to flatten it slightly and unwrap it from the cling film. Repeat for the remaining potato balls.

Heat the 500ml of vegetable oil in a wok or frying pan until it reaches 180°C on a cooking thermometer. If you do not have a thermometer you can drop a small piece of bread in the oil; when it begins to fry and turn golden brown you will know that the oil is ready.

While the oil is heating up, tip the semolina on to a plate and dip each cutlet into it, ensuring an even coating all over. Then dip the cutlets into the beaten egg, again ensuring the egg fully coats each one.

Fry the cutlets one by one for 4 minutes, turning half way through the cooking time, until they are golden brown on the outside and piping hot inside.

600g potatoes (such as Maris Piper – a good mashable potato), peeled and roughly diced
2 tablespoons ghee or vegetable oil
2 small green chillies, finely chopped
1 teaspoon ginger–garlic paste (see page 43)
1 small white onion, finely chopped
1 teaspoon garam masala (see page 46)
1½ teaspoons salt
½ teaspoon cracked black pepper
6 tablespoons coconut and coriander chutney (see page 65)
3 eggs boiled for 8 minutes, peeled and halved lengthways

FOR COATING AND FRYING
500ml vegetable oil, for frying
200g semolina (I prefer coarse semolina for texture)
3 eggs, beaten

See overleaf, images i–iv.

People are either born hosts or born guests.
-- Max Beerbohm

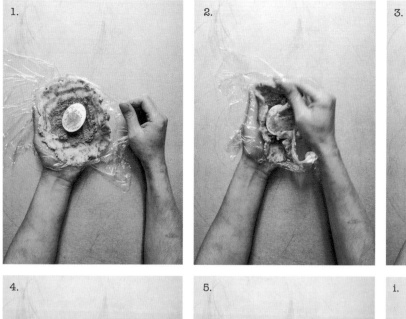

KHEEMA PATTICE
MINCED LAMB AND POTATO CUTLETS

MAKES 6

600g potatoes (such as Maris Piper – a good mashable potato), peeled and roughly diced

2 tablespoons ghee or vegetable oil

4 small green chillies, finely chopped

1 teaspoon ginger–garlic paste (see page 43)

1 small onion, finely chopped

1 teaspoon garam masala (see page 46)

1½ teaspoons salt

½ teaspoon freshly cracked black pepper

6 tablespoons kheema (see page 216)

500ml vegetable oil, for frying

250g semolina (I prefer coarse semolina f or texture)

3 eggs, beaten

 For me this is the quintessential Parsi cutlet; it's the snack that all aunties will cook when you are coming over, and I was fortunate enough to have aunties that could cook delicious pattice. My aunties on my dad's side of the family came to London from Kenya in the early 80s. There were four sisters and a brother living together, and boy could they cook. I have fond memories of going to visit them as a child, and the minute I ran in the door, the smell of frying kheema pattice, samosas and patrel would fill the nose and excite the stomach. My job was to turn the pattice in the frying pan, and in my 8-year-old head I thought, 'well if I'm cooking them all, I should be allowed to eat them all!', but much to my disappointment this was not the case.

Bring a pan of well-salted water to the boil, then add the potatoes and boil for about 10–12 minutes, until tender to the point of a knife. Drain them in a colander, then spread them out on a baking tray and leave them to steam dry for 5 minutes (the less moisture there is in the potato, the easier it will be to work with). Then tip the potato back into the pan and mash until smooth.

Heat the 2 tablespoons of ghee or vegetable oil in a frying pan over a medium heat. Add the chillies, ginger–garlic paste and onion and fry for 8 minutes, until the onion has browned. Remove from the heat and stir in the garam masala to absorb the residual heat.

Tip the mashed potato into a large bowl with the chilli and onion mixture and the salt and pepper. Mix to evenly combine and divide the mixture into 6 equal-sized balls.

Place a thumb into each ball and make a cup shape big enough to place a tablespoon of the kheema inside. Form the sides of the cup over and around the mince, closing and sealing everything inside. Very gently flatten the ball to form a burger shape. Repeat for the remaining balls. (You can use the cling-film technique on page 107 if you don't want to get your hands messy.)

Heat the 500ml of vegetable oil in a wok or frying pan until it reaches 180°C on a cooking thermometer. If you do not have a thermometer you can drop a small piece of bread in the oil; when it begins to fry and turn golden brown you will know that the oil is ready.

While the oil is heating up, tip the semolina on to a plate and dip each cutlet into it, ensuring an even coating all over. Then dip the cutlets into the beaten egg, again ensuring the egg fully coats each one.

Fry the cutlets one by one for 4 minutes, turning half way through the cooking time, until they are golden brown on the outside and piping hot inside.

ROASTING PAPAD

There is more than one way to skin a cat, and so too there is more than one way to cook a papad. Roasting papad on an open flame is a very satisfying experience – watch the disc bubble, crisp and darken under the heat, singeing around the edges to add that roasted flavour. Try this method next time you have your barbecue lit.

Place the papad on a medium–low flame, leaving an overhang closest to you so that you have something to hold and use to turn. When the papad begins to blister and darken, flip it over and place the flame on a different part of the disc.

When that portion chars, turn it over again, again aiming the flame on an uncharred portion of the papad. Repeat the process until you have a papad that is crispy, blistered and slightly charred. The intensity of the flame dictates the rhythm of the turns. So play around with the heat until you find the right timing.

SALI
CRISPY POTATO STRAWS

 These thin, crispy potato sticks are a staple at the Parsi table and bring a savoury crunch to many dishes, as well as being quite moreish just on their own... as my mother will tell you! One large potato will make enough sali to garnish the meals of 6 people.

SERVES 6 AS A GARNISH

1 large potato, peeled
500ml vegetable oil,
    for frying
salt

If you have a mandolin, this will be very useful; if not, a sharp kitchen knife will do just as well. Slice the potato into slices about as thick as a 2-pence coin – don't worry too much if a few slices veer off and become too thin or thick. Layer a few slices neatly on top of each other and slice the stack into matchsticks, also as thick as a 2-pence coin. For those with limited knife skills, use a fine cheese grater to shred your potato for similar – if more rustic – results.

Place your potato sticks in a colander or sieve and rinse them under cold water, giving them a good tickle with your fingers. You want to rinse as much starchiness off the surface as you can. After rinsing, press as much moisture out of the potatoes as possible and lay them on a tea towel to dry.

Heat the oil in a medium pan to 180°C. If you don't have a cooking thermometer, drop a small piece of bread into the pan – the oil is ready to use when the piece of bread begins to fry and go golden.

When the oil is ready, add a small handful of the potato sticks into the pan. Use a fork to separate them from each other, so that they fry evenly. Keep the potato sticks moving for about 3 minutes, until they become golden brown. Use a slotted spoon to remove the cooked sticks from the oil and set them aside to drain on kitchen paper. Repeat, in batches, until all the potato is cooked.

Leave to cool, then season with proud sprinkles of salt and store them in an airtight container. Best kept in the cupboard, the sali will last a week before it starts to lose its crunch.

Potatoes rule the home
and so the world.
    –– Irish proverb

ROTLI

about 200g wholemeal
   chapatti flour, plus 100g
   for dredging
1 teaspoon salt
1 tablespoon ghee or
   butter, softened, plus
   100g, melted, for
   brushing

*My mother reminisces about growing up in Gujarat and my
grandad's daily trip to the market to buy the whole wheat for
rotlis. Once he had the wheat, he would take it to the mill man,
who would turn it into flour. My grandad would return home
with freshly milled flour, still warm to the touch and with its
distinctive aroma. This process is still commonplace in many
parts of India and is said to be the key to the softest rotlis.*

*Of course, for you and me, and as lovely as this anecdote is,
milling your own flour is not an option. I suggest, though, you
do go out of your way to find a store that stocks chapatti flour,
usually coarsely ground wholemeal flour and available in
Asian supermarkets.*

Measure 180ml of water into a small saucepan and bring it to the boil.

Place the 200g of flour, the salt and the tablespoon of softened ghee
or butter in a bowl large enough that you can knead inside it. Stir all
the ingredients together. Make a well in the centre of the mixture and
gradually start pouring in the hot water, using a spoon to stir it in.

Once you have added all the water, use your hands to fully combine the
flour and water and knead it together to form a dough. My kneading
technique is to form a fist, push down on the dough, then push forward,
bring it together and repeat this action for 5 minutes, until the dough
is starting to form and hold its shape. If you feel the dough is too wet
and sticking to your fingers and the bowl too much, dust a little extra
flour you have to hand over both the dough and your fingers and work
it in. Cover the bowl with a cloth or lid and allow the dough to rest for 15
minutes.

Divide the dough into 10 equal pieces and, one by one, roll each between
your palms into a tight ball with no cracks. Flatten each ball into a disc
and dredge it in the extra flour.

On a well-floured surface, use a rolling pin to roll out the discs. One by
one, start at the centre and push out, turn the disc through 45 degrees
and roll out from the middle again. Repeat this a few times, then flip the
rotli over and repeat, until you have a flat, round rotli about 15–18cm in
diameter and the thickness of a penny.

Heat a frying pan or skillet, large enough to fit a single rotli, over a
medium–high heat. When hot, but not scorching, brush a light layer of
melted ghee or butter around the pan and add a rotli, using your fingers
to gently twist the rotli clockwise every 10 seconds for 30 seconds, until it
is hot and blistered. Flip over the rotli and repeat for the other side, until
blistered. Flip the rotli back to the first side and give it a final 30 seconds
in the pan to cook through. You'll need to keep adjusting the heat under
the pan to keep the sweet spot – too hot and the rotli will become too dry

and crisp; too low and it will not cook enough. The timings are not set in stone – practise to find how your hob and your pan work with the rotli and to find your rhythm for turning them over. Finally, if you're using a gas flame, place the cooked rotli directly on the flame for 10 seconds for it to puff up with steam. Repeat on the opposite side.

As each rotli comes off the pan, brush one side with the melted ghee or butter for extra flavour and keep covered with a cloth until all the rotlis are cooked. Serve fresh and warm – but if you have any left over, you can keep them in an airtight container for about 2–3 days. You can reheat your rotlis by warming them through in a dry frying pan, or by wrapping them in foil and placing them in a hot oven for 5 minutes.

KOLMI NA KAVAB
PRAWN KEBAB

MAKES 12

FOR THE KEBAB
2 teaspoons salt
500g potato, peeled and
cut into 2cm chunks
500g raw prawns, peeled
and deveined
2 tablespoons masala
paste (see page 44)
50g frozen peas
1 large carrot, peeled and
diced small
a small handful of
coriander, leaves picked
and chopped
1 teaspoon cumin seeds,
lightly crushed

FOR COATING AND
FRYING
500ml vegetable oil
200g coarse semolina or
dried fine breadcrumbs
4 eggs, beaten

 Although I have specified raw prawns in this recipe as they will give you the best flavour and soft texture, it is not at all unheard of to use cooked, frozen prawns. Just ensure you use the same weight and that they are well defrosted and patted dry from any water before you use them.

Bring a pan of water to the boil, add 1 teaspoon of the salt and the potatoes. Boil for about 10 minutes, until the potatoes are cooked through and tender. Drain in a colander and tip them on to a tray to cool and steam off.

Place the prawns and the masala paste in a food processor and give them a few pulses – you want to chop the prawns up and mix them with the masala paste, but you don't want to turn it into a homogeneous, smooth paste; you want some coarseness in there, for texture.

Tip the potatoes, prawn mixture, a teaspoon of salt and all the remaining kebab ingredients in a large bowl and, using your hands or a large spoon, mix everything together until you have a uniform mixture. Set aside while you heat the oil for frying.

Pour the vegetable oil into a sturdy-bottomed pot or sturdy frying pan and heat it to 180°C (or until a small piece of bread dropped into the oil sizzles and turns golden within 60 seconds). At this point, you know your oil is ready to cook with. Keep the pan over low–medium heat.

Divide your kebab mixture into 12 equally sized balls. Roll the balls in the semolina or breadcrumbs until fully coated, then slightly flatten each ball into a disk then the beaten egg. A few at a time, carefully place the balls in the hot oil, using a slotted spoon to move and turn the kebabs, cooking for 4–5 minutes, until golden all over and piping hot through the middle. Set each batch aside to drain on kitchen paper while you cook the remainder.

Serve your kebabs hot from the fryer with lime wedges for squeezing over and a pot of mango pickle mayonnaise (see page 55) for dipping.

The only thing that can be said
against eating is that it takes
away one's appetite.
-- Frank Schloesser

BANDRA-STYLE SWEETCORN

As the sun lowers on the beaches of Mumbai, faint glows emanate across the promenade from tiny coal fires, stoked by hand-cranked fans that spew bright embers on to the sand. Carts loaded with sweetcorn sit alongside the fires – you go and peruse the corn, stripping back the husk to inspect the plump, golden kernels.

Once you have chosen your cob, the makka wala will strip away its husk and throw the bare corn into the coals. When it emerges again it is charred and ready for a thorough rub down with lemon dipped in salt and chilli powder. The popping sounds and the smell of the blistering kernels, along with the heat of the coals, are a prelude to the joy of biting into the juicy, sweet, salty, spicy corn.

For me, sweetcorn is the best part of a summer barbecue at home. Once the coals have settled down and are glowing hot, place the raw corn on to the coals, turning the cobs from time to time to allow them to char and blister. After about 3–4 minutes of turning on hot coals, they should be ready to eat.

To season the corn, in a small bowl mix 1 teaspoon of salt and ½ teaspoon of chilli powder (mild or hot, as you like). Halve a lemon and dip it, cut side down into the chilli-salt. Rub and squeeze the lemon up and down the cob, seasoning the kernels as you go.

This is a delicious side to any meal or a snack while you are waiting for your food to cook on the barbecue. The stripped kernels also make for a wonderful salad ingredient (see page 135).

If you have a gas hob at home, you can char your corn by placing it over a medium–high flame, diligently turning the corn as it colours and blisters.

SALADS

KACHUBER

**SERVES 6 AS A
SMALL PLATE**

1 large red onion, halved
   and very finely sliced
   (with a mandolin if you
   have one)
½ cucumber, sliced
   lengthways into eighths
   and finely chopped
a small handful of
   chopped mint and
   coriander leaves
2 small green chillies,
   thinly sliced into rounds
1 teaspoon cumin
   seeds, crushed (use
   a pestle and mortar,
   or roughly chop on a
   chopping board)
1 tablespoon apple cider
   vinegar
juice of 1 lemon
1 large ripe tomato (about
   the same size as your
   onion), finely chopped
sea salt flakes and freshly
   cracked black pepper

 This is what I refer to as a pounded salad. One where you place all the ingredients in a bowl and get to work with your hands, lightly crushing and massaging the ingredients until they release all their juices, allowing them to mingle together to create a tangy, herby salad. You'll likely see a salad like this on the dinner table at any of my Parsi dinners – its fresh acidity cuts through spice, making it the perfect accompaniment to fiery dishes.

Place the onion, cucumber, herbs, chillies, cumin seeds, vinegar and lemon juice in a bowl and season with a large pinch of sea salt and a few cracks of black pepper.

Get your hands into the bowl and start squishing the onions and cucumber together with the herbs and seasoning – you're not looking to obliterate the onions, only lightly bruise them to release their juices.

Add the tomato, and with a much more gentle touch, mix it through. You want the tomato pieces to hold their shape and be a part of the salad. Season to taste with more salt and black pepper. Enjoy!

Good, sound cooking, even the simplest,
makes a contented home.

-- Auguste Escoffier

SPROUTING LENTIL SALAD

For Zoroastrians and many other cultures, the New Year falls on the spring equinox, or Nowruz. At home during Nowruz, lentils and seeds are washed, soaked and left to sprout over a few days – the emerging shoots symbolising the coming of spring.

This salad celebrates this tradition and ushers in the start of spring – although of course you can eat it at any time of the year.

I enjoy the salad stripped back, just as it is, but you can add your own creativity to it with leaves, chopped vegetables, and herbs, if you wish. You'll need to do some forward-planning if you're intending to make it for a specific meal, as it takes a few days for the lentils and seeds to sprout. Once sprouted, they will keep in an airtight container in the fridge for 2–3 days.

SERVES 2

20g fenugreek seeds
20g mung beans
20g masoor dal
100ml lemon and cumin
    dressing (see page 136)
sea salt flakes and freshly
    cracked black pepper
20g ripped flat leaf parsley

First, sprout your pulses. Rinse the fenugreek seeds, mung beans and masoor dal together in a sieve for 1 minute to rinse off any surface dust.

Tip them into in a large bowl and fully submerge them in plenty of fresh, cold water. Leave the pulses to soak at room temperature for 8–10 hours or overnight (I find soaking overnight works best, as then the next morning, you can carry on with the next step).

Drain the pulses and give them another rinse, then lay them in a layer on a tray. Soak a clean tea towel in cold water and wring out the excess – you want the towel to be damp, not soaking. Place this over the pulses.

Place the covered pulses somewhere cool to moderately warm – sprouting happens best at between 15°C and 20°C. My mum always used to leave the seeds by the kitchen window during summer with excellent results.

At the end of the day, rinse the pulses, drain them well and return them to the tray. Moisten the towel again and place it over the top. (The towel must stay moist throughout this whole process, so do keep checking that it hasn't dried out.)

After the first 24 hours you will notice small shoots starting to emerge from the pulses. After day two, these will be much more prominent, and by the end of day three you will be ready to harvest your crop. If you like, you can let the pulses sprout for another day or two, after which they will start to shoot small leaves.

Gather up your sprouts and place them in a bowl with the lemon dressing and parsley, a few healthy pinches of salt and a few cracks of black pepper. Toss the sprouts through the dressing until fully coated. Then serve.

PEA, FENNEL AND PANEER SALAD

SERVES 6–8

400g fresh podded peas

2 fennel bulbs, thinly shaved on a mandolin

a generous handful of rocket or baby spinach leaves

a handful of mint, leaves picked and torn

100ml lemon and cumin dressing (see page 136)

1 recipe quantity of paneer (see page 75)

sea salt flakes and freshly cracked black pepper

 This salad summons the start of summer and the arrival of an abundance of summer vegetables and fruits. Early on in the season, the peas are smaller, sweeter, and perfect for eating raw. Fennel planted in early spring yields an early summer harvest – just in time for the peas. The unctuous, freshly made curds bring this salad together with their clean, fresh flavour.

Tip all the ingredients except the dressing and paneer in a bowl and season with salt and pepper. Toss together to mix and then mix through the lemon and cumin dressing to taste (reserve a little dressing for the end). Taste to check the seasoning and when you're happy, crumble in two thirds of the paneer and give the salad one final toss.

Transfer your salad to its final serving dish and garnish with the remaining paneer and a final lick of dressing over the top.

It's better to pay the cook than the doctor.

-- Anon

MOOLI, CUCUMBER AND POMEGRANATE SALAD

 Mooli, or mooro as it is known in Gujarati, is a member of the radish family. The long, white root has a fresh, earthy flavour and is popular in east Asian cooking. I love this salad because everything about it is fresh, crunchy and juicy. The fresh herbs provide a delicious contrast against the freshness of the mooli and cucumber, and the pomegranate brings a sweet pop.

Moolis come in all sizes – if yours is particularly large, slice just enough to match the length of your cucumber. Then slice both the mooli and cucumber into wafer-thin slices using either a mandolin or a sharp kitchen knife.

Pick your mint leaves and give them a few good rips. Pick your tarragon and dill, keeping the leaves whole.

Cut your pomegranate in half and hold it over a bowl. Using the back of a wooden spoon, give the skin side a few short, sharp taps – the seeds will fall out pristinely.

In a large enough bowl, mix your mooli, cucumber, herbs, turmeric and half the pomegranate seeds together with a few glugs of dressing, a healthy pinch of salt and a few cracks of black pepper. Give everything a good toss to coat it all in the dressing, adding more if you feel the salad is running the risk of being dry.

Place the salad on a large platter and top it with a few licks of pomegranate molasses. Scatter over the remaining pomegranate seeds to finish.

SERVES 6–8

1 mooli (about 25cm long)
1 cucumber
a bunch of mint
½ bunch of tarragon
½ bunch of dill
1 pomegranate
2–3 teaspoons turmeric pickle (see page 57)
200ml lemon and cumin dressing (see page 136)
pomegranate molasses, for finishing
sea salt flakes and freshly cracked black pepper

There was an old man from Fife
Who was greatly disgusted with life
They sang him a ballad
And fed him with salad
Which cured that old person from Fife.
-- Edward Lear

GREEN BEAN, MINT AND RED ONION SALAD

SERVES 6

2 teaspoons fine salt
600g green beans
1 large red onion, sliced
as thinly as possible
(a mandolin will come
in handy here)
100ml lemon and cumin
dressing (see page 136),
plus extra to taste and
to serve
1 small bunch of mint
½ small bunch of flat-leaf
parsley
½ small bunch of
coriander
½ small bunch of dill
1 recipe quantity of paneer
(see page 75)
2 tablespoons sesame
seeds, black or white
1 teaspoon sea-salt flakes,
plus extra pinches
to season
freshly cracked black
pepper

 This is a fine salad for early summer when green beans are abundant, tender and sweet.

Two-thirds fill a large pan with water and add the fine salt. Bring to the boil over a high heat.

Meanwhile, sparingly trim the knobbly end off the green beans (the end where it grew off the plant). Once the water has come to a rolling boil, add the trimmed beans to the pan and boil for about 4 minutes, or until the beans are tender and cooked through (test one to make sure it is soft – if not, boil for a further minute or two and check again). Remove the cooked beans using a slotted spoon and set them aside on a tray to cool down.

Place the onion slices in a large bowl with a few generous pinches of flaky salt and 1 tablespoon of lemon and cumin dressing. Using clean hands, spend 20 seconds gently massaging and lightly crushing the onions to release all the juices, working the salt and dressing into and around the slices.

Pick through the herbs, discarding any of the tougher stems and leaving the more tender ones. Pile all the picked leaves and stems on top of one another on your chopping board and roughly chop them – a few chops going north to south and a few chops going west to east.

Place the herbs, green beans and teaspoon of sea salt flakes, a few cracks of black pepper and the remaining dressing in the bowl with the onions and toss everything together. The dressing should surround the ingredients, giving the beans a silky gloss and lightly coating the herbs. You can add more dressing if you feel the need.

Taste, taste, taste! Take a good mouthful of all the salad ingredients together, consider, and then adjust the seasoning appropriately – a dash more dressing perhaps? One more crunch of salt, maybe?

Place the salad on a large platter – do not pile it high, more Table Mountain than Mount Fuji. Crumble over the paneer, then generously sprinkle over the sesame seeds, ensuring an even distribution so that everyone gets a scoop of everything. Finish with a final crunch of salt and pepper and a final lick of dressing.

GRILLED SWEETCORN, CARROT AND PANEER SALAD

 This is a late-summer riff on the pea salad, using grilled sweetcorn from page 119.

Stand a grilled corn upright like a totem pole on your chopping board and with a sharp knife and a swift, downward stroke from the top, run the blade between the corn and the cob, stripping the cob of its kernels. Repeat for the remaining 3 corns, gathering the kernels in a bowl as you go.

Add the carrots to the bowl with the corn, then add the chopped herbs, chilli flakes and a few glugs of dressing. Season with a healthy pinch of salt and plenty of black pepper. Taste the salad and adjust the seasoning as necessary (maybe a pinch more chilli for extra heat, or a glug more dressing for acidity?).

Place the salad on to your preferred platter and crumble the paneer evenly over the top. Finally, sprinkle over the sesame seeds to give a pop with every bite.

SERVES 4 AS A SMALL PLATE

4 cooked corns on the cob (see page 119)
4 large carrots, peeled and grated
a few fistfuls of mixed herbs, such as mint, dill, coriander and parsley, leaves picked and chopped
1 teaspoon chilli flakes
100ml lemon and cumin dressing (see page 136)
1 recipe quantity of paneer (see page 75)
2 tablespoons black or white sesame seeds
sea salt flakes and freshly cracked black pepper

LEMON AND CUMIN DRESSING

MAKES ABOUT 170ML

1 teaspoon cumin seeds
juice of 1 large lemon
120ml extra-virgin olive oil
1 tablespoon apple cider
    vinegar
sea salt flakes and freshly
    cracked black pepper

 If your salads need a lift, this versatile, tangy dressing does just the job – and is a cinch to make!

Place a frying pan over a low heat and add the cumin seeds. Toast them for 2 minutes, or until fragrant. Tip them into a spice grinder or pestle and mortar and grind to as fine a powder as you can.

In a bowl or a jug, whisk together the lemon juice, oil and vinegar and season with a few pinches of salt and pepper. Add the ground toasted cumin and whisk everything together.

Store in a bottle or jam jar in the fridge for up to two weeks.

I like to drizzle the dressing on cooked sliced beetroot, shredded raw cabbage, coleslaw (without the mayo), cold pasta salads, grilled or baked fish, crushed chickpeas with coriander and sesame seeds, or really anything that needs a lift!

RICE
AND
LENTILS

RICE

One of my earliest kitchen memories is of helping my mother measure and wash the rice for dinner. We kept the grains in a big ice-cream tub in the kitchen cupboard and would periodically top up the tub from the even bigger drum of rice in the garage. We used a coffee mug to measure out the portions – one full mug was more than enough for two people, leaving enough cooked rice behind for a late-evening snack. Once we'd measured the quantity, my mother performed a little ritual of putting a pinch back in the tub – a symbolic gesture that meant there would always be rice left for the next meal. In our house, we treated every grain with care and wasted nothing. Respect the rice and in turn it will nourish you.

The shops and markets throughout India brim with so many varieties of rice, but basmati is the grain of choice in the Parsi household. That's why it's the only rice you'll find in this book. For me, basmati – with her elegant, long grains and punctuating aroma that stirs the heart and summons you to the dinner table – is queen.

As a rule of thumb, an 'official' cup measure, such as that used in US cookery (packed level this is equivalent to 185g of rice), will feed two people – or a cup and half each if you are hungry. I always like to cook a little bit more than I need for the meal – leftover rice is a great cure for midnight munchies. The important thing, though, is to work by volume, rather than weight. You can measure your rice in whatever cup or mug you like, as long as you stick to the rule that you cook it in one-and-a-half times the same cup or mug of water.

ENHANCING THE AROMAS

The fancy name for the source of basmati rice's wonderful aroma is 2-acetyl-1-pyrroline. It's the same compound that's found in pandan leaves. Cooking your rice with a small piece of pandan leaf reintroduces any key aromas that may be lost during washing and boiling, and boosts what's there.

Fresh pandan leaves are readily available in Asian grocery stores, but if you can't find them, use kerwa water, an essence made from pandan and also found in most Asian supermarkets (usually next to the rose water). A drop or two in your rice cooking water will have similar results.

Thunder will not strike one when eating rice.
— Chinese proverb

WASHING YOUR RICE

To wash or not to wash?

Washing rice rinses off powdery starches on the surface of the grain that can give cooked rice that gluey, porridge-like texture. Apart from being a therapeutic task that gives us time to ponder life's bigger questions, a good rice wash allows for a loose, fluffy grain when the rice is cooked. So, in short: dodge the stodge and always wash your rice! A word of caution, though – you need to strike a compromise between just enough washing and too much. Over-rinsing can wash away some of those key flavours that make basmati rice so distinctive.

To get the washing just right, place your rice into a suitably large bowl or saucepan and cover it with cold water so that the water is about 2.5cm higher than the top of the rice. Use your hand to gently agitate and stir the rice in the water for 10 seconds, then pour off the milky water, using a sieve to catch any grains that try to swim away. Repeat this process two more times (three times altogether), then drain all the rice well through the sieve.

There is another slightly quicker method, which is to place the measured rice in a sieve and gently rinse it under the cold tap, agitating it with your fingers. You are looking for the same semi-clear water to run off.

COOKING WHITE BASMATI RICE

 If your rice does not turn out as you wish the first time, make small adjustments until you get it perfect. If it's slightly wet, cook it for longer; if it's burned on the bottom, cook it for less time at each stage. Not all pots and hobs are equal, so it's to be expected that you may need to make adjustments to the heat and timings. Every rice-eating household has their preferred rice pot, so try different options until you find the one that works for you – and, remember, cooking perfect rice comes with much practice and much more patience.

SERVES 2

1 cup white basmati rice, washed (see page opposite)
1½ cups water

Use a pot with a study bottom and a tight-fitting lid. A glass lid is best, if you have one, as you can see what is happening inside.

Place the washed rice in the pot and add exactly one-and-a-half times the amount of water to rice by volume; this means for every cup or mug of rice you use, you need 1½ cups or mugs of water. (Remember it's the volume that's important, rather than the weight.)

Place the pot on the hob over a high heat and watch intently for the surface of the water to begin shimmering and the first wisps of steam to emanate. Now, place the lid on the pot and lower the heat just below medium. After 10 minutes, turn the heat to its lowest setting and keep it there for a further 5 minutes. Turn off the heat. Take note of the aromas at this stage – as you become more in tune with cooking rice, you begin to notice the subtle differences in the aromas of raw rice as it transforms into cooked rice.

Do not lift the lid at any point during the cooking or resting process, not even for an anxious peek to see how things are going. Because we are using the absorption method to cook the rice, every bit of steam inside the pot is crucial for cooking that amount of rice to perfection. This is also the reason we reduce the heat towards the end of the cooking, as the moisture in the pot reduces, so should the heat, to avoid burning. This is where I find the change in aroma from raw to cooked rice a useful marker – you can smell what's happening without needing to lift the lid.

Leave the rice to rest for 10 minutes with the lid still firmly in place. This is an important stage as, even though the rice is off the heat, there is still plenty of hot steam in the pot and the rice is absorbing it to become proud and plump. After the resting period you can lift the lid – be sure to have your face close to the pot when you do, to take in all the wonderful aromas that billow forth (if there is a loved one nearby, offer them the ceremonial steam). Fluff the rice using a thin, flat paddle or spoon, gently cutting into the rice to loosen the grains from each other, but be gentle enough as not to turn them to mush. You can even add a spoonful of melted ghee or butter as you do this to coat and enrich the grains and help them stay separate.

Continued overleaf...

AROMATS

Nothing brings rice to life more than spices. Choose them in the right combination and use them deftly and they will add subtle character and nuance to your rice. In turn, these flavours should complement the flavours of the dish your rice is to accompany. You are limited only by your creativity (and what you have in your cupboard), but to get you started, and although this list is anything but exhaustive, here are a few of my own much-loved combinations.

SERVES 2

1 cup white basmati rice, washed (see page 142)
1 whole star anise
2.5cm cassia bark or cinnamon stick
3 cardamom pods, cracked
4 cloves
1 tablespoon ghee
1½ cups water

THE (W)HOLY 4: STAR ANISE, CINNAMON, CLOVE AND CARDAMOM

To me, these are the holy four spices that, in their correct quantities, will elevate rice to mouthwatering heights. This is my go-to rice at home or at work – once you try it, you will see why.

Based on 1 cup of rice, add 1 whole star anise, 2.5cm of cinnamon or cassia bark, 3 cracked cardamom pods and 4 cloves to a pan with 1 tablespoon of ghee. Gently fry the spices on a medium heat for 1 minute, then add the washed and well-drained rice and carry on frying for a further minute, until the rice smells nutty and the grains become very slightly translucent around the edges. Add 1½ cups of water and immediately cover the pan with a lid. Follow the cooking process as on page 143.

SERVES 2

1 cup white basmati rice,
  washed (see page 142)
a pinch of saffron
1½ cups water

SAFFRON

Aah, saffron. Nothing speaks more of our Persian heritage than the combination of saffron and rice – the ultimate in decadence and a must for any celebration. Saffron rice pairs very well with light fish or crab dishes, as well as mutton or lamb stews.

Following the cooking instructions on page 143, just add a pinch of these crocus stigma before you put the lid on the pan and your dinner guests will surrender to the aromas coming forth from your kitchen.

SERVES 2

1 cup white basmati rice,
  washed (see page 142)
1½ cups water
or
1½ cups coconut water
or
1 tablespoon grated
  coconut flesh
or
1 tablespoon unsweetened
  desiccated coconut
or
1 tablespoon creamed
  coconut

COCONUT

The flavour of coconut complements fish, prawn and chicken curries very well. There are several forms and ways to introduce coconut into the rice, which I suggest for you here.

First, you can use the coconut water as part of the liquid to cook the rice... if you can resist the temptation to drink it.

Or you can use grated fresh coconut, which is the grated flesh from the inside of the whole coconut (the type you get at a fête having bean bags thrown at them). You can cook the grated flesh in the rice (about 1 heaped tablespoon per 1 cup of rice), just following the instructions on page 143.

Alternatively, you can use desiccated coconut in a way similar to the grated flesh – it will yield comparable results, but it won't be as tender in its texture. If I use desiccated coconut, I like to brown it in the pot with a tablespoon of ghee before I add the rice and water for a deeper flavour.

Processed from mature coconuts, and sold in hard, white blocks in many supermarkets, one tablespoon of creamed coconut, melted and lightly brown in the pot before the rice and the water goes in, will give you that distinct, coconut flavour, but without the bits. This is my favourite method, as the coconut cream browns during the frying, adding a certain depth to the flavour of the rice.

SERVES 2

1 cup white basmati rice,
  washed (see page 142)
¼ teaspoon ground
  turmeric
1½ cups water

TURMERIC

Turmeric adds a vibrant yellow hue, as well as a distinctive taste to rice that is intended to accompany fish or prawn curries.

Following the cooking instructions on page 143, just add ¼ teaspoon of ground turmeric to the pan before cooking.

COOKING BROWN BASMATI RICE

 Brown rice is the less processed grain form – with the bran and germ attached. It has a wonderfully nutty aroma and flavour, as well as those delicious characteristics anyway found in white basmati rice. Look for the best-quality brown basmati rice you can find, steering clear of packets that proclaim health benefits and that they do wonders for your body. These are usually inflated in price – we know eating the whole grain is better for us nutritionally, but rice is still a staple ingredient and we want it in its humblest form. A good place to find good brown basmati is in wholefood stores where it is sold loose by weight.

Cooking brown rice requires an almost slapdash approach. Because the grains are still enveloped in the bran, the rice takes a lot of water and cooking time to penetrate and get to them. Soaking the rice can help, but dry, unsoaked rice allows for a better fry in the first steps of cooking, which gives a deep and nutty flavour.

SERVES 2

1 whole star anise
2.5cm cassia bark or
     cinnamon stick
3 cardamom pods,
     cracked
4 cloves
1 tablespoon ghee, plus
     1 teaspoon to finish
1 cup brown basmati rice
3 cups water

Start by toasting off the holy four spices in a healthy dollop of ghee and add your 1 cup of rice (there's no need to wash brown rice as it is unprocessed and therefore has no residual starch or powder). Fry the rice in the ghee and spices on a medium heat for 2 minutes, to help the bran yield more readily and pronounce the nutty flavour.

Add three times the amount of water to rice – you're going to need to do a lot of boiling to cook the rice through to the grain. For the first two thirds of the cooking time, keep the lid on and allow that water to really boil into the rice. For the last third, allow the excess water to evaporate, leaving you with somewhat dry rice as the end result. Cooking times will vary according to how much rice you're cooking, but generally you need to allow 30 minutes for 1 cup of brown rice.

Once you're happy the rice is cooked, strain off any excess water. Stir through a teaspoon of ghee or butter for a fuller flavour.

Tasting is the key to success – learn to distinguish between the hard, uncooked grain and the firm bite of the cooked grain. Don't let the different textures put you off – it brings contrast to the dinner table and a workout for your jaw!

COOKING RICE FOR BIRIYANI

SERVES 4

1 tablespoon ghee
2 green chillies, split
2 whole star anise
4 cardamom pods,
   cracked
6 cloves
6 black peppercorns
2.5cm cassia bark or
   cinnamon stick
1 large dried bay leaf
2 cups white basmati rice,
   washed (see page 142)
pandan leaf (optional)
1 teaspoon salt

 Baking the rice in the final stages of cooking the biriyani means that it is important to undercook it in the first (boiling) stage. Use a large pot that allows for lots of water and lots of space for the rice to boil in – just like cooking pasta.

Melt the ghee in a large pan. Add the green chillies, star anise, cracked cardamom pods, cloves, black peppercorns, cassia bark or cinnamon stick and bay leaf and leave to fry for 1 minute.

Add cold water so that it comes two thirds of the way up the sides of the pan and bring it to the boil. Add the basmati rice to the boiling water, a piece of pandan leaf if you have it, and the salt.

Boil the rice uncovered for about 4–5 minutes, until the grains are tender but not cooked through – there should still be a noticeable chalkiness to the bite. Strain the rice through a sieve and lay it flat on a tray to cool. Once cool, it is ready to layer into your biriyani (see page 155).

DHANSAK NA CHAWAL
PARSI BROWN RICE

 This classic preparation is an essential accompaniment to a traditional Parsi dhansak (see page 48). The term brown rice derives from the colour of the rice once cooked and not, as you might think, from the type of rice you're using. Caramelising sliced onions until they are dark brown and then adding jaggery to the pot to caramelise alongside the onions colours and transforms the cooking water, imparting hue and flavour to the rice. Cumin and caraway balance out the sweetness of the caramelised onions and jaggery to create an utterly moreish rice dish.

Heat the ghee or oil in your favoured rice cooking pot over a medium heat. Add the onion and keep stirring until it becomes dark brown, but not black. This step should be done at a slow and controlled pace and can take anywhere from 10 to 15 minutes. Be bold – the dark, almost burnt flavour of the onions will dissipate through the rice as it cooks, imparting a beautiful caramel-like flavour and that eponymous brown colour.

When you're happy with the colour of your onion, add the cumin, caraway, star anise, cassia bark or cinnamon, cardamom and cloves. Stir the spices through the onion for 1 minute, then add the jaggery or sugar. As the jaggery or sugar heats up, stir and crush it into the onion and wait for it to darken and eventually caramelise, on a low–medium heat. This can take about 3 minutes. A good indication of caramelisation are thick bubbles 'blooping' from the pot.

Add the washed rice and 3 cups of water and cook over a low–medium heat with the lid on for 12 minutes (don't remove the lid to test the rice, but know that at this stage it will still have a bit of bite). Then remove the pan from the heat and leave the rice to rest, with the lid still on, for a further 10 minutes. For the rice to cook perfectly the lid must stay in place all through the cooking and resting period.

The finished rice will have a beautiful brown colour and a unique, caramelised depth of flavour. The cumin and caraway add a delicious savouriness to the rice that complements meaty curries, especially lamb or chicken dhansak.

SERVES 4

2 tablespoons ghee or vegetable oil

1 medium onion, thinly sliced

1 teaspoon whole cumin seeds

1 teaspoon whole caraway seeds

2 whole star anise

5cm cassia bark or cinnamon stick

5 cardamom pods, cracked

5 cloves

1 teaspoon grated jaggery or dark brown soft sugar

2 cups basmati rice, washed (see page 142)

3 cups water

PERSIAN SCORCHED RICE

 This is a version of tahdig, a Persian rice dish that has always fascinated me. I remember the first time I made this in my small flat – for the next three days that fragrant aroma awaited me every time I got home. When you present Persian scorched rice at the table for a dinner party, the 'wows!' will make you blush. Find yourself a round, heavy-based baking dish to bake your rice in to get that perfect crust and shape.

First, make the crispy onions. Heat 2 tablespoons of ghee or oil in a frying pan over a medium–high heat. Add the onion and fry for about 4–5 minutes, until golden and crispy. Scoop out the onions and set them aside to drain on kitchen paper.

Using the same pan, add the remaining tablespoon of ghee or oil and place it over a medium heat. Add the flaked almonds and barberries and gently stir them until they turn gold. Immediately scoop them out of the pan and place on kitchen paper to drain.

Preheat the oven to 180°C/160°C fan. Bring a large saucepan of salted water to the boil over a high heat. Add the rice and the cardamom pods and cook for about 5 minutes, until the rice has only the slightest bite to it (you don't want it completely tender at this point). Strain the rice immediately into a sieve and gently run it under some cold water for only a moment to halt the cooking. Discard the cardamom pods. Set the rice aside, allowing any excess water to run off.

In a bowl, mix together the onions, yoghurt, egg and egg yolk, kerwa water, rose water and pomegranate molasses. In a pestle and mortar, grind the saffron to a powder and add the hot water. Add the saffron water to the bowl with the onion mixture, followed by the rice. Stir the rice through the sauce until all the grains are coated. Season well with salt.

Rub the melted butter all over the bottom and sides of a medium-sized, round baking dish (it needs to be no larger than a dinner plate as you're going to invert the rice on to a plate later). Pile the rice into the dish and level it out, gently pushing it down with the back of a spoon. Cover tightly with a lid or foil, and place the rice in the oven to bake for a little over 1 hour – don't be hasty and rush the rice as you want to allow enough time for that gorgeous golden crust to form evenly.

When the rice is ready the bottom will have baked golden brown and become crispy. Remove the dish from the oven and place it directly onto a damp tea towel (this helps to release the rice). Use a knife to prise the rice away from the sides of the dish, then place a plate on top of the dish. Say a quick prayer to the rice gods, and with one swift movement turn the dish upside down so the rice turns out on to the plate in one piece. Garnish with the toasted almonds, pomegranate seeds, barberries, a scattering of fresh herbs and a flourish of lemon and cumin dressing (see page 136).

SERVES 2

3 tablespoons ghee or vegetable oil
1 small onion, thinly sliced
20g flaked almonds
10g barberries
1 cup basmati rice, washed (see page 142)
5 cardamom pods, cracked
6 tablespoons full-fat natural yoghurt
1 egg, plus
1 egg yolk
1 teaspoon kerwa water
½ teaspoon rose water
2 teaspoons pomegranate molasses
a generous pinch of saffron
2 tablespoons hot water
a knob of butter, melted
salt

To serve
a handful of pomegranate seeds
a handful of barberries
fresh herbs
lemon and cumin dressing (see page 136)

TARKARI NO PULAO
PARSI VEGETABLE PULAO

SERVES 4

4 tablespoons ghee or
vegetable oil

1 whole star anise

4 cardamom pods,
cracked

5 cloves

2.5cm cassia bark or
cinnamon stick

1 onion, chopped

1 tablespoon ginger–garlic
paste (see page 43)

1 teaspoon caraway seeds

1 teaspoon cumin seeds

250g potatoes, unpeeled
and cut into 1cm chunks

1 carrot, unpeeled and
roughly chopped

100g frozen or fresh peas

100g frozen or fresh green
beans

100g frozen or fresh
sweetcorn

4 small green chillies,
slit open

1½ cups basmati rice,
washed (see page 142)

1 large overripe tomato,
roughly diced

1 heaped teaspoon garam
masala (see page 46)

1 heaped tablespoon
dhansak masala (see
page 48)

a generous pinch of
saffron

½ teaspoon ground
turmeric

3 teaspoons salt

a handful of coriander,
leaves picked and
chopped

 *This is a delicious one-pot wonder, packed full of amazing
flavours yet unfussy and simple to make. My version of a pulao
is made exclusively with vegetables you may have at home in the
freezer, but feel free to express yourself or, if needs be, empty
the fridge – there are no hard-and-fast rules on which vegetables
you can use.*

*I also make versions of this pulao with chicken breast, meaty
white fish and even prawns. Just cut the meat into small chunks
(leave prawns whole in the shell, which add more flavour) and
add them to the pan at the same time as the spices and rice.*

Heat the ghee or oil in a saucepan large enough to hold all the
ingredients (bearing in mind the rice will triple in volume once cooked).
Add the star anise, cardamom, cloves and cassia bark or cinnamon, and
allow to fry in the oil for 1 minute, until fragrant.

Add the onion and cook for about 3 minutes, until it starts to turn light
brown. Add the ginger–garlic paste and cook for a further 1 minute,
stirring everything together so that it cooks evenly. Once the onions are
golden, add the caraway seeds and cumin seeds and stir them through
the onion for 1 minute.

Add the vegetables, chillies and rice and fry for a further 2 minutes, then
add the tomato, garam masala, dhansak masala, saffron, turmeric and
salt. Fry for a further 2 minutes.

Add 2¼ cups of water and stir everything together, pushing the rice
under the water (the vegetables can poke above the water, but the rice
needs to be submerged to cook properly). Increase the heat to high,
bring the liquid to the boil, then place a tight-fitting lid on the pan to stop
the steam escaping. Reduce the heat to medium–high and cook for
5 minutes, then reduce the heat again, to medium–low, and cook again
for 5 minutes. Finally, reduce the heat again to the lowest setting and
cook for a final 5 minutes. Turn off the heat, but leave the lid on the pan,
allowing the rice to absorb the steam for 10 minutes, until the rice is fully
cooked through. For the rice to cook perfectly, the lid must stay in place
all through the cooking and resting period.

Remove the lid from the pan and take in all those wonderful aromas. Stir
through the coriander and serve with spoonfuls of pickled turmeric (see
page 57), lemon wedges and thinly sliced red onion.

PARSI-STYLE BIRIYANI

 There is a certain ceremony involved around making, serving and eating a biriyani. The love and attention that goes into its creation reflect the feelings you have for those who will eat it. The intricate aromas and flavours found in a biriyani are like no other – black cardamom, cloves and cinnamon balanced with saffron, rose and kerwa. This is the perfect dish to make for celebrations and special occasions. Say 'I love you' with a biriyani.

If you like, you can brine the meat (see page 203) before you begin. This will keep the meat succulent as the biriyani bakes and make for the most juicy and mouthwatering morsels.

Tip the meat into a bowl and sprinkle over the salt, garam masala, chilli powder, ginger–garlic paste, puréed onion, half the chopped chillies, the lemon juice and the yoghurt. Stir to coat the meat in all the spices and yoghurt and leave to marinate, covered in the fridge, for at least 3 hours to tenderise and absorb all those flavours.

When you're ready to cook, pour the 300ml of vegetable oil for frying into a deep, large saucepan. Place over a high heat and, when hot, add the sliced onion. Reduce the heat to medium and fry, stirring continuously to move the onion slices around the pan, for about 3–4 minutes, until golden and crispy. As soon as the onions are ready, remove the pan from the heat to make sure they don't burn. Set a metal sieve over a heatproof bowl and strain the oil, catching the onions in the sieve and the oil in the bowl. Tip out the onions on to some kitchen paper to drain. Sprinkle with salt and set aside while you partly cook the rice.

You need to cook the rice for a biriyani in a different way to the methods elsewhere in the book – it needs to be undercooked at first, because you're going to bake it later to finish it off. Three-quarters fill a large saucepan with water (the rice needs lots of space to move around, like cooking pasta, so if you don't have a pan big enough, cook the rice in stages). Add all the salt, whole spices and the bay leaves and place the pan over a high heat. Bring the water to the boil.

Add the washed rice and boil, uncovered, for about 4–5 minutes, until tender but not fully cooked through – there should still be a noticeable firmness to the bite. Immediately drain the rice and spread it out in a layer on a tray to stop it overcooking. Set aside.

Preheat the oven to 200°C/180°C fan.

Using your hands, remove the pieces of meat from the marinade, squeezing off as much of the yoghurt back into the bowl as possible. (I find squeezing each piece of meat through my closed fist works perfectly.)

Continued overleaf...

SERVES 8

2kg chicken or mutton, diced on the bone into 2–5cm pieces

2 tablespoons salt, plus extra to season

3 tablespoons garam masala (see page 46)

2 teaspoons chilli powder (mild or hot, as you like)

2 tablespoons ginger–garlic paste (see page 43)

2 large onions, 1 blitzed to a purée, 1 halved and very finely sliced

8 small green chillies, roughly chopped

juice of 1 large lemon

1kg full-fat natural yoghurt

100g ghee or vegetable oil, plus 300ml vegetable oil for frying

3 teaspoons kerwa water

4 teaspoons rose water

2 tablespoons whole milk

a very healthy pinch of saffron (about 0.5g)

a small handful of coriander, leaves and stems roughly chopped

a small handful of mint, leaves picked and roughly chopped

FOR THE RICE

1 teaspoon salt

2 whole star anise

4 cardamom pods, cracked

6 cloves

6 black peppercorns

2.5cm cinnamon stick

2 large bay leaves

2 cups basmati rice, washed (see page 142)

Heat the ghee or vegetable oil in a sturdy-bottomed pot over a medium heat. When hot, bit by bit, add the meat to the pan – the gradual process is so as not to take all the heat out of the pan at once. Fry the meat for about 3 minutes – it won't brown as much as you may expect or want because the marinade will abate this process. After about 3 minutes of steady frying, add the marinade from the bowl, increase the heat and allow it to bubble, stirring and scraping continuously, cooking the meat for 3 minutes (or 1 minute if you're using chicken breast – you don't want it to overcook during baking and become dry).

Make a layer of half the part-cooked rice in the bottom of a large baking dish. Level it out but do not press it down. Tip in all the meat and the sauce, distributing it evenly over the top. Again, level out the layer, but don't squash anything down. Top with the remaining rice, spreading it out to cover all the meat. Evenly sprinkle the kerwa water and rose water over the top layer of rice.

Pour the milk into a small saucepan and place it over a low–medium heat, warming it until it is steaming (but not boiling) hot. Meanwhile place the saffron in a small cup. When the milk is ready, pour it into the cup over the saffron. Infuse for 1 minute, then sprinkle the infused milk and saffron strands over the rice. Alternatively, sprinkle a few teaspoons of the saffron infusion from page 41 over the rice.

Scatter the fried onions over the top of the dish, followed by the chopped coriander and mint leaves and the remaining chopped chillies.

Place two layers of foil over the top of the baking dish, crimping the edges tightly so that no steam can escape. If you are using a cast-iron baking dish with a tight-fitting lid, use the lid.

Place the dish in the middle of the preheated oven and bake for 1½ hours, until the meat at the centre of the dish is cooked through and comes away easily from the bone.

I like to serve a biriyani in the dish I used for baking, placing it with pride in the centre of the table. Use a large spoon to dig up and turn the rice so the meat and layers of flavour mix and mingle. Serve with wedges of lemon, pickles and a kachuber salad (see page 124).

KHICHDI

Khichdi is a simple preparation of rice cooked with lentils, beans or vegetables. It is meant to be a sustaining and comforting staple and can take many forms depending on the cook's temperament. Add a dash of cumin–coriander powder in the cooking water, a handful of chopped vegetables and a finish of fresh herbs, such as coriander, mint and dill and you have a meal in itself. Or, use it as a companion rice to bring substance to other dishes. Think of this recipe as a template and add your own flair and creativity. Khichdi should be uncomplicated and as simple to make as it is to eat. My mum likes to sprout mung beans (see page 127) and use this in lieu of red lentils.

For me, this dish is a must alongside kadhi (see page 163).

SERVES 4

2 cups basmati rice, washed (see page 142)
180g red lentils or split yellow mung beans, washed
½ teaspoon ground turmeric
½ teaspoon cumin seeds
¼ teaspoon salt
3 cups water

Place all the dry ingredients in a pan with a tight-fitting lid. Pour in 3 cups of water and place the pan over a high heat for 5 minutes, until steam starts to push past the lid, then lower the heat to medium and continue to cook the rice for 5 minutes. Then lower the heat to its lowest setting and let the rice cook for a further 5 minutes. After the 15 minutes of cooking, remove the pan from the heat and leave to rest for 10 minutes with the lid on before serving (don't lift the lid at any point during cooking).

See overleaf for images.

Khichree ne patyo, pait bharine chatio.

— Gujarati saying

DHAN DAR
PLAIN DAL

SERVES 6

FOR THE DHAN DAR
200g red split lentils
200g split yellow mung
    beans
½ teaspoon ground
    turmeric
a pinch of hing (asafoetida)
1½ teaspoons salt

FOR THE CHAUNK
    VAGAR
2 tablespoons ghee or
    vegetable oil
5 garlic cloves, sliced
    wafer thin
4 small green chillies,
    sliced into thin rounds
1 teaspoon cumin seeds
8 fresh curry leaves

 This is a simple bowl of lentil gravy for simple afternoons. The dish is finished with chaunk vagar – tempered garlic, chilli and curry leaves.

Place both the red lentils and the mung beans together in a bowl and soak them in cold water for 20 minutes, then rinse twice in cold water, using your hand to agitate and stir. Drain them off.

Place the soaked lentils and beans in a large saucepan with 500ml of water, as well as the turmeric, hing and salt. Bring to the boil over a high heat, then lower the heat to medium–low and simmer the lentils for 40 minutes until they are soft. (You can do this in a pressure cooker, if you prefer – it will take about 15 minutes).

While the lentils are cooking, make the chaunk vagar. Heat the ghee or oil in a small frying pan over a medium heat. When hot, add the garlic and fry for 1–2 minutes, until golden. Add the chillies and stir for 30 seconds, then lower the heat and add the cumin seeds and curry leaves. Stir for another 30 seconds, then remove from the heat and tip the mixture into a bowl to cool. Set aside.

Use a stick blender or food processor to pulse the cooked lentils to a semi-smooth purée; or do as my grandma did – give it a good beating with a whisk, which works just as well.

To serve, pour the dhan dar into a large serving bowl and spoon the crispy, tempered garlic and spice over the top, along with the flavourful ghee or oil in the pan.

This is a wonderfully simple dish – enjoy it with some rotli (see page 114) or rice, and sliced red onion. You can also eat dhan dar the Parsi way with prawn patyo (see page 199) and khichdi rice (see page 159).

You can cook this dish with some of your leftover whey from other recipes for a delicious and nourishing dal.

MASOOR DAR
BROWN LENTILS

On special occasions this dish is made with pig trotters or goat lungs. Here, it is presented in its simplest form.

Tip both types of lentil into a bowl. Pour over cold, fresh water to cover and soak the lentils for 15 minutes, then drain them in a sieve, rinse them under cold water and let them drain again for a moment.

Meanwhile, put the chillies, cumin seeds and garlic in a spice grinder or a pestle and mortar and grind to a coarse paste.

Heat the ghee or vegetable oil in a deep, large saucepan over a medium heat. When hot, add the paste and let it sizzle for 2 minutes, until aromatic. Add the tomatoes and cook for 5 minutes, then stir in the jaggery, allowing it to dissolve into the tomatoes.

Add the drained lentils, along with the onion, potato, turmeric, salt and 1 litre of water. Bring to the boil, reduce the heat to low and simmer for 30 minutes, stirring every 5 minutes, until the lentils are cooked. (To check, take a bite of a lentil – there should be no chalkiness or textured 'bite' – a well-cooked lentil should be soft like rice but not mushy.)

To prepare the tangy onions, peel a small red onion, cut in half, then thinly slice using a mandolin or sharp knife. Sprinkle the salt and cracked black pepper. Sprinkle the apple cider vinegar over the onions and, using your fingers, massage together.

Stir through the chopped coriander and serve with fresh rotlis (see page 114), tangy onions and a bowl of cooling yoghurt.

SERVES 8

250g masoor dal (brown lentils)
50g toor dal or channa dal
4 small green chillies
1 teaspoon cumin seeds
3 garlic cloves
3 tablespoons ghee or vegetable oil
2 small tomatoes, chopped, or 200g tinned chopped tomatoes
1 tablespoon grated jaggery
1 small red onion, chopped into 1cm pieces
1 small potato, peeled and roughly chopped into 3cm chunks
1 teaspoon ground turmeric
1 tablespoon salt
1 small bunch of coriander, leaves and stems chopped

FOR THE TANGY ONIONS
1 small red onion
2 generous tablespoons apple cider vinegar
1 teaspoon salt
1 teaspoon black pepper

KADHI

 Kadhi is a yoghurt-based dish eaten all over India, where it takes many forms depending in which state you eat it. Although it's not a Parsi dish as such, Parsis who reside in Gujarat cook a delicious version with a soothing and slightly sweet nature – the qualities that made it my mum's go-to dish whenever I was ill as a child and currently at the top of my 'last meals'. Do go out of your way to hunt down a small tub of hing (asafoetida) – it brings a quintessential flavour.

In a large bowl, whisk together the yoghurt and chickpea flour with 750ml water, until smooth. Add the ginger, chilli, salt, sugar and turmeric and stir it all through.

Heat the ghee in a large saucepan over a medium heat. When hot, add the curry leaves, cumin seeds and the mustard seeds. When the mustard seeds begin to pop and jump around (about 2 minutes), add the hing and stir for 5 seconds. Add the yoghurt mixture, reduce the heat to medium–low and cook for 15 minutes, stirring continuously, until the mixture bubbles and thickens to the texture of double cream (if it gets too thick, add some water to loosen it). Take care not to let the yoghurt catch on the bottom of the pan. Add the chopped coriander leaves, allowing them to wilt in the heat of the kadhi. Top with chaunk vagar (see page 160), then serve with khichdi rice (see page 157) and tangy onions (see page 161).

SERVES 4–6

450g full-fat natural yoghurt (see page 74 for homemade)
5 tablespoons chickpea flour
2cm fresh ginger, peeled and grated
2 green chillies, finely chopped
1 teaspoon salt
1 tablespoon caster sugar
½ teaspoon ground turmeric
2 tablespoons ghee
8 fresh curry leaves
1 teaspoon cumin seeds, lightly ground in a pestle and mortar
½ teaspoon black mustard seeds
¼ teaspoon hing (asafoetida)
a handful of coriander, leaves picked and chopped
chaunk vagar (see page 160)

Buy it with thought
Cook it with care
Use less wheat and meat
Buy local foods
Serve just enough
Use what is left
Do not waste it.
–– US Food Administration, 1917

VEGETABLES

PAPRI
WING BEAN AND SWEET POTATO STEW

SERVES 6

120ml vegetable oil

20 garlic cloves, unpeeled

2 red onions, peeled and
cut into small wedges

5 small green chillies,
slit open

1 aubergine, chopped into
bite-sized chunks

2 large potatoes, peeled
and chopped into bite-
sized chunks

1 large sweet potato,
peeled and chopped
into bite-sized chunks

1kg surti papri, de-stringed
on both sides

6 tomatoes, finely
chopped

200g fresh or frozen peas

5 teaspoons dhansak
masala (see page 48)

2 teaspoons sambhar
masala (see page 46)

2 teaspoons ground
turmeric

4 teaspoons salt

1 teaspoon ajwain

a handful of each of
coriander and fenugreek
leaves, chopped

juice of 1 small lemon

Named for the surti papri (a variety of winged bean) it contains, this spicy vegetable stew has its origins in what today's Iranians would call khoresh, a general name for stew. The bean is readily available in Asian grocery stores, but you can substitute it with runner beans, English green beans, which all work just as well.

Ajwain, also known as carom seed, has a pungent aroma that reminds me of thyme, oregano and citrus. It has a slightly bitter flavour, but used in the right quantities brings a certain uplifting nuance to this stew.

Rather curiously, we leave the skin on the garlic during cooking, to give a soft, caramelised-garlic flavour weaving throughout the stew – you can pop each clove out of its jacket as you eat. I learned this trick of leaving the skin on only recently from my aunty, whose mum cooked this traditional way. Before my aunty Zarine's revelation, I'd always peeled my garlic. Both options yield exceptional results.

Pour the vegetable oil into a cast-iron saucepan over a medium heat. When hot, add the garlic cloves and put the lid on the pan. Leave the garlic to sizzle away for about 3 minutes, removing the lid to stir every now and then, until the garlic cloves have taken on an even golden colour. Add the onions and chillies and fry for a further 8 minutes, lid on, stirring occasionally, until the onion begins to caramelise.

Add the aubergine, potatoes and sweet potatoes to the pan and cook them, stirring for 5 minutes, then add the beans, tomatoes and peas, all the spices and salt. Rub the ajwain in the palm of your hand with your thumb to release its aromas and then add this to the pan, too.

Stir everything together, place the lid on the pan and lower the heat to just below medium. All the juices from the tomatoes and vegetables will release so that the vegetables can stew, while the lid keeps the steam and flavours locked inside the pan. Cook the stew like this for 30–45 minutes, lifting the lid every 10 minutes to give things a good stir. When you lift the lid, tilt the lid into the pan so all the condensed water goes back into the pot. Ensure the potatoes are cooked through but not mushy (all the vegetables must keep their integrity).

Stir through the coriander and fenugreek and a generous squeeze of lemon juice to finish. Serve with fresh, warmed rotlis (see page 114) and kachuber salad (see page 124).

KORU NE KOPRA NI CURRY
PUMPKIN AND COCONUT CURRY

 Parsis are not known for their love of vegetables. Nonetheless, I wanted to create a dish that had all the signature ingredients and flavours of Parsi cooking, and also celebrated a much-admired and widely available vegetable. The humble pumpkin is sweet and delicious and holds its own against the fiery spices and the flavours of coconut. You can, of course, use any suitable pumpkin – or squash – that is available to you seasonally.

Place the oil and creamed coconut in a wok or large frying pan over a low heat, crushing the creamed coconut with the back of a spoon. Once the fats have melted, add the cumin–coriander powder and desiccated coconut and gently fry for 5 minutes, until the coconut has browned and become intensely fragrant. Add the curry leaves and allow them to pop and sizzle in the heat for 30 seconds.

Add the coconut milk, then half fill the empty tin with water and add that to the wok, too. Add the squash or pumpkin, tomato, chilli powder, turmeric and salt, increase the heat to medium and bring the liquid to the boil. Reduce the heat again and simmer for 45 minutes, until the squash or pumpkin is tender (use a small, sharp knife to give it a poke). Add the vinegar, jaggery and saffron and stir everything through until the jaggery has dissolved into the sauce. Serve with freshly made rotlis (see page 114) or plain basmati rice.

SERVES 4

about 2 tablespoons vegetable oil
40g creamed coconut
2 tablespoons cumin–coriander powder (see page 48)
30g unsweetened desiccated coconut
10 fresh curry leaves
1 400g tin of full-fat coconut milk
500g peeled, deseeded and chopped butternut squash or pumpkin (other squashes and softer pumpkins will work, too)
1 large ripe tomato, finely diced
1 tablespoon chilli powder (mild or hot, as you like)
1 teaspoon ground turmeric
2 teaspoons salt
1 tablespoon apple cider vinegar
1 tablespoon grated jaggery
a large pinch of saffron

It is a great mistake to suppose that in order to do good cooking it is necessary to be extravagant in one's use of ingredients.
— Auguste Escoffier

SEKTA NI SING NI CURRY
DRUMSTICK CURRY

SERVES 2 AS A SIDE

2 large drumsticks
1 tablespoon vegetable oil
1 tomato, chopped small
1 teaspoon sambhar
   masala (see page 46)
¼ teaspoon garam masala
   (see page 46)
salt

 My grandad used to have a tall tree directly outside his house in Gujarat that grew drumsticks (or moringa, as they are also known) – very long, bean-like pods that held seeds inside. When I visited as a child, I would hang over the edge of the top floor balcony (with my mum or uncle keeping a firm grip on my waist) and pick the pods off the tree to cook up for dinner.

I have noticed that drumsticks have become increasingly common in Asian fruit and veg shops in the UK – even though they are one of those vegetables that you pick up with curiosity and put back down with fear of the unknown! Indeed, you do need to eat them with a certain amount of skill and understanding. They have long, tough fibres running down their length that no amount of cooking will break down. So, in order to get that tasty, soft flesh out from the inside, you need hold the piece of drumstick firmly at one end and, using your front teeth, clamp down at the same end and drag the drumstick through your teeth, forcing all the deliciousness from the inside into your mouth.

This recipe is a great introduction to cooking drumsticks and with some creativity can lead on to more involved and elaborate dishes. Imagine what other vegetables you could simmer alongside the drumsticks, or what other sauces the drumsticks could simmer in.

Using a vegetable peeler or sharp knife, peel the drumsticks to trim away the outer part of the fibrous layer. Wash the drumsticks, then chop them into 5cm pieces.

Heat the vegetable oil in a saucepan over a medium heat. When hot, add the tomato and both masalas, and season with salt. Reduce the heat to low–medium, and simmer, stirring occasionally, for about 5 minutes, until the tomato breaks down. Add 150ml of water and the chopped drumsticks, increase the heat to medium and simmer for 5 minutes with the lid on. Remove the lid, give everything a stir, then lower the heat, replace the lid, and leave the drumsticks to cook for a further 10 minutes, until they are soft and cooked through. Taste the sauce and add more salt if you feel it needs it.

Serve as a great sidekick to fish and prawns to complement the spice and flavours, and with rotli (see page 114) and rice to mop up all the sauce.

MASALA NI PAPETA
MASALA POTATOES

This is a fine side dish. A common seasoning for snacks in India, the chaat masala adds a unique, spicy, salty tang. As an alternative you could combine ¼ teaspoon of kala namak (powdered black salt) with a tablespoon of cumin–coriander powder (see page 48) and use that instead. The black salt gives that quintessential minerally, sulphurous flavour that makes these potatoes so moreish. I like to keep the steam on for extra earthy flavour.

SERVES 6 AS A SIDE OR SNACK

2.5kg large potatoes (such as Maris Piper or King Edward), unpeeled and chopped into even, bite-sized chunks
1 tablespoon salt
500ml vegetable oil, for frying
2 teaspoons chaat masala
juice of 1 large lemon
4 small green chillies, finely chopped
1 bunch of spring onions, finely sliced
a handful of coriander, leaves and stalks chopped

Tip the potatoes into a large saucepan and add the salt. Cover the potatoes with water and place over a high heat. Bring the water to the boil and cook the potatoes for about 8–10 minutes, or until they are soft all the way through (use a pointed knife to poke the chunks every now and then – they are ready when there's no resistance). Carefully drain the potatoes and leave them to steam off and cool down in the colander for 10 minutes.

Pour the oil into a large, sturdy-bottomed pot so that it comes about two thirds of the way up the sides. Place the pot over a medium–high heat until the oil reaches 170°C on a cooking thermometer. If you don't have a thermometer, drop a cube of day-old bread into the oil – if it browns and rises quickly to the surface, the oil is ready.

Once the oil is at the right temperature, carefully lower in a handful of potatoes and fry over a medium heat for about 4–5 minutes, gently moving them around, until golden and evenly cooked. Scoop out the cooked potatoes using a slotted spoon and set them aside to drain on kitchen paper while you cook the remainder in batches.

Place all the fried potatoes into a large bowl and liberally dust them with the chaat masala – toss them around until they are evenly coated. Add the lemon juice, chillies, spring onions and coriander and give everything a final few tosses. If you haven't already, taste the potatoes and add some extra chaat masala or lemon juice to balance them out, if you feel the need.

Serve piping hot as an accompaniment to a main meal or as a tempting snack.

Top: masala potatoes
Middle: sweet potato cakes (see tip, page 173)
Bottom: sweet potato mash (see page 174)

MASALA NA KAN
SWEET POTATO MASH

SERVES 2 AS A SIDE

1 large sweet potato
(about 500g), peeled
and chopped into
large chunks

½ teaspoon of cumin–
coriander powder
(see page 48)

¼ teaspoon ground
turmeric

1 teaspoon lightly crushed
caraway seeds

½ small bunch of
coriander, leaves picked
and chopped

120g cheddar, grated
(optional)

salt and freshly cracked
black pepper

A quick one to knock up when you are in a hurry, and a great substitute for rice as an accompaniment to grilled fish or other dishes. Equally, on its own it makes for a comforting snack. My version is simple, but feel free to add whatever you have available – make this your own.

Bring a large saucepan of water to the boil and add the sweet potato. Boil for about 10–15 minutes, until soft (alternatively do this in a pressure cooker for 6 minutes). Drain the sweet potato chunks in a colander and sit the colander in the empty pan, allowing the potatoes to steam off and dry out a little.

Tip the sweet potato chunks back into the pan and add all the remaining ingredients. Season well with a good pinch of salt and a few cracks of pepper, then smash (with a masher, whisk or even a fork) everything together until smooth and fully combined.

If you have any leftovers, make them into sweet potato cakes and pan fry them until crispy on the outside, then top with a fried egg.

CHUTNEY BHARELU VENGNU
AUBERGINES STUFFED WITH COCONUT AND CORIANDER CHUTNEY

 This recipe is a contribution from my mother, who loves aubergines and first taught me how to make coconut and coriander chutney.

Make a large slit all the way down the length of each aubergine, keeping each attached at the top, so that it looks like a wooden clothes peg. Sprinkle a light pinch of salt inside the slits.

Fill each aubergine with a tablespoonful of coconut and coriander chutney – use enough to fit between the slit but not so much that it's spilling out.

Heat the oil in a wok or a heavy-based frying pan over a medium heat. Add the onion and fry for about 3–4 minutes, until translucent. Add the ginger–garlic paste and fry for a further 2 minutes, or until the mixture begins to take on some colour and become fragrant.

Add the tomatoes, garam masala, chilli powder and turmeric and stir. Leave to simmer over a medium heat for 1 minute, allowing the flavours to come together.

Add 2 tablespoons of water to the pan, then nestle the stuffed aubergines into the sauce. Place a lid on the pan and gently simmer the aubergines for 5 minutes. Then remove the lid and flip the aubergines over. Replace the lid and simmer again for a further 5 minutes, or until the aubergines are soft and cooked through. (If you are using slightly bigger aubergines, you may need to allow a few more minutes each side.)

These are beautiful served with fresh rotlis (see page 114) and lagaan nu achar (see page 59).

SERVES 2

6–8 small aubergines (often in Asian vegetable stores)
2 teaspoons fine salt
6–8 tablespoons coconut and coriander chutney (see page 65)
2 tablespoons vegetable oil
1 small onion, diced
2 teaspoons ginger–garlic paste (see page 43)
2 small tomatoes, chopped
1 teaspoon garam masala (see page 46)
½ teaspoon chilli powder (mild or hot, as you like)
½ teaspoon ground turmeric
¼ teaspoon jaggery or a pinch of caster sugar

Khanar pinar ne khodai apnar.
God gives in abundance to those who eat well.
–– Parsi proverb

See overleaf for images.

FISH

MASALA MACCHI
MASALA FRIED FISH

SERVES 4

2 teaspoons cumin seeds,
   lightly ground in a pestle
   and mortar, plus extra
   if needed
1 teaspoon hot chilli
   powder, plus extra
   if needed
1 teaspoon ground
   turmeric, plus extra
   if needed
½ teaspoon salt
enough of your chosen
   fish, skin on, to feed
   4 people
vegetable oil, for shallow-
   frying
1 lemon, cut into wedges,
   to serve
a small handful of
   coriander, leaves picked
   and chopped, to garnish
1 large red chilli, sliced into
   thin rounds, to garnish

 For Parsis living in India, pomfret is a popular choice of fish. The firm, white flesh and small, saucer-like body make it ideal for shallow-frying. There is no hard-and-fast rule about which type of fish you use for this dish, though, and (when in season) sardines and mackerel are fantastic; sea bream and sea bass are exceptional; and, for something different, a small sea trout is quite a delight. In short, you can choose whether you want to cook this dish with filleted fish, or for a small fish whole on the bone, such as a sardine.

Mix the cumin, chilli, turmeric and salt together in a large bowl and judge whether there is enough to generously coat your fish – if not add a dash more of each ingredient.

Make small incisions in the flesh of the fish about 5mm deep and 2cm across. Throw the fish into the bowl with the spices and rub thoroughly, making sure the spices get into all the crevices and slits. Leave the fish, either covered or uncovered, for 20 minutes at room temperature to allow the spices and salt to permeate the flesh. (Keeping the fish out of the fridge allows the temperature to mellow for a more even cook and succulent flesh.)

Heat the oil in a wok or frying pan over a high heat until the surface of the oil begins to shimmer. Gently add the fish and, as a guide, fry for 2 minutes on each side, until the skin is crispy and the fish is cooked through (the precise frying time will depend upon the type, size and thickness of fish you choose). Transfer the cooked fish to a plate lined with kitchen paper to soak up the excess oil. Fry all your fish in this manner.

Serve promptly while still hot, squeezing generous amounts of lemon juice all over the fish and garnishing with the chopped coriander leaves and sliced red chilli.

For a summery feel, serve your fish with mooli, cucumber and pomegranate salad; or for something more comforting, set the fish on top of plain basmati rice (see page 131) with some pickled turmeric (see page 57).

During the summer months, or when the weather permits, the glowing coals of a hot barbecue offer a unique and exciting way to cook your fish. Season the fish as in the method above and rub it with oil. Wrap it in foil and place it on the hot coals. Alternatively, you can grill the fish without wrapping it directly on the barbecue, but remember to oil the grill first to stop the fish from sticking.

SAAS NI MACCHI
FISH IN A SWEET AND SOUR SAUCE

 This dish is traditionally served at weddings to symbolise good luck and prosperity. The fish is gently cooked in sauce that is a beautiful balance between sweet and sour. Flat fish are best, as they are easier to cook in the thin layer of sauce. However, that's not to say that a well-filleted piece of hake, pollock or haddock would not suit. Even a skate wing would be a great twist to this classic dish.

Heat the ghee or butter in a frying pan over a medium heat. When hot, add the onion and garlic and fry for 6 minutes, or until the onion turns soft and translucent. Add the cumin, chilli and curry leaves and stir for 2 minutes to release the flavours.

Stir the flour into the pan to form a paste, then, bit by bit, add 500ml of water, stirring it into the paste to create a smooth sauce as you go. Do not be tempted to add too much water in one go, as this will create a lumpy sauce – an egg cup at a time is a good reference.

Crack the egg into a bowl and beat it together with the vinegar, sugar, salt and turmeric.

Lower the heat under the frying pan and add the egg mixture, stirring it in thoroughly.

Place the fish in a pan. As the sauce gently simmers around the fish, it will thicken and turn glossy. Cook the fish for 5 minutes on each side, regularly basting the sauce over the top to help the fish cook evenly, until cooked through.

As Parsi food is a balance between sweet, sour and salty, you must constantly taste your food to correct any imbalance. Have a taste of your sauce now and adjust it with a sprinkle of sugar, a dash of vinegar and/or a pinch of salt, as necessary, to bring harmony to the dish.

Once the fish is cooked through and you are happy with your sauce, place the fish on a large platter and smother it with the sauce. Arrange the cherry tomatoes around the platter and serve, preferably with steaming hot rice and kachuber salad (see page 124).

SERVES 2

2 tablespoons ghee or butter
1 small onion, finely chopped
3 garlic cloves, thinly sliced
1 teaspoon cumin seeds, lightly crushed in a pestle and mortar
1 small green chilli, thinly sliced
6 fresh curry leaves, roughly chopped
1 tablespoon rice flour (or chickpea flour or cornflour)
1 large egg
2 tablespoons apple cider vinegar, plus extra to taste
1 teaspoon caster sugar, plus extra to taste
1 teaspoon salt, plus extra to taste
½ teaspoon ground turmeric
1 whole flat fish on the bone, such as plaice, lemon sole or Dover sole (about 300g)
5 cherry tomatoes, halved

In the music of the kitchen,
the sauces are the melodies.
-- Alexandre Dumaine

Left: Gandhidham fish market
Right: Dinaz Aunty making fish curry

DINAZ AUNTY'S COCONUT AND TAMARIND FISH CURRY

The first time I ate this curry was after a 12-hour overnight train ride from the bustling city of Mumbai through the dusty desert state of Gujarat, to visit my grandfather. By the time the train pulled in to Gandhidham, it was midday and my aunt was preparing lunch for our arrival.

We were ushered straight into the kitchen to sit at the dining table overlooking the sunny back garden, sheltered from the scorching dry heat of midday. I have always known my aunty Dinaz is a fantastic cook – she prepares three meals a day for a family of five and takes immense pride in what she puts on the table. She follows the recipes and techniques handed down to her from her mother with the utmost rigour. I will never forget those first few mouthfuls of spicy, tangy sauce infused with the flavours of coconut and toasted coriander seeds. I knew immediately that this was a recipe I needed to add to my repertoire.

If you're using tamarind pulp rather than paste, prepare it by placing it in a small bowl and covering it in boiling water. Stir to separate the pulp from the seeds (you can use your fingers to do this once the water is cool enough). Strain the dark brown liquid and discard the seeds – use the liquid in the method as indicated.

For the best results, cook this dish in a wok.

Grind the coriander seeds, cloves, cinnamon or cassia bark, chillies, poppy seeds and sesame seeds together in a food processor to a semi-fine powder. Add the chopped coconut and the ginger–garlic paste and blitz to give a coarse paste.

Heat the vegetable oil in a wok over a low–medium heat. When hot, add the paste and fry it, continuously moving the paste around with a wooden spoon, for 8 minutes to give an even cook. You want the paste to become fragrant.

Add the coconut water and tomatoes and stir through, crushing the tomatoes as you go. Allow everything to come to a simmer over a low–medium heat, stirring every now and again.

As the liquid reduces it will start to lightly catch on the bottom of the wok. This is a good thing and will bring depth of flavour to your curry – use a wooden spoon to scrape, stirring the caught sauce back into the liquid and letting it catch again. If you feel the sauce catching on the bottom of the pan too quickly, and burning, just lower the heat a little

Continued overleaf...

SERVES 6

a golf-ball-sized piece of tamarind pulp, or 2 tablespoons tamarind paste

45g coriander seeds

8 cloves

5cm cinnamon stick or cassia bark

8 dried Kashmiri chillies

2 tablespoons white poppy seeds

2 tablespoons white sesame seeds

1 coconut, cracked open, coconut water reserved, peeled and chopped into small pieces (see page 32)

2 tablespoons ginger–garlic paste (see page 43)

125ml vegetable oil

8 large ripe tomatoes, chopped (the softer and squidgier, the better)

1 teaspoon hot chilli powder

1 teaspoon ground turmeric

4 teaspoons salt

800g firm, white fish (such as hake, cod or pollock), cut into bite-sized chunks

3 small green chillies, slit open

a generous handful of coriander, leaves picked and chopped

more and add a splash of water as you scrape those bits off. After about 20 minutes of catching and scraping, a wonderful aroma will fill your kitchen as the oils are drawn out of the coconut and spices.

Add the tamarind liquid or the tamarind paste, then 1 litre of water, the chilli powder, turmeric and salt and simmer for 20 minutes over a low–medium heat. Every now and then, return to the wok, stir, and make sure nothing is catching on the bottom.

Using a hand-held electric blender (or by transferring the sauce to a food processor), blitz the sauce until smooth (tip the sauce back into the wok from the food processor). It's not vital to blitz, but it does bring all the flavours together in a wonderful way.

Add the fish and the chillies and simmer for a further 10 minutes, or until the flesh of the fish is firm, opaque and cooked through. Remove from the heat and stir in the coriander. Serve to your weary travellers, family or friends with mounds of basmati rice and some pickled turmeric (see page 57).

No human being, however
great or powerful, was ever
so free as a fish.

-- John Ruskin

KEDGEREE – A PARSI VERSION

 I have fond memories of cooking kedgeree at St. John Bread and Wine. The aromas of steaming basmati rice, subtly spiked with cinnamon, cardamom and cloves, and of haddock fillets poaching in a milky bath tinted orange from saffron, all created smells that punctuated the restaurant in the early morning as we prepared to delight our lunchtime punters. I've put together this version with a hint of Parsi flair.

Heat a little ghee or butter in a large frying pan over a medium–high heat. Add the onions and fry, continuously moving them, for about 6–8 minutes, until they are dark golden and crisping at the edges.

Pour the milk into a large saucepan and add the bay leaves, saffron and turmeric. Place over a medium heat and bring to a gentle simmer.

Meanwhile, cut the haddock into pieces small enough to fit in the pan.

Turn down the heat under the pan to its lowest and add the haddock. If the pieces are not fully submerged, top up with more milk. Gently simmer the haddock for 2 minutes, or until the flesh turns from translucent to opaque and shows the first signs of giving. Leaving the milk on the heat, use a slotted spoon to remove the fish to a plate, skin side up, to cool. When the fish is cool enough to handle, peel away the skin and discard.

Pour the milk into a heatproof jug and tip the cooked rice straight into the same pan. Spoon the milk back into the pan, bit by bit, stirring it through and adding just enough so that the rice becomes damp, but not soupy. (You can freeze any leftover milk for the next time you make the kedgeree. It will keep, frozen, for up to 3 months.)

Place the onions and haddock in the pan, and place it over a low heat. Put a lid on the pan and leave it for about 5 minutes, until everything is piping hot, removing the lid to fold and gently tumble the ingredients together every minute. Take care to be gentle – you want the fish pieces to stay as whole as possible. If the kedgeree becomes dry or catches on the bottom of the pan at any point, add a few more splashes of the reserved milk and lower the heat a little more if possible.

Once the kedgeree is piping hot, fold in the lemon juice, and season with plenty of freshly cracked black pepper, and enough sea salt flakes to bring out the flavours. Finally, throw in a few fistfuls of chopped coriander and fenugreek leaves, and give everything one last fold. Serve the kedgeree on a platter and garnish with the boiled eggs.

Serve Gujarati-style with a warm bowl of kadhi (see page 163) and lagaan nu achaar (see page 59).

See overleaf for images.

SERVES 6–8

a little ghee or butter, for frying

2 large red onions, thickly sliced

1 litre whole milk, plus extra if needed

2 bay leaves

a generous pinch of saffron

¼ teaspoon ground turmeric

3 fillets of naturally smoked, skin-on, undyed haddock (about 800g total weight)

6 servings of khichdi rice, cooked with the holy four spices (see page 157)

12 eggs, boiled for 7 minutes, then peeled and halved

juice of 1 large lemon

a handful of coriander, leaves picked and chopped

a handful of fenugreek, leaves, picked and chopped

sea salt flakes and freshly cracked black pepper

PATRA NI MACCHI
FISH BAKED IN A BANANA LEAF WITH CORIANDER AND COCONUT CHUTNEY

SERVES 6

6 small firm white fish or
  fish fillets (see recipe
  introduction)
lemon juice
coconut and coriander
  chutney (see page 65)
6 banana leaves
sea salt and freshly
  cracked black pepper

This is a quintessential Parsi fish dish, favoured at weddings and other special occasions – and for good reason. Imagine, if you will, a succulent chunk of firm, white fish, coated in a paste of ground coconut, fresh coriander leaves and sour mango, then wrapped in a banana leaf and steamed until the fish flakes away from itself. Now imagine having that fragrant parcel gifted on your plate. And the excitement of unwrapping the green leaf to find a moist piece of fish, coated in the most flavoursome tangy green paste. I think it is the best present anyone could receive at the dinner table.

You will find the recipe for the coconut and coriander chutney on page 65, and this is also a perfect opportunity to use the brine recipe on page 203.

There are no hard-and-fast rules for choosing the fish you serve. Typically, Parsis would use pomfret, which you may be able to get hold of frozen, but I always think it's better to use fresh. In that case, hake, mullet, coley, bream and sea bass are all fantastic options. You can prepare small fish (around the size of your hand) whole; bigger fish (such as hake and coley) are better prepared as fillets, which makes it easy to judge portions. I prefer to leave the skin on – once the fish has cooked in the leaf, the skin becomes soft and delicious.

You'll find banana leaves readily available in Asian supermarkets. They are usually trimmed and ready to use, but a wipe with a damp cloth for good measure won't hurt. If they still have the spines running down them, trim these away, as they hinder the folding. Banana leaves are waxy, so they need a lick of heat to make them more pliable – pass your leaves over an open flame, or warm them in a dry frying pan, as if they were a rotli. Alternatively, use frozen. Frozen banana leaves (also readily available in Asian supermarkets) tend to be softer and easier to fold once they've defrosted than they are when the banana leaves are fresh.

If you can't find banana leaf, baking paper will achieve similar results – although it not as appealing to the eye. Depending on the size of the fish you are wrapping, for each fish, cut a piece of banana leaf into a rectangle roughly three times bigger than the piece of fish itself.

Season the fish well with salt, pepper and a squeeze of lemon juice, then liberally apply the chutney all over the fish, coating it in a layer a few millimetres thick.

Place the fish in the centre of a banana-leaf rectangle and fold in the sides to create a parcel. You can tie the parcel with string so that it holds, or just flip it over to keep the folds pinned underneath. Repeat for each piece of fish.

There are a few ways to cook the fish. The first is the classic: in a bamboo steamer (a saucepan of water topped with a steaming basket and a lid will do the trick if you don't have a bamboo version). Depending on the size of the fish, steaming should take 10 minutes, until the fish is opaque, flaking apart and cooked through.

I really enjoy the flavour of roasting the fish in the oven. Preheat the oven to 200°C/180°C fan. Place a shallow tray of water on the floor of the oven to heat up at the same time (this will create steam to help cook the fish and keep it moist). Lay the wrapped fish on a baking tray, then quickly open the oven door and pop the baking tray inside, trying not to let too much steam escape. Depending on the size of the fish, this method should take about 15 minutes.

Patra ni macchi is usually served with a whole plethora of side accompaniments, such as lagaan nu achar (see page 59), lentils and rice, but I like the idea of this as a small starter on its own or a dish to share at the table.

During the summer months, try grilling the fish parcels on the barbecue and serve them alongside grilled sweetcorn (see page 119) and fennel salad (see page 128).

See overleaf for images.

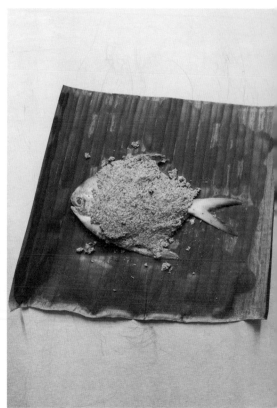

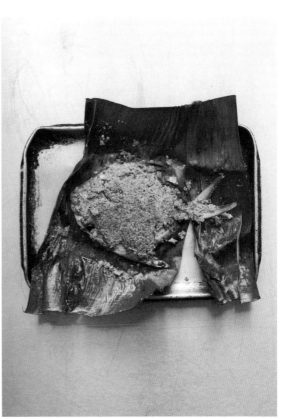

KOLMI NO PATYO
PRAWNS IN A RICH TOMATO GRAVY

 I ate this dish quite a few times growing up, but I only recently learned to cook it – Sunita, my uncle's cook in Mumbai, taught me. We made a basic version without the prawns and served it, the traditional Parsi way, alongside dhan dar (see page 160) and plain boiled rice. This trio is usually eaten the night before a Parsi wedding as it is simple to rustle up, yet unfailingly satisfying, readying the family before the big day. A neat little trick I learned from Sunita was to cut the tomatoes in half and grate the cut surface on the coarse side of a cheese grater. You end up with beautifully shredded tomato flesh (do it over a bowl to catch the juice, too) and the bare tomato skin left in your hand can be discarded.

First, make the sauce. Heat the vegetable oil in a wok over a medium heat. When hot, add the onions and garlic and cook for about 5 minutes, until the onions turn translucent and start to colour. Add the remaining sauce ingredients and reduce the heat to medium–low. Place a lid on the wok, leaving it slightly ajar, and simmer the sauce for 30 minutes, until the tomato has broken down and become one with the sauce.

While the sauce is simmering away, tip the salt, turmeric and chilli powder into a bowl and add the prawns. Add the lime juice and stir to coat the prawns in the marinade. (Do the same whether the prawns are raw or cooked.)

Heat the vegetable oil in a frying pan until hot. Add the prawns and fry for 1–2 minutes to cook out the spice coating.

Once the sauce has been bubbling away for 30 minutes, add the prawns, then simmer for 5 more minutes, until the prawns are cooked through and everything is piping hot. Scatter with the coriander, to garnish. Serve with dhan dar and steaming hot basmati rice.

There are plenty of other things that you could cook in the sauce (patyo) than prawns. Chunks of fish, such as cod, hake, pollock and mullet; chunks of sea bream cut on the bone; and skate cheeks; cooked and peeled brown shrimp; or green beans, peas, corn and other such vegetables. Alternatively, try fish roe, cut into chunks and pan-fried in hot oil for 4 minutes before adding to the sauce.

SERVES 4

FOR THE SAUCE
100ml vegetable oil
2 medium onions, finely chopped, or blitzed in a food processor
8 garlic cloves, grated
8 firm medium tomatoes, grated, or 2 400g tins of chopped tomatoes
1 tablespoon sambhar masala (see page 46)
½ teaspoon ground turmeric
1 tablespoon cumin–coriander powder (see page 48)
½ teaspoon chilli powder (mild or hot, as you like)
2 teaspoons salt
75ml apple cider vinegar
60g jaggery, chopped, or dark brown soft sugar

FOR THE PRAWNS
2 teaspoons salt
½ teaspoon ground turmeric
1 teaspoon hot chilli powder
500g raw peeled prawns (or 500g cooked)
juice of 1 lime
2–3 tablespoons vegetable oil
a handful of coriander, leaves picked and chopped, to garnish

CRAB AND COCONUT CURRY

SERVES 4

100ml vegetable oil

2.5cm cassia bark or cinnamon stick

4 cardamom pods, cracked

6 cloves

1 red onion, chopped

3 large garlic cloves, thinly sliced

7.5cm fresh ginger, peeled and cut into slivers

1 large red chilli, sliced into thin rounds

6 new potatoes, quartered and thickly sliced (skin on)

4 tomatoes, chopped

500ml crab cooking water or tap water

80g creamed coconut, chopped or grated

1 teaspoon ground turmeric

2 teaspoons sambhar masala (see page 46)

4 teaspoons cumin–coriander powder (see page 48)

¼ teaspoon fenugreek seeds, crushed in a pestle and mortar

a pinch of saffron

3 teaspoons sea salt

4 crabs, ideally Dorset crabs (about 600g each), cooked and picked; or 150g white and 100g brown crab meat

juice of 1 lime

a handful each of coriander and mint, leaves picked and roughly chopped

For the best results with this dish, try to get hold of live crabs – most fishmongers will source them with a bit of warning; large Asian supermarkets are likely to have them, too. When you buy your crabs, check that they are showing signs of life – look for movement as well as firm and intact limbs. When you get the crabs home, place them in the freezer for 1 hour to put them to sleep, then transfer them to a pan of very salty boiling water (salty as the sea – about 30g of salt per litre of water). Put the lid on the pan and boil the crabs for 12 minutes, then carefully transfer them to a tray to cool, collecting up any limbs that have detached themselves in the cooking process and reserving a few cups (about 500ml) of the flavourful crab water. Once the crabs are cooled, prise the top shell away from the body and the legs and use a teaspoon to scoop out the brown meat from inside the shell. Discard the spongey gills resting on the leg portion. Crack open the limbs (you may need to raid the tool box for a hammer or pair of pliers) and pick out all the flaky white crab meat; take your time and be thorough while moving through the many crevices to gather all your bounty.

Alternatively, you can, of course, save yourself the trouble and buy fresh crab meat from your local fishmonger or supermarket! For the best results, make this dish in a wok, if you have one.

Heat the oil in a wok over a medium heat. When hot, add the cassia or cinnamon along with the cardamom and cloves and allow to sizzle and become fragrant (about 1–2 minutes).

Add the onion, garlic, ginger and sizzle and sizzle for a further 3 minutes, until they are all soft, but not coloured – you want to maintain the fresh vibrancy of the ginger. Add the potato slices, increase the heat to high and fry for 1 minute, then add the tomatoes, crab water or tap water, creamed coconut, the rest of the spices and the salt (if using the salty crab water, taste before adding the salt). Bring the liquid to the simmer and adjust the heat to allow it to gently tick over for 20 minutes, or until the potatoes are cooked through and the pools of red oil from the creamed coconut float to the surface.

Stir in the white and brown crab meats, the lime juice and the chopped herbs and simmer for 2 more minutes to heat through. Serve with mounds of fluffy white rice.

MEAT

A FEW WORDS ON BRINING

Divide by 100 and multiply by 3 for effortless deliciousness.

I was never the biggest advocate for brining – the lazy cook in me just said get on with it and cook the meat! I was put off because there were percentages to calculate, timings were never consistent and recipes always differed – and most would never really explain the point of such a time-consuming process.

Then I found out about the equilibrium brine. I really got into this one as it was so simple to do. 'What is it for, though?' you ask. Put simply, proper brining paired with a good cooking technique can turn a lesser cut of meat into an unforgettably mouthwatering meal. Once cooked, a mundane piece of meat, through simple brining, can become a juicier, more flavourful, perfectly seasoned and much more tender chunk.

Brining does take time (anywhere from 6 to 24 hours), but none of those hours involve any effort and the payoff is huge. Truly convinced, I now brine fish and meat, especially if the meat is going to stew in a curry for a long time. I have found great success in brining chicken and recommend this as a starting point: the difference in flavour and texture for a brined versus non-brined chicken breast, thigh or drumstick will be enough to convert you. Before I make patra ni macchi (see page 192), I brine the fish so it stays perfectly moist during cooking, and even if it spends moments too long in the oven.

First, you'll need a set of scales (unless you already know the weight of what you're brining and have a marked measuring jug). Place a container on your scales that is big enough to take the piece of meat or fish you're intending to brine, as well as enough water to cover it.

Zero the scales so you are not taking into account the weight of the container. Place the fish or meat into the container and cover it with water (I also like to use any leftover whey from making paneer or shrikhand; see pages 75 and 278). Note the combined total weight of the meat or fish and the water. Divide this weight by 100 and multiply that number by 3. This is the amount of salt you need to add to the water for the brine to work (3%).

Place the 3% of salt into a jug and pour out some of the water that is in the container of meat or fish. Stir it through the salt until the salt has completely dissolved, then pour the mixture back to the container, ensuring all the salt is in the container and there are no grains left lurking behind.

Cover the container and place it in the fridge – overnight for smaller cuts of meat and for fillets of fish, or for 24 hours for large joints of meat.

Once the meat or fish has brined, rinse it in plenty of fresh, cold water before using – now you are ready to start cooking according to the recipe, just as you normally would.

A general rule of thumb is 6 hours for diced chicken breast or fish fillets. 12 hours for whole chicken, diced lamb or mutton. 24 hours for whole joints of lamb or mutton on the bone.

CHICKEN FARCHA
PARSI-STYLE FRIED CHICKEN

SERVES 6

1 whole chicken (about
    1.4kg), skin removed
    and broken into wings,
    drumsticks and thighs
    and each breast cut into
    3 pieces on the bone
a few shakes of
    Worcestershire sauce
1 bunch of coriander
5 bird's-eye chillies
4 tablespoons ginger–
    garlic paste (see
    page 43)
3 teaspoons salt
2 teaspoons ground
    turmeric
2 teaspoons hot chilli
    powder
2 tablespoons dhansak
    masala (see page 48)
1 litre vegetable oil,
    for frying
200g fine semolina
6 eggs, well beaten

 The most memorable chicken farcha I ever ate was at the Globe Hotel in Udvada. This small, dusty town set along the Arabian Sea is frequented by Zoroastrians from all over India and the world, who go there to visit the Iranshar Atash Behram, our holiest of Fire Temples.

Enterprising Parsis set up many hotels to accommodate those Parsis making the pilgrimage from far and wide to this small town. They knew that serving three hot meals a day of the most typical Parsi fare would clinch the deal – the quality of breakfast, lunch and dinner is the only way to choose a hotel. And so it was, at the renowned Globe Hotel, I bit into a piece of chicken farcha so delicious I've spent many years trying to replicate it. What follows is the version I'm most pleased with, although there are lost nuances that makes a trip to Udvada all-the-more worthwhile.

Of course, you can find fried chicken all over the world. What excites me about this Parsi style is the order in which the chicken is coated. More usually, the chicken is dipped in the egg to help the crumbs stick to the surface for a crunchy end product. Parsis, though, to show their affinity towards eggs, dip the chicken into the beaten egg last to create a perfectly golden and lightly crisp omelette casing. Genius!

I urge you to take the time to brine your chicken (see page 203) for the juiciest, most mouthwatering bite.

Tip the chicken pieces into a large bowl and prick them all over with a fork. Shake over the Worcestershire sauce, until all the pieces have a light coating.

Blitz together the coriander, chillies and ginger–garlic paste in a food processor to form a paste.

Using your hands, rub the paste into every crevice and fold of the chicken, making sure every surface is coated.

Add the salt (omit if you have brined the chicken), turmeric, chilli powder and the dhansak masala to the bowl, and rub some more. Cover the bowl and refrigerate for at least 1 hour, or overnight if possible, for the flavours to seep into the chicken.

Remove the chicken from the fridge at least 1 hour before cooking to allow it to come up to room temperature.

Pour the oil into a deep, heavy-based pot so that it comes two thirds of the way up the sides. Place the pot over a medium–high heat and heat the oil to 170°C on a cooking thermometer (or until a cube of bread dropped into the oil sizzles, rises to the surface and turns golden within 60 seconds).

Tip the semolina into a shallow tray and the eggs into a deep bowl. Piece by piece, roll the chicken pieces into the semolina until they resemble wet thighs on a sandy beach, followed by a dip in the beaten egg, then straight into the frying pot. Fry the chicken a few pieces at a time (don't overload the pot), turning every so often with a slotted spoon, until the chicken is golden and cooked through (about 8–9 minutes per batch).

Using the slotted spoon, remove each batch of chicken and set aside to drain on kitchen paper and cool until hot, but not scalding. Season each piece with a light pinch of salt and serve with wedges of lemon for squeezing, mango pickle mayonnaise (see page 55) and some coconut and coriander chutney.

ALETI PALETI
SPICY CHICKEN LIVER AND GIZZARDS

SERVES 4

600g chicken livers

400g chicken hearts

100ml vegetable oil, plus
  2 tablespoons

1 large onion, thinly sliced

5 small green chillies,
  thinly sliced

2 tablespoons ginger–
  garlic paste (see
  page 43)

2 large tomatoes, finely
  chopped

1 teaspoon cumin seeds,
  lightly crushed

2 teaspoons dhansak
  masala (see page 48)

2 teaspoons garam masala
  (see page 46)

20g jaggery, chopped, or
  caster sugar

2 tablespoons apple cider
  vinegar

2 tablespoons
  Worcestershire sauce,
  plus extra if needed

a handful of coriander,
  leaves picked and
  chopped

salt

This popular dish, traditionally of chicken gizzards and livers, is often eaten during a Parsi wedding feast. However, from the many chickens that are prepared for a Parsi wedding, there's usually not enough offal to feed all the hundreds of guests – only a select lucky few. Guests are fed in sittings – with out-of-towners fed first, followed by friends and family. As a reward for their patience, the bride and groom and their close family – the last sitting of all – get to eat the aleti paleti.

I prefer to use hearts instead of gizzards – they are easier to get hold of, simple to clean and much more forgiving during cooking. If you can't find them, though, all is not lost – this dish is still delicious with livers on their own. It's best cooked in a wok or large frying pan.

Before you begin, clean the livers and hearts. To clean the livers, slice away any sinew and white bits that hold the different lobes of the liver together. For the hearts, you just want to slice away the first few millimetres of white fat and sinew at the top of the heart.

Rinse the livers and hearts in cold water and drain them in a colander. Use some kitchen paper to dry off the last of the water.

Pour the oil into a large frying pan or a wok and heat it over a high heat.

Meanwhile, season the livers and hearts with salt. When the oil is hot, add the hearts to the pan and fry for 1 minute, then add the livers and fry for a further 2 minutes (the hearts are denser muscle and take that little bit longer to cook and colour up). Tip the contents of the pan into a bowl and set aside.

Add the extra 2 tablespoons of oil to the pan. Reduce the heat to medium–low and add the onion, chillies and ginger–garlic paste. Fry for 3 minutes, then add all the juices and oil from the livers and hearts that have collected in the bottom of the bowl. Continue to cook for a further 3 minutes, until the onions soften and become translucent.

Add the tomatoes, cumin, dhansak masala, garam masala, half a cup of water and ½ teaspoon of salt. Cook for a further 10 minutes, with a lid placed loosely over the top, until the tomatoes have cooked down and given. If things start to catch during that time, lower the heat and add a splash more water.

Continued overleaf...

Add the jaggery or sugar, vinegar and Worcestershire sauce, giving everything a moment to mingle together.

Return the livers, hearts and any juices that have accumulated in the bowl to the pan and cook for a further 3 minutes, to heat through. Stir through the coriander leaves to finish.

Taste the sauce and adjust the seasoning – I sometimes find a dash more Worcestershire sauce or pinch more salt refines the balance. Serve with warmed rotlis (see page 114) and a bowl of tangy onions (see page 161).

I also like to serve aleti paleti as a pie. In this case, don't return the livers and hearts to the pan for the final stages of cooking, as they will overcook as the pie bakes. Instead, at the stage where the jaggery has dissolved, add the vinegar and Worcestershire sauce and let it cook out for 2 minutes. Turn off the heat and stir the livers and hearts through with the coriander. Place the mixture in a pie dish or bowl and top with a pie lid (see page 257). Make a hole in the top of the pastry to allow the steam to escape and bake in the oven for 30 minutes at 200°C/180°C fan, or until the pie lid is golden brown.

ADU LASAN NI MURGI
ROAST CHICKEN WITH GINGER AND GARLIC

Give your Sunday roasts a Parsi twist with this simple – yet rewarding – one-tray wonder that's certain to impress family and friends alike.

Bring a large saucepan of salted water to the boil over a high heat. Add the potatoes and boil for 8–10 minutes, until tender but not falling apart. Drain and set aside.

Sprinkle the chicken pieces all over with salt (unless the chicken has been brined). Spoon the ghee or vegetable oil into a sturdy baking tray or cast-iron pot and place it over a high heat. Fry the chicken pieces for about 4 minutes, turning regularly to give a golden colour all over the skin and flesh.

Remove the chicken pieces from the tray or pot and reduce the heat to low. Add the onion, ginger–garlic paste, chillies, all the whole spices, the garam masala and a good sprinkling of salt. Cook gently for a good 10 minutes, until the onion has softened and is beginning to turn light brown. During this time the ginger–garlic paste will start to catch in the tray or pot and darken – this is a good thing. Add a few tablespoons of water over the caught areas and scrape them free. The water will evaporate and the process will start again – repeating it over the 10 minutes will add an aromatic and caramelised depth to the dish.

Preheat the oven to 190°C/170°C fan.

Add the jaggery and vinegar to the tray or pot, squashing the jaggery down with the back of your spoon to break it apart and help it dissolve.

Return the chicken pieces to the pan and nestle the potatoes around them. Pour the chicken stock over the top but do not submerge the meat or potatoes (think chicken icebergs poking above a sea of stock). For spectacularly golden potatoes, brush the parts poking above the stock with oil or ghee and finish the tray with a final flourish of salt and a generous crack of black pepper.

Bake, uncovered, for 1½ hours, or until the chicken is cooked through. Serve with kachuber (see page 124), wedges of lemon, and some cooling bowls of yoghurt.

See overleaf for images.

SERVES 6–8

6 medium potatoes, peeled and quartered
1 large chicken (about 1.8kg), divided into pieces on the bone
4 tablespoons ghee or vegetable oil, plus extra for brushing
1 large onion, thinly sliced
4 tablespoons ginger–garlic paste (see page 43)
3 small green chillies, split
2 whole star anise
½ teaspoon cloves
1 teaspoon cardamom pods, cracked in a pestle and mortar
7.5cm cassia bark or cinnamon stick
1 tablespoon garam masala (see page 46)
1 tablespoon jaggery or dark brown soft sugar
70ml apple cider vinegar
1 litre hot chicken stock
salt and freshly cracked black pepper

One need not devour a whole chicken
to know the flavour of the bird.
-- Chinese proverb

BADAM NI MARGHI
CHICKEN IN RICH ALMOND GRAVY

SERVES 6

1 large chicken (about 1.8kg), divided into pieces on the bone

1kg full-fat natural yoghurt

2 tablespoons ginger–garlic paste (see page 43)

200g ground almonds

a few tablespoons ghee or unsalted butter

1 teaspoon cardamom pods, lightly cracked in a pestle and mortar

7.5cm cassia bark or cinnamon stick

1 teaspoon cloves

3 whole star anise

3 medium red onions, thickly sliced

1 tablespoon caraway seeds

a generous pinch of saffron

5 small green chillies, split

a large handful of coriander, leaves picked and chopped

salt and freshly cracked black pepper

 I have seen different versions of this dish in many old Parsi cookbooks. It's sometimes referred to as chicken with 100 almonds. There is something very quaint about the idea that a dish must be made with 100 of something – where 99 just won't do and 101 will tip the balance. To save you counting, though, I've given the quantity of almonds by ground weight, (you can buy them whole and grind them yourself in a spice grinder if you prefer).

Place your chicken pieces in a large bowl followed by the yoghurt, ginger–garlic paste, ground almonds, and a few good sprinkles of salt and black pepper to season. Massage the chicken pieces, evenly coating them with the yoghurt mixture. Cover the bowl and leave the chicken to sit out at room temperature, while you prepare the rest of the dish.

Melt the ghee or butter in a large, cast-iron pot over a medium heat. Once melted, throw in cardamom pods, cassia or cinnamon, cloves and star anise. Allow the spices to sizzle for a minute or two to become fragrant, then add the caraway seeds, giving them 1 minute to sizzle with the spices.

Add the onions and turn up the heat slightly. Leave to cook for 5 minutes. When they begin to sizzle and take on some colour, add the saffron.

Take the chicken out of the marinade, squeezing it through your fingers to remove as much yoghurt coating as possible. Reserve the marinade in the bowl.

Turn up the heat under the pot and add the chicken, stirring it through for 5 minutes, until it begins to take on some colour. Stir in the marinade and when the sauce begins to bubble, turn down the heat to low and add the chillies.

Place a lid on the pot, keeping it ever so slightly ajar, and cook the chicken for 45 minutes, returning to the pan every 5 minutes to give things a stir.

Alternatively, preheat the oven to 180°C/160°C fan. Place the pot in the oven without a lid for 45 minutes, returning every 10 minutes to give things a stir.

By the end of the cooking time, the yoghurt should have reduced so that it looks as though it has split and is slightly bobbly, but coats the chicken. Stir through the coriander leaves. Serve, ideally with fresh rotlis (see page 114) and kachuber salad (see page 124).

PARSI MARGHI NO RAS
MEHERJI UNCLE'S PARSI-STYLE CHICKEN CURRY

 Cooking meat on the bone will bring the most flavour to a dish. It is no wonder, then, that Parsis love to eat their meat, especially chicken, like this. I like to crack the bones of the drumsticks open with a meat cleaver, allowing all the flavour from within to simmer into the sauce as it stews.

Traditional Parsi cookbooks often refer to this dish as 'poor man's curry' – an indication that adding meat is optional, for when the budget allows. So, feel free to make it without the chicken, if you prefer – it will be delicious nonetheless. One of my uncles in Mumbai taught me this particular recipe.

Heat the vegetable oil in a wok or sturdy-bottomed pot over a medium heat. When hot, add the onion and 1 teaspoon of salt and fry for 5 minutes, until the onion shows the first signs of turning brown. Stir in the ginger–garlic paste and continuously agitate and scrape the bottom of the pan with a wooden spoon for 5 minutes, until the onion and ginger–garlic paste are golden. You may need to add a dash of water to the pan to release anything that has caught on the bottom.

Add the creamed coconut and jaggery or sugar, stirring it in for 30 seconds, until everything has dissolved, then add the cashew and coconut masala and thoroughly stir again. Reduce the heat to medium–low and cook the masala for 2 minutes to bring out the flavours in the spices.

Add the tomatoes, turmeric and vinegar with 250ml of water and stir everything together. Place a lid on the pan and allow the sauce to simmer gently for 30 minutes, stirring everything every 5 minutes or so, until it has reduced and thickened.

Meanwhile, place the chicken pieces in a large saucepan and cover with water. Add the remaining salt and place over a medium–low heat. Bring to the simmer and very gently simmer for 30 minutes, until cooked through. (Reserve the cooking water to use as stock another day.)

For the best results, giving the most tender meat that falls from the bone, cook the chicken legs in a pressure cooker for 15 minutes.

Add the cooked chicken to the tomato sauce and simmer for 10 minutes, allowing the chicken to sup up all the flavours from the sauce and until the liquid has reduced so that the sauce is thick and chunky and the creamed coconut has formed a deep red oil that sits on the surface.

To finish, stir through the coriander, then serve immediately with plain rice and toasted papads (see page 111).

SERVES 6

100ml vegetable oil
1 white onion, blitzed in a food processor or very finely chopped
3 teaspoons salt
2 tablespoons ginger–garlic paste (see page 43)
50g creamed coconut
20g jaggery, grated, or 1 teaspoon caster sugar
4 tablespoons cashew and coconut masala (see page 47)
8 large tomatoes, chopped small
1 teaspoon ground turmeric
2 tablespoons apple cider vinegar
12 chicken drumsticks, or 6 thighs and 6 legs
a small bunch of coriander, leaves and stems chopped

KHEEMA
A PARSI VERSION

SERVES 6

100ml vegetable oil
4 cloves
2.5cm cassia bark or
  cinnamon stick
3 cardamom pods,
  cracked
1 teaspoon cumin seeds,
  lightly crushed in a
  pestle and mortar
8 fresh curry leaves
1 medium onion, chopped
3 tablespoons ginger–
  garlic paste (see
  page 43)
4 small green chillies,
  slit open
1 teaspoon sambhar
  masala (see page 46)
2 teaspoons garam masala
  (see page 46)
1 teaspoon ground
  turmeric
3 teaspoons salt
1 teaspoon caster sugar
3 tablespoons apple
  cider vinegar
3 teaspoons
  Worcestershire sauce
  (about 9 dashes)
1 400g tin of chopped
  tomatoes
500g minced meat
  of choice
200g frozen peas
a handful of coriander,
  leaves picked and
  chopped
a handful of mint, leaves
  picked and chopped

Kheema, a dish of spiced ground meat, is not uniquely Parsi: communities throughout India and farther afield eat it voraciously in many forms – scooped up in rotli, stuffed inside mashed potato and deep-fried, or baked with eggs.

When it's in season, I like to use venison mince for my kheema. The meat is lean and lends a deep flavour that is not overly gamey, but quite enjoyable. Typical Parsi cafés would make this using goat, but don't feel restricted in choosing the type of meat you use – beef, lamb, venison or pork, any will work. My mum even used to make it with minced turkey when I was growing up.

Heat the vegetable oil in a wok over a medium heat. When hot, add the cloves, cassia bark or cinnamon stick, and cardamom pods and sizzle for 2 minutes, until fragrant. Add the cumin seeds and curry leaves and sizzle for a further 1 minute.

Add the onion and fry for 3 minutes, then add the ginger–garlic paste and chillies. Fry for a further 5 minutes, or until the onions begin to turn golden.

Lower the heat and add the sambhar masala, garam masala, turmeric, salt and sugar and stir through for 30 seconds, then add the vinegar, Worcestershire sauce and tomatoes. Half fill the empty tomato tin with water, give it a swirl, and add the water to the wok.

Bring everything to a gentle simmer, then add the minced meat and stir through well, breaking up any big clumps.

Bring the mixture back to the simmer over a medium–low heat and add the peas. Cook for about 25 minutes, stirring occasionally – you want the liquid to reduce during the cooking, which will thicken up the dish.

Remove the wok from the heat, throw in the coriander and mint and stir through. Serve immediately with rotlis (see page 114) and a kachuber salad (see page 124).

They dined on mince and slices of quince.
-- Edward Lear

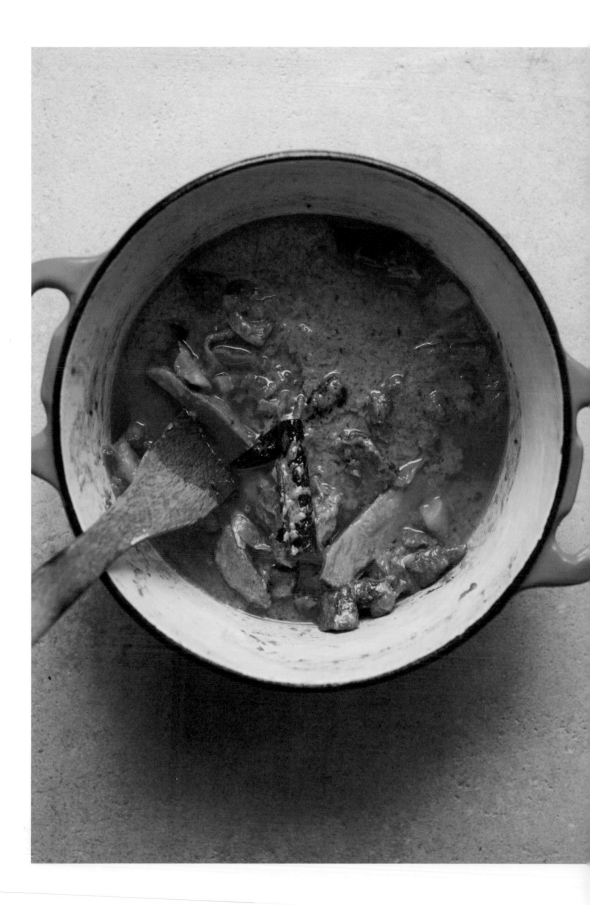

PAPETA MA GOS
MEAT AND POTATO STEW

This classic Parsi stew is traditionally made with goat meat
in India, but you can improvise and use mutton or lamb which
bring exceptional flavour, or try veal for something different.
Whichever animal you decide on, choose a cut that is suited to
slow cooking – shank, leg, shoulder and brisket are all great
choices. Most butchers will give you the option of meat on the
bone and this is what you want – the flavours imbued during
a slow braise from the bone and its marrow are distinctive and
delicious; it's a trick not to be missed.

This recipe makes good use of the brining technique (see page
203). For something more exotic, you can substitute the cream
for coconut milk, which any Parsi would always be delighted
to eat. In this case, though, I prefer the richness of cream, and
the way it reduces down as the meat cooks and coats the chunks
makes for a very comforting and hearty stew.

I like to keep the skin on my potato when frying as it gives a
real earthy flavour to the braise and a slight chew for the tooth,
which is a lovely contrast to the soft and unctuous meat. Just
give them a good wash beforehand if they are muddy, which
some varieties of small potatoes can be.

SERVES 4

500g diced meat of choice
(preferably on the bone
for flavour)
1 tablespoon ginger–garlic
paste (see page 43)
¼ teaspoon ground
turmeric
2 teaspoons salt
200ml vegetable oil
300g potatoes (Jersey
Royals or new potatoes
are good), halved if
small, or quartered,
skin on
3 dried Kashmiri chillies
5 cardamom pods,
cracked
6 black peppercorns
5 cloves
1 teaspoon cumin seeds,
lightly crushed in a
pestle and mortar
2.5cm cassia bark or
cinnamon stick
1 large onion, finely sliced
350ml single cream
pinch of saffron (optional)
½ bunch of coriander,
leaves picked and
chopped

Tip the meat into a large bowl and add the ginger–garlic paste, turmeric
and ½ teaspoon of the salt (omit the salt if you have brined the meat
beforehand). Rub the marinade all over the meat, cover and let it sit at
room temperature for 30 minutes.

Towards the ending of the marinating time, heat the vegetable oil in
a large, sturdy cast-iron pot over a medium heat. When hot, add the
potatoes and fry for about 2–4 minutes, turning regularly, until golden.
Using a slotted spoon, remove the potatoes from the pot and set aside,
leaving the oil in the pot.

Add the meat to the hot oil in the pot and fry, turning regularly, for
3 minutes, or until the meat has evenly coloured. Using a slotted spoon,
remove the meat from the pot and set aside. Reduce the heat under the
pot to low.

Add the chillies, cardamom pods, peppercorns, cloves, cumin seeds
and cassia bark or cinnamon to the pot and sizzle the spices for a few
minutes, until fragrant. Add the onion and cook for 5 minutes, or until
the onion slices turn golden brown.

Continued overleaf...

Return the meat and any resting juices to the pan. Add the remaining salt and stir everything together, allowing the onions and the spices to coat the meat.

Pour in the cream – there should be just enough that it does not completely submerge the meat, but leaves a few chunks showing above the surface. Bring the cream to a gentle simmer and place the lid on the pot, leaving it slightly ajar. Gently simmer the meat like this for 30 minutes, then return the potatoes to the pot, stirring them through.

Bring the liquid back to the simmer and cook, with the lid ajar, for a further 30 minutes, until the meat is completely tender and the potatoes are cooked through.

Remove the stew from the heat, stir in a pinch of saffron if using, and rest the stew for 20 minutes, allowing the meat time to relax and absorb all the flavours in the sauce. Finish with the coriander and serve with piles of basmati rice, and tangy onions (see page 161).

If you prefer, you can cook the stew in the oven (I find that it gives a more even, controlled cook). Preheat the oven to 180°C/160°C fan and use the cooking and resting times given in the method.

During the months when fresh broad beans, runner beans and peas are in season, you can make a summer version of this stew: instead of using potatoes, use a mixture of these beans and peas, adding them after the meat and just before the cream. This is a riff on another classic Parsi stew called papri ma gos.

MASOOR MA JEEBH
LAMB'S TONGUE, MASOOR DAL AND SPINACH

 Far be it for any discerning Parsi to shy away from offal. A lamb's tongue offers flavours and textures that no other cut of meat can match. The tongue has qualities that pair well with the mixture of spices in the dish and the gentle nature of slowly braised lentils. You'll need to prepare your tongues the day before you intend to cook.

The day before you intend to cook, place the lamb tongues in a large bowl or airtight container and generously sprinkle with the coarse sea salt to coat. Cover with cling film or the lid and refrigerate for 8 hours. During this time the tongues will expel some moisture and impurities as the salt penetrates the flesh, seasoning it to perfection.

The following day, rinse the lamb tongues under cold water to wash away the salt. Your tongues are now salted and ready to cook.

Place the rinsed tongues in a saucepan and totally submerge them with fresh, cold water. Throw in the bay leaf and 1 teaspoon of salt, and place over a high heat. Bring the liquid to the boil, then reduce the heat and gently simmer the tongues for about 2½ hours, or until they are tender and giving. (A pressure cooker will do this job in just 30 minutes, leaving you with the most tender tongues.)

Use tongs or a slotted spoon to remove the tongues from the cooking water and leave them to cool. Reserve the cooking water as stock to cook the lentils later. Once the tongues are cool, peel away the thick, outer skin. Slice each tongue along its length to about 3mm thick, keeping those long, elegant contours.

Heat the vegetable oil in a wok over a medium–high heat. Add the onion and gently fry for about 1 minute, then add the ginger–garlic paste. Fry for about 3 minutes, until the onion is translucent but not coloured. Then add the tomatoes, rinsed and drained lentils, the split chillies and all the dried spices, and season with salt. Stir everything through and leave on the heat for about 10 minutes, until the tomato has broken down.

Little by little, add the reserved tongue stock – don't swamp the lentils, let them gently cook and slowly absorb the liquid after each addition of stock. Keep adding more liquid as they cook – you want the end result to be cooked lentils with a little bit of stock, not lentils in broth. The whole process will take about 15–20 minutes.

SERVES 4

8 lamb tongues
200g coarse sea salt
1 bay leaf
100ml vegetable oil
1 large onion, thinly sliced
1 tablespoon ginger–garlic paste (see page 43)
3 medium tomatoes, finely diced
200g masoor dal (brown lentils), soaked for 20 minutes and rinsed
3 small green chillies, split
½ tablespoon garam masala (see page 46)
1 tablespoon dhansak masala (see page 48)
1 teaspoon ground turmeric
250g spinach leaves
about 500g full-fat natural yoghurt, for dolloping
salt and freshly cracked black pepper

Continued overleaf...

Once you are happy that your lentils are cooked through, add the tongue slices and gently stir them through for a few minutes to take in the heat. Taste for seasoning and add more salt, if necessary, as well as freshly ground cracked pepper, which is always welcome, too.

Remove the pan from the heat and throw in the spinach, folding it through to wilt. Pour the mixture on to a large platter and add generous dollops of yoghurt to cut through the richness. Serve with warmed rotlis (see page 114) and a large bowl of tangy onions (see page 161).

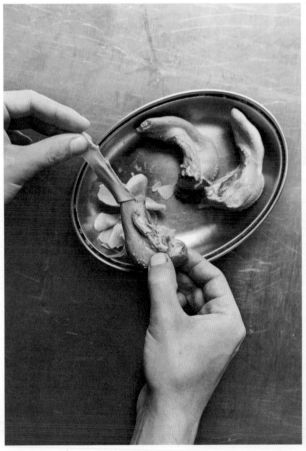

LAMB AND
HERB KAVABS

 These tasty kebabs are traditionally prepared to be served alongside dhansak, nestled among the brown rice. They make a tasty snack if you have friends coming over... or also when you don't.

MAKES 20

1 small onion, finely
    chopped
4 small green chillies,
    finely chopped
a handful of mint, leaves
    picked
a handful of coriander,
    leaves and stems torn
500g lamb mince
2 teaspoons salt
½ teaspoon freshly
    cracked black pepper
250g fine semolina
500ml vegetable oil,
    for frying

Blitz the onion, chillies, mint and coriander together in a food processor to make a paste.

In a large bowl, mix together the minced lamb, salt, pepper and the blitzed mixture.

Divide the kebab mixture into 20 small pieces and roll each into a ball.

Tip the semolina on to a plate or tray and roll the balls through it a few at a time to coat them in the semolina, then lightly flatten.

If serving alongside dhansak, this is all you need to do. If serving as a snack, it a nice touch to dip them in beaten egg after, just like chicken farcha (see page 204).

Pour the oil into a medium heavy-based saucepan so that it comes two thirds of the way up the sides. Place the pan over a medium–high heat and heat the oil to 170°C on a cooking thermometer (or until a cube of bread sizzles, rises to the surface and turns golden within 60 seconds). Add the kebabs a few at a time to the hot oil, taking care not to overcrowd the pan. Fry each batch for about 3 minutes, turning frequently, until the kebabs are a darker shade of gold all over. Remove each batch with a slotted spoon and set aside to drain on kitchen paper while you fry the remainder.

They are delectable served with a generous squeeze of lemon juice and alongside mango pickle mayonnaise (see page 55).

MASALA CHORA NE KHARIA
SPICY BLACK-EYED BEANS AND TROTTERS

SERVES 4

120g dried black-eyed
   beans
4 sheep's trotters or 2 pig's
   trotters, split lengthways
   and halved (your
   butcher will oblige)
1 tablespoon ghee or
   vegetable oil
1 medium onion, finely
   chopped
2 teaspoons ginger–garlic
   paste (see page 43)
3 small green chillies,
   split open
1 tablespoon sambhar
   masala (see page 46)
½ teaspoon ground
   turmeric
5cm cassia bark or
   cinnamon stick
200ml full-fat
   coconut milk
1 tablespoon tamarind
   paste
salt and freshly cracked
   black pepper

 The culinary use of trotters is popular in cultures across the world, bringing a gelatinous, lip-smacking texture to dishes of many cuisines. In the UK, sheep's trotters are readily available in Halal butchers and pig's trotters in Chinatown markets, or a well-stocked local butcher. A trotter cooked with care and attention is a joy to gnaw on. Past the thin layer of soft skin comes a bounty of tender meat and a satisfying crunch of cooked cartilage. In this classic dish the trotters bring those qualities together with black-eyed beans and hearty spices, tempered with soothing cassia bark and coconut milk to create a memorable stew with bold character.

You can also make the dish with lamb's or pig's tongue (a tongue per person is plenty) instead of trotters, or without either if you fancy a meat-free meal.

First, place the beans in a bowlful of water to cover and soak for at least 1 hour. Use an extremely sharp knife or disposable razor to trim away any patches of hair from the trotters, and then give them a thorough wash.

Place the trotters in a large pot and cover with cold water. Place the pot over a high heat and bring the water to the boil. Remove the trotters to a plate and discard the water. (This pre-boil ensures the trotters are thoroughly cleaned and ready to cook.)

Heat the ghee or oil in a large, sturdy-bottomed pot over a medium heat. When hot, reduce the heat to low and add the onion, ginger–garlic paste and chillies. Fry for 6 minutes, until the onion is translucent, then add the sambhar masala, turmeric and cassia bark and stir everything through.

Add the drained beans, coconut milk and 2 teaspoons of salt, along with 400ml of water. Increase the heat and bring the liquid to the boil, then lower the heat to a simmer and add the trotters. Simmer with the lid on for 1½ hours (check the contents of the pot after 30 minutes, turning the trotters over; if the liquid has gone down below the line of the beans, top up with some more water).

If you have a pressure cooker, you can cook this meal in less than half the time – take all the same steps using the pressure-cooker pan as the sturdy pot and cook under pressure for only 40 minutes.

Once the beans are soft and the meat on the trotters is tender and falling from the bones, add the tamarind paste and stir it through. Have a taste and adjust the seasoning accordingly.

To serve, spoon the beans on to a platter and place the trotters on top for everyone to help themselves. Every person should have a trotter to gnaw on. Fresh rotli (see page 114) and tangy onions (see page 161) are excellent accompaniments.

MASALA MA BUKKA
SPICED LAMB KIDNEYS

 Kidneys – you either love them or hate them, but if it's the latter hopefully this recipe will convince you otherwise. Kidneys are widely eaten within the Parsi community, revered for their nutrients and protein, and loved for their own delicious flavour and the affinity they have with spices.

Lamb kidneys are readily available, even in supermarkets. They should smell fresh with only the notes of raw meatiness – people who have been put off by the strong, unpleasant smell of kidneys have not had the opportunity to eat them fresh.

Season the kidneys well with ½ teaspoon of salt.

Heat half of the fat, vegetable oil or ghee in a wok over a high heat. When hot, add the kidneys, cut side up, and fry them for 1 minute, until they take on a dark brown colour. Tip the contents of the pan into a bowl and leave the kidneys to rest.

Wipe the wok clean with a piece of kitchen paper and return it to the heat with the remaining fat, oil or ghee. When hot, add the onion and fry for 3 minutes, or until the onion begins to turn translucent, add the crushed cumin seeds, then the garlic. Fry for 3 minutes, then add the ginger and chillies and cook for 2 minutes, until aromatic.

Add the tomatoes, turmeric, both masalas and 1 teaspoon of salt to the pan. Bring the sauce to the simmer, then reduce the heat to low and simmer everything for 10 minutes, stirring every now and then to break up the tomato, until the sauce begins to thicken.

Return the kidneys to the pan, including any oil and resting juices, and add the vinegar. Simmer over a low heat for a further 3 minutes, until the kidneys are fully heated through and the flavours have melded. Finally, stir through the coriander, then remove from the heat and serve immediately with fresh rotlis (see page 114) and tangy onions (see page 161).

SERVES 4

500g lamb kidneys,
  cleaned and halved
100g suet or kidney fat
  (from the lamb), or
  100ml vegetable oil
  or ghee
1 medium onion,
  thinly sliced
½ teaspoon cumin seeds,
  lightly crushed
5 large garlic cloves,
  thinly sliced
2cm fresh ginger, grated
4 small green chillies,
  finely chopped
2 large, overripe tomatoes,
  finely chopped
½ teaspoon ground
  turmeric
1 teaspoon garam masala
  (see page 46)
1 teaspoon dhansak
  masala (see page 48)
2 tablespoons apple cider
  vinegar
a large handful of
  coriander, leaves
  chopped
salt

ROAST LEG OF LAMB WITH GARLIC AND TURMERIC

SERVES 6–8

1 leg of lamb (about 1.5kg)
8–12 large garlic cloves, halved lengthways
2 tablespoons ground turmeric
1 teaspoon cumin seeds, lightly ground
1 teaspoon caraway seeds, lightly ground
2 teaspoons salt
1 teaspoon freshly cracked black pepper
100ml melted ghee or vegetable oil

During the Iranian midsummer festival of Tiregan, those who made the pilgrimage to the Zoroastrian holy shrines would often take with them pieces of lamb or goat. The meat would be studded with cloves of garlic and rubbed all over with salt and turmeric before being roasted on open fires and served to fellow pilgrims.

You can recreate the essence of this ancient roast at home either in an oven or on a barbecue. Cooking this leg should be part of a festive occasion, surrounded by family and friends and with myriad other dishes to accompany it – Persian scorched rice (see page 151), papri (see page 166) and mooli, cucumber and pomegranate salad (see page 131) would be welcome guests at the table.

If you want something extra-special, brining the leg overnight (see page 203) will keep the lamb succulent throughout the roasting period.

Preheat the oven to 190°C/170°C fan.

With the tip of a sharp knife, poke 1cm-deep holes all over the lamb and push the halved garlic cloves into the cuts.

Place the turmeric, cumin, caraway, salt and pepper in a bowl with the ghee or vegetable oil and mix it together to form a paste. Rub the paste all over the lamb leg. (You may want to use gloves, as the turmeric will stain your hands – though I find this is a good look!)

Place the lamb in a baking tray and roast for 1 hour 20 minutes, turning it every 20 minutes and basting it over the top with any juices to keep it succulent, until the lamb is cooked through. Remove from the oven, cover the leg in foil and leave the lamb to rest for 20 minutes away from the heat to give the juices a chance to ease back into the meat, making your leg of lamb all the more juicy and delicious. Use a long, sharp knife to cut the meat into thin slices to serve.

To barbecue the meat, heat your barbecue until moderately hot (you should be able to hold your hand about 5cm above the grill for 5 seconds before it feels too hot) and without any flames or hot spots. Place the leg on the grill, turning every few minutes to ensure that the leg cooks evenly and the spices don't burn, for about 45 minutes, until cooked. A great tip is to push the hot coals to one side of the barbecue and place the leg on the opposite side – this will stop the direct heat from the coals overcooking or burning the meat.

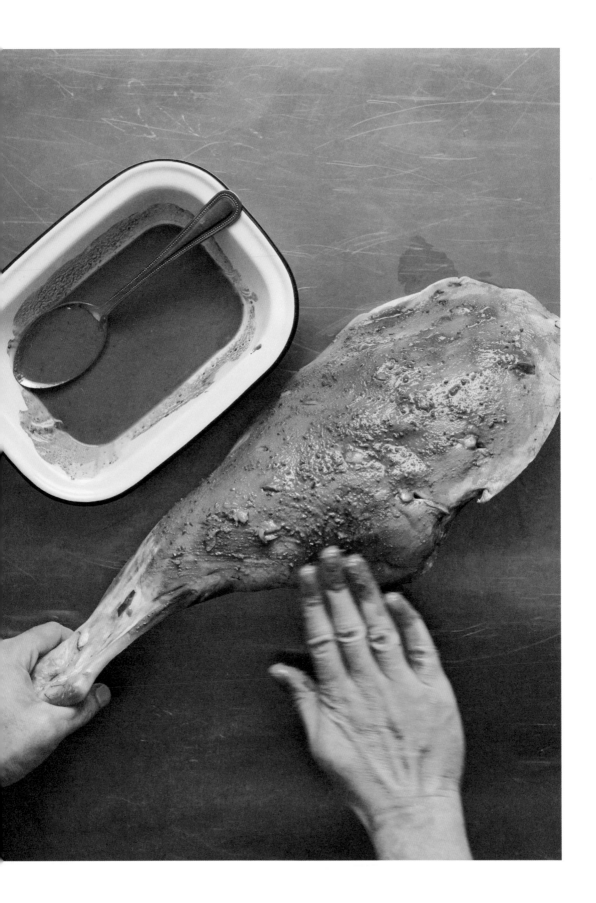

MUTTON DHANSAK
MUTTON IN A RICH LENTIL GRAVY

 Dhansak is a quintessential Parsi dish found on the Sunday lunch table in Parsi households all around India (though never on auspicious days) – the equivalent of the Sunday roast, if you will. Served alongside are its faithful companions: basmati rice steamed with caramelised onions (known to Parsis as 'brown rice' because of the colour after cooking) and kebabs made from minced mutton or lamb (see page 225).

Dhansak – a mixture of different lentils, fiery spices and slow-cooked mutton – was much loved by the British in India, so they brought it to the UK and it became a mainstay of curry houses up and down the country. However, a trait of Anglo-Indian cooking during those early years was to take favoured aspects of different regional dishes and apply them to all. Inevitably, then, along the way dhansak lost its identity as it became twisted into a dish that tried to please everyone, but then pleased no one. I doubt there are many curry houses in the UK today that serve a dhansak anything like the original Parsi recipe. Let this recipe restore your faith in dhansak and prove how sophisticated and utterly delicious a dish it truly is!

I find the results are not only faster, but tastier, by making this curry in a pressure cooker, as all the flavours stay locked inside. I've used that method here, but having said that, a pressure cooker is a relatively modern gadget and dhansak has been cooked for centuries in pots over open wood fires.

SERVES 8

1kg diced mutton on the bone (or use chicken), brined for 24 hours if possible

3 tablespoons salt, plus extra to season if necessary

3 tablespoons dhansak masala (see page 48)

50g toor dal

50g channa dal

150g split mung dal

150g split red dal

4 tablespoons ghee, unsalted butter or vegetable oil, plus optional extra ghee or butter for blending

1 medium onion, thinly sliced

4 tablespoons ginger–garlic paste (see page 43)

1 large tomato, chopped

1 tablespoon sambhar masala (see page 46)

½ aubergine, roughly chopped

100g red pumpkin or ½ small butternut squash, peeled, deseeded and roughly chopped

½ sweet potato, peeled and roughly chopped

1 potato, peeled and roughly chopped

5 small green chillies, split

1 tablespoon garam masala (see page 46)

½ tablespoon ground turmeric

a handful of coriander, leaves picked and chopped

a handful of fenugreek leaves, chopped

Place the mutton in the pressure cooker and add water to just cover the meat. Add 1 tablespoon of the salt, 1 tablespoon of dhansak masala and pressure cook for 20 minutes. (Alternatively, simmer the mutton in a normal saucepan for 1 hour, until the meat is tender – take care to not let the water boil vigorously as this will toughen the meat.) Take the meat out of the saucepan and set aside. Pour the liquid into a measuring jug. Make the liquid up to 1.2 litres, using tap water if necessary – this will be your stock to cook the lentils in later.

(Note that if you're using chicken, pressure cook only the thighs and drumsticks for 15 minutes – or simmer for 35 minutes in a pan. The breast will cook from raw quite easily in the finished dish.)

Meanwhile, soak all the lentils together in a large container in plenty of cold water for 25 minutes. Then rinse the lentils in cold water twice, so that the murky water becomes clearer.

Next, we will need to cook the lentils. Heat the ghee, butter or oil in the pressure-cooker pan or a large, heavy-bottomed pot over a medium

Continued overleaf...

heat. Once hot, add the onion and fry for about 10 minutes, until translucent. Then add the ginger–garlic paste and cook for a further 10 minutes, until everything is brown. Each time the ginger–garlic paste sticks to the bottom slightly, add 1 tablespoon of water and scrape up all that caramelised flavour from the bottom of the pot with a wooden spoon to deepen the flavour of the final dish. Add the tomato and cook for a further 3 minutes, then add the remaining dhansak and the sambhar masalas, stirring them through for 1 minute to form a paste.

Drain the lentils, if necessary, and add them to the pan with the chopped vegetables, chillies, garam masala, turmeric and remaining 2 tablespoons of salt. Add the 1.2 litres of reserved stock (enough to come 2.5cm above the lentils) and put the lid on the pressure cooker or pot. Cook for 30 minutes in the pressure cooker or for 1–1½ hours in the pot, until the larger lentils are mushy. (If you're making this in a pot, remove the lid to stir the lentils every 5 minutes, to make sure they don't sink to the bottom and burn, then replace the lid.)

Once the lentils are soft and all the vegetables are breaking apart, remove the lid and stir through the chopped coriander and fenugreek leaves, letting them wilt in the heat. Add a few spoonfuls of ghee or butter, if you're feeling decadent and want a velvety smooth texture, then using a hand-held electric blender, blitz the contents of the saucepan to a smooth purée (my grandmother always used to use a whisk to beat everything to a coarse purée, but I find the flavours really come together when properly blended). Dhansak should not be watery, nor should it be so thick that it is a chore to eat – look for a happy medium, like the texture of a split-pea soup.

Add the cooked mutton (or cooked chicken, as well as the raw diced chicken breast) to the pot and gently simmer over a low–medium heat for a further 10 minutes so that the meat gets to know the gravy. Adjust the seasoning with salt, as necessary. Serve hot with brown rice, kebabs and kachuber (see page 124).

A vegetarian dhansak is commonplace on many Parsi dinner tables – the lentil gravy is delicious enough to stand on its own. Simply make it without the meat and use water instead of the meat stock. I like to roast off some chopped pumpkin or squash that has been lightly seasoned with garam masala and add that to the gravy instead of the mutton or chicken.

JARDALOO MA GOS
MUTTON STEW WITH HUNZA APRICOTS

 Here is a dish that harks back to the time of the Zoroastrians in Persia. It's a stew of meat and dried apricots, subtly flavoured with whole spices to create a balance between savoury, sweet and spiced. Like many Parsi stews, it is up to you what meat you decide to use. I prefer leg or shank meat from either an older lamb or a goat, as the rich flavours bring character to the dish. Chicken works very well, too, but use thighs and drumsticks, as the nature of the cut lends itself to long, slow cooking. Hunza apricots are quite unique in flavour – they come from wild apricot trees where the fruit is left on the tree to dry before being plucked. I would implore you to go out of your way to find them.

This dish itself is a relatively simple one-pot wonder (use a sturdy, cast-iron pot) that will fill your kitchen with mouthwatering aromas.

SERVES 4

500g diced mutton or lamb, preferably on the bone
1 tablespoon ginger–garlic paste (see page 43)
200g Hunza apricots
1 teaspoon caster sugar
2 tablespoons ghee or vegetable oil, plus extra if needed
3 dried Kashmiri chillies
4 cardamom pods, lightly cracked
4 cloves
1 teaspoon cumin seeds, lightly crushed in a pestle and mortar
5cm cassia bark or cinnamon stick
1 large onion, thinly sliced
300g small waxy potatoes, such as Pink Fir Apple or new potatoes, skin-on, quartered
½ bunch of coriander, leaves picked and chopped
salt

Tip the meat and spice into a large bowl and add the ginger–garlic paste and ½ teaspoon of salt. Rub the paste and salt into the meat until well coated, then set aside and leave it to absorb the flavours for 1 hour.

Place the apricots in a small bowl with the sugar and cover them with boiling water. Allow to sit for 20 minutes to rehydrate.

When the meat is ready, heat the ghee or oil in a large, sturdy-bottomed pot over a medium–high heat. When hot, add the meat and fry, turning regularly, for 5 minutes, or until the meat has evenly browned. If the meat starts to catch on the bottom of the pot, add a spoonful of water where it's catching and scrape to release the flavours. Use a slotted spoon to transfer the meat to a plate and set aside. Lower the heat under the pan.

Add the chillies, cardamom pods, cloves, cumin and cassia bark or cinnamon and sizzle the spices for a few minutes, allowing them to become fragrant. Add the onion and cook with the spices for 5 minutes, or until they turn golden brown (add an extra glug of oil, if necessary).

Return the meat and any resting juices to the pan, and add the potatoes. Stir everything together, allowing the onions and the spices to coat the meat and potatoes.

Add the apricots and any soaking liquid that still remains in the bowl, then pour in just enough water that it barely covers the meat (if you

Continued overleaf...

have any whey left from making paneer, then use this instead). Add 1 ½ teaspoons of salt and bring the liquid to a gentle simmer. Once simmering, put the lid on the pot, leaving it slightly ajar.

Gently simmer the meat for 1½ hours over a low heat – you're looking for just a few 'blub blubs' like lava every now and then, rather than a constant bubble. The stew is ready when the meat is tender enough to break apart when pulled.

Remove the pot from the heat and leave the stew to rest for 20 minutes with the lid on (this allows the meat to relax, making it more tender and allowing it to take in the flavours) before finishing with a fold of chopped coriander leaves. Serve with either warm rotlis (see page 114) or basmati rice and pickled turmeric (see page 57) to contrast the savoury sweetness with some acidity.

**Greet the guest
with a sincere heart
and good food.**
   -- Persian proverb

SALI GOS
BRAISED GOAT WITH CRISPY POTATO STRAWS

 On the Indian subcontinent, the term mutton refers to goat meat, which is readily available and widely enjoyed. It has a rich and delicious flavour with beautiful depth, especially when slowly braised, allowing all the flavours to meld together.

Goat meat is readily available in Asian butchers, some of which actually specialise in it. Be sure to specify that it is goat you want and not what, in the UK, we call mutton (a female sheep typically over a year old). Although, the UK's mutton makes a suitable alternative if you can't find goat.

Preheat the oven to 190°C/170°C fan. Season the shanks with salt. Heat the oil in a sturdy, ovenproof cast-iron pot over a medium heat. Add the shanks (or do this one by one, depending on the size of your pot), turning regularly until browned all over (about 3 minutes; if you're using diced meat don't overload the pot, which will lower the heat and the meat will stew rather than brown). Remove the shanks from the pot and set aside.

Reduce the heat to low and add the chillies, cassia bark or cinnamon, cardamom and cloves, allowing the whole spices to sizzle in the hot oil for a moment before adding the cumin and sizzling for a further 30 seconds, keeping the heat low and taking care not to burn any of the spices.

Increase the heat to a medium and add the onion, stirring for about 5 minutes or so, until golden. Add the ginger–garlic paste and carry on stirring for a further 3 minutes, until it also starts to brown.

Add the vinegar and let it bubble away for 30 seconds, then add the tomatoes, turmeric, garam masala, dhansak masala and 1 teaspoon of salt. Stir everything together, then add 500ml of water. Increase the heat to high and bring the liquid to the simmer.

Return the shanks to the pan, nestling them tightly against each other as if being laid to bed. Don't push the shanks down so that they become fully submerged; allow just a portion to be poking above the sauce, like icebergs (10 per cent above the level of the liquid to brown beautifully). Add up to another 500ml of water, if necessary. Sprinkle the sugar on top of the exposed meat to caramelise and sweeten during the cooking process.

Bring the liquid in the pot back up to the simmer and place in the oven, uncovered, as you want the exposed meat to darken and caramelise, bringing depth to the finished dish. Cook for 1½ hours, until the meat slips easily from the bone when firmly poked. (Cook for a further 20 minutes, testing regularly, until it does, if necessary.)

To serve, place the shanks on a platter and cover in the thick, tomato-stew gravy. Sprinkle with the coriander and pile generous amounts of sali over the top.

SERVES 4

2 goat shanks (each weighing 750g on the bone, although about 800g of the diced meat off the bone will work just as well)
150ml vegetable oil
4 dried Kashmiri chillies
2.5cm cassia bark or cinnamon stick
6 cardamom pods, cracked
8 cloves
2 teaspoons cumin seeds, crushed
1 large red onion, chopped
2 tablespoons ginger–garlic paste (see page 43)
3 tablespoons apple cider vinegar
4 tomatoes, chopped
2 teaspoons ground turmeric
2 teaspoons garam masala (see page 46)
4 teaspoons dhansak masala (see page 48)
1 teaspoon caster sugar
a small handful of coriander, leaves picked and chopped
1 recipe quantity of sali (see page 113)
salt

MASOOR MA GOS
BRAISED KID SHANK AND BROWN LENTILS

SERVES 2

2 kid shanks (about
    250g each)
4 tablespoons vegetable
    oil
6 cloves
5 cardamom pods, lightly
    cracked
5cm cassia bark or
    cinnamon stick
1 medium onion,
    thinly sliced
2 small green chillies,
    slit open
6 garlic cloves, crushed
2.5cm fresh ginger, peeled
    and grated
2 tablespoons apple
    cider vinegar
1 teaspoon grated jaggery
4 medium tomatoes, finely
    chopped, or 1 400g tin of
    chopped tomatoes
1 tablespoon dhansak
    masala (see page 48)
1 tablespoon cumin–
    coriander powder
    (see page 48)
1 teaspoon ground
    turmeric
about 180g masoor dal
    (brown lentils), boiled
    in seasoned water until
    soft to the bite
salt
fresh mint, to serve
fresh coriander, to serve

 There is something quite satisfying about having a whole shank on your dinner plate, knowing that it's all yours to grapple with. Goat, and especially kid, is a great choice for depth of flavour, but you could try this dish with lamb shanks instead. Sometimes, when I want to make this braise and I can't get hold of a shank, I use diced mutton and approach the recipe in the same manner.

Preheat the oven to 180°C/160°C fan. Season the shanks all over with fine salt.

Heat the vegetable oil in a heavy-based ovenproof pot over a medium heat. When hot, add the shanks and sear them, turning regularly, until evenly browned all over. Concentrate your efforts on the back of the shank where the larger portion of meat is, and also give some love to the base of the shank (more browning means more of that delicious roasted flavour).

Remove the shanks from the pot and set aside, leaving behind the oil. Add the cloves, cardamom, cassia and onion, stirring everything together for 5 minutes over a medium heat, until the onion is softened a little and any caramelised bits on the bottom of the pan from browning the meat have scraped off. Then add the chillies, garlic and ginger and continue to stir for a further 3 minutes, or until the onion turns golden brown.

Add the vinegar and jaggery, stirring them through until the jaggery dissolves. Then add the tomatoes, dhansak masala, cumin–coriander powder and turmeric, along with 2 cupfuls of water. Season well with salt, then return the shanks to the pot, lying them down with the meatiest parts facing up. The liquid should not be so much that the shanks are completely submerged, but just enough to show a cheek of flesh above the liquid. The exposed part will roast, while everything submerged braises, giving an accomplished contrast in texture and flavour.

Place the pot, uncovered, in the oven for 2–2½ hours, or until the meat no longer protests and moves freely away from the bone. Remove from the oven, take the shanks out of the pot, add your cooked lentils and stir them through to sup up the hot, flavourful juices.

Serve adorned with chopped mint and coriander leaves and thinly sliced red onions, and rotlis (see page 114) on the side to mop up all the gravy.

BHEJA NA CUTLETS
CRISPY SPICED BRAINS

 Lightly spiced and crunchy nuggets that give way to a custard-like texture within – the more of these brain nuggets you eat, the smarter you get... or so my aunties will tell you.

Mild and creamy, brains are very much about the texture – the light and soft. They are a fantastic vehicle for carrying flavour to your mouth. Calf brains are larger than lamb, but both are equally delicious. To buy them, you need to know where to look or who to ask: check with your butcher or on the meat counter at your local Asian supermarket. The effort it takes to procure them will make the first bite all the more satisfying.

SERVES 2–4, DEPENDING ON THE BEAST

1 calf brain or 2 lamb brains
1 tablespoon dhansak masala (see page 48)
4 eggs, beaten
200g of fine semolina or fine dried breadcrumbs
500ml vegetable oil, for frying
salt and freshly cracked black pepper

Place the brains in cold water for 30 minutes to purge them of any blood and impurities. Remove from the water and, using a small knife, begin peeling away any membrane and bits of blood – if you peel away carefully, much of the membrane will come off in one piece. Trim sparingly as everything is good to eat, even if it is a bit visceral at this point. I promise things get better.

Bring a saucepan of salted water to the boil over a high heat. Add the brains and poach for 1 minute, then remove them with a slotted spoon and transfer to a plate to drain and cool. Once cool enough to handle, cut the brain into bite-sized nuggets. Lightly sprinkle the nuggets all over with salt and pepper and sprinkle over the dhansak masala.

Tip the beaten eggs into a wide bowl and the semolina into a shallow tray or a plate. Piece by piece, dip the brains into the egg. Using a fork, scoop out the piece and allow as much egg to drain off as possible. Finally, dip each piece into the semolina, rolling it around to coat. (Dab a bit of egg on any bald spots and coat again.)

Pour the oil into a medium, heavy-based saucepan so that it comes two thirds of the way up the sides. Place the pan over a medium–high heat and heat the oil to 170°C on a cooking thermometer (or until a cube of bread dropped into the oil sizzles, rises to the surface and turns golden within 60 seconds). A few pieces at a time, taking care not to overcrowd the pan, carefully lower the nuggets into the hot oil, using a slotted spoon to keep them moving until they are golden (about 3–4 minutes per batch). Remove the cooked nuggets using the slotted spoon and set them aside to drain on kitchen paper.

Once you have cooked all the nuggets, season liberally with salt and pepper. Serve the nuggets hot and crispy next to healthy dollops of herby mayonnaise (see page 54) and pickled tindora (see page 56).

For something different, you can season the fried brains with chaat masala, a spice blend made with black salt, which adds a unique, mineral flavour. It is typically used on snacks in India and is readily available in Indian grocery stores.

See overleaf for image.

BHEJA PER TOAST
BRAINS ON BUTTERED TOAST

SERVES 2

1 calf brain or 2 lamb brains

3 tablespoons ghee or
   vegetable oil

1 small shallot, finely
   chopped

1 teaspoon ginger–garlic
   paste (see page 43)

1 small tomato, finely
   chopped

¼ teaspoon ground
   turmeric

1 heaped teaspoon
   dhansak masala (see
   page 48)

2 small green chillies,
   finely chopped

a small handful of
   coriander, leaves picked
   and chopped

4 slices of well-buttered
   toast of choice

salt and freshly cracked
   black pepper

 Parsis are very fond of brains – their soft texture and mild, creamy flavour closely resemble gently scrambled eggs and, like scramble, take well to a light spicing. I like to cook with calf brains, as they are larger than goat or lamb brains and therefore slightly easier to handle, although all are equally delicious.

Toast comes down to preference. I'm a big fan of a piece of rustic sourdough. For something a bit different, though, like the pav bhaji vendors, you could slice open and butter soft white buns or hot-dog rolls, then place them, butter side down, on a hot pan until each side has formed a delicious, golden crust.

Place the brains in fresh, cold water for 30 minutes to purge them of any blood and impurities. Then remove them from the water and, using a small knife, begin peeling away any membrane and bits of blood – if you peel away carefully, much of the membrane will come off in one piece. Trim sparingly as everything is good to eat, even if it is a bit visceral at this point. I promise things get better. Chop the cleaned and trimmed brains into bite-sized chunks.

Heat the ghee or oil in a large frying pan over a medium heat. When hot, add the shallot and fry for 2 minutes, until softened a little. Add the ginger–garlic paste and cook for a further 2 minutes, until everything starts to turn a light golden colour.

Turn up the heat to high and add the brains, gently folding them in the pan to combine – be careful as too much stirring will turn the delicate chunks to mush. Fry the brains for 1 minute, then add the tomato, turmeric, dhansak masala and a few generous pinches of salt and ground black pepper. Gently fold and turn the brains for 3 minutes, allowing the tomatoes to simmer and break down and the flavours to intensify.

Your brains will now have the appealing texture and appearance of scrambled eggs. Take the pan off the heat, throw in the chilli and coriander and fold everything through. Spoon the mixture on to the lavishly buttered toast and scoff while piping hot.

Human life is truly a
short affair. It is better
to live doing the things
that you like.
  -- Yamamoto Tsunetomo

See previous page for image.

MASALA DUKKAR GOS
PORK CHOP CUTLET

Hindu and Muslim religious beliefs mean that pork is not a meat commonly found at the dinner table in much of India – and by extension, nor is it an ingredient common in Parsi cookery. It is therefore my pleasure to write this recipe with a pork chop in mind. A well-chosen chop will yield mouthwatering results. Dhansak masala lifts and transforms the delicate flavours of a chop from a rare-breed pig, with the delicious butter-like fats melting under the semolina crust to transform the flavours as they reach your tongue. This dish is simple and life-affirming.

Choose the best-quality pork available (ask your butcher). Breeds such as Tamworth, Saddleback and Middle White all have great-quality fat that is rich and buttery, an essential attribute for such a simple plate of food.

SERVES 1

1 best-quality pork chop, trimmed of the skin and cut from the bone
1 teaspoon ginger–garlic paste (see page 43)
1 teaspoon dhansak masala (see page 48)
1 tablespoon vegetable oil, plus 200ml for frying
1 egg, beaten
a handful of fine semolina or dried breadcrumbs
lemon wedge
salt

Lay the chop on a chopping board and place a piece of greaseproof paper over the top. Using a rolling pin, firmly bash the chop from top to tail to flatten it to roughly half its original thickness.

Combine the ginger–garlic paste, dhansak masala, ¼ teaspoon of salt and the tablespoon of oil in a bowl to form a paste.

Season the chop generously with the paste, massaging the paste well into both sides. Leave the chop to rest for 20 minutes at room temperature to absorb all the flavours.

Heat the 200ml of vegetable oil in a heavy-based frying pan over a medium heat. Tip the beaten egg and the semolina or breadcrumbs into separate wide, shallow bowls.

Dip the chop into the semolina or breadcrumbs until evenly coated, then into the egg. Allow any excess egg to drop off and transfer the chop to the hot oil in the pan. Fry for about 4–5 minutes, turning every 30 seconds, until golden and cooked through. Remove from the pan and set aside to rest on a warm plate for a further 5 minutes to allow the fats and juices to mingle with the spices in the masala.

Slice the chop into bite-sized mouthfuls and arrange on the plate. Season with salt. Finally, squeeze over the lemon wedge, and serve with a small pile of tangy onions.

See overleaf for images.

BHARELA TITTER
QUAILS STUFFED WITH RICE

MAKES 6

12 tablespoons cooked biriyani or other flavourful rice

6 quails, cleaned and innards removed

6 quail eggs, boiled for 3 minutes, then drained and peeled (not essential but a nice touch)

3 tablespoons ghee, melted, or vegetable oil, plus extra oil for frying

3 teaspoons dhansak masala (see page 48)

2 teaspoons salt

 I created this dish for a Parsi dinner at a friend's restaurant. It went down very well. On the night, we decided not to put knives and forks on the table, so it was a joy to watch the revellers grapple the birds with their bare hands and tear into the quails to get at the rice. Be prepared to get hands-on to eat this one!

I made the dish using biriyani rice specifically, as I wanted to give the quails as much flavour as possible. I recommend going out of your way to use something flavourful – biriyani rice, vegetable pulao or Parsi brown rice are all good options.

Quails are accessible birds. If you are lucky enough to get your hands on birds that still have their insides intact, you can chop up the heart and liver, season with salt and pepper and mix through your rice before stuffing.

Before you begin, gather some butcher's string and a large meat needle – neither is absolutely essential, but they help.

Spoon 1 tablespoon of cooked rice into the open cavity of each quail. Using your fingers, push it right to the back of the bird, as far as it will go. Push in 1 boiled quail egg, if using, and then another spoonful of rice (or however much more will fit in there). Using the butcher's string and meat needle, if you have them, sew 2 stitches in the back of the bird, sealing off the cavity so the rice is secured inside. If you have neither, just take extra care with the bird during cooking, so that the rice does not fall out.

Preheat the oven to 220°C/200°C fan.

Combine 2 tablespoons of the melted ghee or the vegetable oil in a bowl with the dhansak masala and salt to form a paste. Rub the paste all over the outside of the quails, massaging it over the surface to coat.

Heat the remaining ghee or vegetable oil in a large frying pan over a medium heat. When hot, add the quails and fry for 3–4 minutes, turning regularly, until golden brown all over. Lower the heat if at any time you feel the spices might be burning.

Transfer the quails to a baking tray (or two if you don't have a tray big enough) and pour over any cooking juices from the pan. Place the baking tray in the oven and roast the quails for 10 minutes, until they are cooked through. Remove from the oven and leave to rest, uncovered, for 10 minutes.

Serve the quails whole with wedges of lemon, beetroot and mustard seed chutney (see page 64) and dollops of mango pickle mayonnaise (see page 55). (Imagine making this dish with a whole roast chicken... hint, hint!)

OOMBARIYOON
GREEN BEAN AND QUAIL STEW

This is a Parsi adaptation of a Gujarati dish called undhiyu (the odd-sounding name comes from the Gujarati word for upside-down). It is traditionally cooked in earthenware, vase-like pots called matkis that would be filled with field beans or papri beans, vegetables, and ground herbs and spices, then sealed with mango leaves and cooked upside down on a fire of burning hay, dried cow dung, and leaves. The Parsis added meat – birds like pheasants and quails being the norm, as well as much-loved mutton – although this can still be a lovely stew of beans and vegetables alone, if you choose it to be.

We won't be using earthenware pots nor burning hay and dung, so I recommend using a sturdy cast-iron crock pot, which will be great at retaining an even heat during the slow cooking.

If the quails still have their offal inside them, pluck it out and give the birds a rinse, reserving the offal. With a large knife or cleaver, chop the quails each into 4 pieces – 2 legs and 2 breasts. Rub with the vegetable oil and ginger–garlic paste. Set aside.

Make the paste. Blitz all the ingredients (including the stalks of the coriander) together with 3 tablespoons of water in a food processor.

Transfer the paste to a large bowl and add the all the chopped vegetables, as well as the surti papri or beans and the peas. Mix everything to coat it in the paste.

Preheat the oven to 180°C/160°C fan.

In a sturdy, cast-iron pot with a tight-fitting lid, make a layer using half the vegetables. Layer the pieces of quail on top of the vegetables, and scatter the offal around the pieces of bird, if you have it. Gently place the raw, unpeeled eggs around the meat, then cover all this with the remaining vegetables. Keep things loose and take care not to crack your eggs – don't pack anything down, the loose spacing will allow the heat to make its way through the pot.

Cut a piece of baking paper the same diameter as your pot and run the paper under the tap to make it wet. Place this over the top and put the lid on the pot. Bake the stew for 1½ hours, until the meat is cooked through and the vegetables are tender. Remove from the oven and leave to rest with the lid on for 20 minutes – this resting period allows the meat to relax and become even more tender.

Just before serving, pick out the eggs and stir everything through. Then transfer the stew to a platter and place the eggs, unpeeled on top. Give each of your guests the enjoyment of peeling and eating their own egg with their meal. Serve with warmed rotli (see page 114) and yoghurt for spooning over.

SERVES 4

4 oven-ready quails
2 tablespoons vegetable oil
1 tablespoon ginger–garlic paste (see page 43)
1 large red onion, peeled and cut into 8 wedges
1 aubergine, cut into bite-sized pieces
1 small sweet potato, unpeeled and cut into bite-sized pieces
2 large potatoes, unpeeled and cut into bite-sized pieces
500g surti papri or green beans or runner beans, trimmed and de-stringed if necessary
200g fresh or frozen peas
8 quail eggs, or 4 hen's eggs

FOR THE PASTE
1 large bunch of coriander
1 teaspoon cumin seeds
1 teaspoon ground turmeric
½ teaspoon ajwain seeds
8 small green chillies, split
2 teaspoons salt

MASALA SASLU VATENA
SPICED RABBIT, PEAS AND YOGHURT

SERVES 4

2 large rabbits, preferably
   wild, offal intact
1 tablespoon dhansak
   masala (see page 48)
a glug of vegetable oil, plus
   extra for frying
6 shallots, peeled
1 tablespoon ginger–garlic
   paste (see page 43)
2 large tomatoes,
   diced small
2 tablespoons apple
   cider vinegar
500ml chicken stock
2 handfuls of frozen peas
a handful of fenugreek
   leaves, roughly chopped
salt

 While working at St. John Bread and Wine early one week, I found myself with the perfect opportunity to add a touch of Parsi flair to this rabbit dish, having some leftover dhansak masala to hand. Frozen peas make this a dish for any time of year. You'll need to begin marinating the meat the day before you intend to serve.

Pull out the offal from inside your rabbits. You will have 2 kidneys, hopefully surrounded by some delicious fat, 2 liver pieces, and digging right to the back of the rib cage, 1 heart. Trim off any gore from the offal and drop the pieces into a small bowl of cold water for 30 minutes to purge out the blood and impurities. Then drain the offal and rinse it under cold water. Keep it to make aleti paleti on page 206.

Break the rabbits down into two sets of front shoulders (slip a sharp knife between the shoulder and the body to separate them easily) and two sets of front legs (a bit more finicky: dislocate the leg from the hip socket, then use the tip of a sharp knife to carve between the leg and body). Finally, with a hefty knife or cleaver, chop each torso into 4 or 5 chunks.

Put the dhansak masala and 1 teaspoon of salt in a large bowl with a glug of vegetable oil. Add the rabbit pieces to the bowl and rub them all over with the marinade. Leave to sit for 2 hours at room temperature (no need to cover) so that the meat can take in all that goodness from the masala.

Preheat the oven to 180°C/160°C fan.

Heat a glug of vegetable oil in sturdy, cast-iron ovenproof pot over a medium–high heat. Add the limbs, a few at a time, and allow them to sizzle in the pan, turning regularly for 5 minutes, until golden on both sides and fragrant. Take care to moderate the heat so that you don't burn the delicate spices. As each limb is coloured, transfer it to a plate and add another in its place, until all the limbs are done. Continue this process with the torso pieces.

Once you've browned all the meat pieces and set them aside, add the shallots to the pot, season with salt, and keep them moving for about 5 minutes, until they begin to turn golden. Add the ginger–garlic paste and keep stirring for 1–2 minutes, until the paste is fragrant and taking on some colour. Add the chopped tomatoes and vinegar and let it all sizzle away for 5 minutes. Introduce the rabbit legs and shoulders back to the pot, nestling them in evenly and tightly so nothing is poking up too much. (Keep back the body pieces for now, as they take much less time to cook.)

Continued overleaf...

Pour in the chicken stock so that it comes two thirds of the way up the rabbit, leaving the last third poking above the stock to colour up in the oven. Bring the liquid to a gentle simmer, then transfer the pot, uncovered, to the oven and cook the rabbit for 1 hour 40 minutes. Then remove the pan from the oven and add the torso pieces and peas, stirring them into the sauce. Return the pot to the oven for a final 20 minutes, until the rabbit is tender and comes away from the bone without much protest. You don't want it to fall off the bone of its own accord – some resistance makes good work for the teeth and firmness is more in line with the nature of wild rabbit. Remove from the oven and stir through the fenugreek leaves.

Serve with generous dollops of yoghurt and warmed rotlis (see page 114) for mopping up the sauce.

More possibilities! Another way to serve this dish is to take the limbs from the sauce once they are cooked, pick all the meat off the bone, returning the chunks of meat to the sauce and discarding the bones. Add the torso pieces and peas to the sauce. Stir through the fenugreek and yoghurt, then place the mixture into a pie dish, using some of the sauce to brush around the edges of the dish. Place a pie lid (see page opposite) over the top and crimp it to seal. Using a sharp knife, make a cross in the top of the pie lid for the steam to escape. Bake the pie for 45 minutes at 210°C/190°C fan, until the top is golden and crisp and the juices are dancing at the top of the pie.

SPICED GAME PIE

Pie-making is a familiar, weekly fixture of working in the kitchens of St. John Bread and Wine, marrying game with seasonal herbs and vegetables and allowing for just the right splash of booze to bring life to the mixture. Each week brings something different – a seasonal ingredient or offer from a supplier tempts us down a slightly different path, while still heading for the same journey's end. If we are pushed for time, we go as the crow flies – chop, season, colour and braise. But, on the rare occasion that time is on our side, taking the scenic route would often throw up something new and exciting. This pie stems from one of those happy moments.

I often wondered to myself why there are no pies in Parsi cuisine. I began to imagine myself as the first Parsi that came across the meat pie, and how would I adapt it to appeal to a fellow Parsi's palate. Balancing sweet and sour flavours with jaggery and Parsi vinegar, incorporating the offal, not shying away from game, using the right masalas to balance with the flavours of the meat. These were all the answers I gave myself. Essentially, I was building layers. I have written this recipe specifically for game. Widely underappreciated and underutilised, game animals are flavoursome and abundant. Here, I've suggested a combination of venison, pigeon and pheasant, but you can use guinea fowl, as well as or instead of any, swapping in and out when the season is right.

Take the time to brine your game (see page 203), as this will help keep the meat succulent and juicy as it cooks in the pie.

MAKES 1 PIE, SERVES 6

1kg venison haunch, cut into bite-sized chunks
6 pigeon breasts, each cut into 3 pieces
2 pheasant breasts, each cut into 4 pieces
1 heaped tablespoon dhansak masala (see page 48)
½ tablespoon garam masala (see page 46)
200ml vegetable oil
1kg shallots, peeled and halved
10 garlic cloves, peeled and very lightly crushed under your palm
3cm fresh ginger, peeled and grated
50g jaggery, chopped
100ml apple cider vinegar, plus extra to season if necessary
100ml Worcestershire sauce
a glug of Madeira wine
1 litre chicken stock
a handful of coriander, leaves picked and chopped
a handful of fenugreek leaves, chopped
salt

FOR THE PIE LID
200g self-raising flour
100g shredded suet
¼ teaspoon salt
a jug of ice-cold water
1 egg yolk beaten with 1 tablespoon whole milk
a healthy pinch each of cumin seeds, fennel seeds and caraway seeds

Preheat the oven to 200°C/180°C fan. Place the pieces of meat in a bowl and sprinkle liberally and evenly with salt (omit this step if you have brined your meat). Add the dhansak masala, garam masala and 50ml of the vegetable oil to the bowl and toss everything together, until the masalas have evenly coated all the pieces. Use your hands to massage the spices into the meat.

Place a large, flameproof baking dish on the hob over a medium heat. Add the remaining vegetable oil. Once it is hot, a few pieces at a time, fry the venison for 2 minutes on each side, until evenly coloured (lower the heat if you feel the spices are burning before you get the chance to turn the meat; or alternatively increase the heat if you feel the meat can take more of a sear). Remove the browned venison to a bowl, and set aside.

Lower the heat under the dish and add the shallots, garlic and a liberal sprinkling of salt. Allow things to sizzle and colour for 5 minutes, then add the ginger and cook for a further 5 minutes, stirring continuously and

Continued overleaf...

adjusting the heat as necessary, until the shallots, garlic and ginger are browned. If you feel that patches in the dish are catching, add a spoonful of stock or water and scratch away the dark bits, allowing them to become part of the sauce.

Increase the heat slightly and add the jaggery, vinegar, Worcestershire sauce and Madeira wine and allow the liquids to bubble and reduce for 2–3 minutes, agitating and scraping away any bits that have caramelised and stuck to the bottom of the dish.

Return only the venison pieces to the dish, then add enough chicken stock so that everything in the tray is at least three-quarters submerged. Bring the liquid in the dish up to a vigorous bubble and taste for seasoning – you may need to adjust with salt or balance with some vinegar (even at this stage the sauce must taste delicious, so be liberal with your seasonings).

Cover the dish with a loose piece of foil (if you cover tightly, the liquid can overheat and boil, resulting in tough meat) and bake for 1 hour 20 minutes, until the meat is cooked through. Remove the tray from the oven, but leave the foil in place so that the steam stays inside the dish and keeps things moist. Allow the meat to cool in the dish like this for about 45 minutes – this will give everything in the tray a good chance to get to know each other.

While the filling is cooling, make the pie lid. In a large mixing bowl rub the flour, suet and salt together with your hands until the suet has crumbled down and is completely coated with the flour. The texture should be that of fine breadcrumbs. Add cold water 50ml at a time, mixing to combine until you have a dough that holds its shape and comes away cleanly from the inside of the bowl. Cover with cling film and let the dough rest in the fridge for 30 minutes.

Lightly dust a clean work surface with flour and, using a rolling pin, roll out the pastry into the shape of your pie dish and until 5mm thick and at least 2cm bigger than the diameter of the tin.

Preheat the oven to 210°C/190°C fan.

Add the pigeon and pheasant breast, chopped coriander and fenugreek leaves to the cooled filling and stir everything together. Have one final taste to make sure you are happy with the seasoning. Spoon the filling into your chosen pie dish and brush the edges and under the rim of the dish with some of the sauce from the filling. Place the pie lid gently over the top and crimp the edges of the pastry to the edge of the dish using your thumb and forefinger – the brushed juices will be the glue holding the lid in place. Brush the top of the pie with the egg and milk mixture, to glaze, and scatter the seeds evenly over the top. Trim off any excess pastry, leaving roughly 1cm over the edge of the rim. With a sharp knife, pierce a cross in the top of your pastry lid to allow the steam to escape.

Bake your pie for 45 minutes, until you have a wonderfully golden, crusty top and the juices are bubbling forth. Allow the pie a moment to cool before serving alongside masala potatoes (see page 173) and kachuber salad (see page 124).

VENISON BERRY PULAO

SERVES 6

1kg diced venison, brined if
possible (see page 203)
1 recipe quantity of plain
patyo (see page 197; just
the sauce, no prawns)
3 cups of basmati rice,
cooked with the
(w)holy four spices, a
very generous pinch of
saffron and ½ teaspoon
ground turmeric (see
page 146)
100g shelled cashews,
fried or roasted until
golden
a dash of rose water and
kerwa water
1 recipe quantity of
kebab mixture (see
page 225), substituting
minced venison for the
minced lamb
100g fine semolina
200ml vegetable oil
a handful of barberries
1 small bunch of coriander,
leaves picked

FOR THE VENISON
MARINADE
2 tablespoons ginger–
garlic paste (see
page 43)
1 teaspoon sambhar
masala (see page 46)
1 teaspoon chilli powder
2 heaped teaspoons
dhansak masala
(see page 46)

FOR THE CRISPY-FRIED
ONIONS
100ml vegetable oil
1 large onion, thinly sliced
flaky sea salt

The long-standing Britannia & Co. restaurant has been serving its chicken berry pulao to the people of Mumbai for decades. It is the masterpiece of the founder's Parsi wife (the founder himself is an Iranian immigrant). What makes this dish stand out is the generous sprinkling of tiny, deep-red barberries on top of the rice, which brings a tart fruitiness to the already fragrant pulao.

My venison berry pulao, which brings together some of the different recipes in this book to create a single, majestic dish, is an homage to the Britannia classic – not an exact recreation in any way, but lovingly reinvented from the mind's eye. I chose venison not only because of its delicious character, but because I feel it is under-utilised for such a plentiful meat. Barberries are usually available in the Persian section of Asian supermarkets.

First, marinate the venison. Tip the diced venison into a large bowl and add all the marinade ingredients. Massage the marinade into the meat, cover the bowl and refrigerate for at least 1 hour.

Meanwhile, make the crispy-fried onions. Heat the 100ml vegetable oil in a wok or heavy-bottomed frying pan over a high heat. When hot, add thinly sliced onion and fry for about 3 minutes, until golden and crispy. Remove from the oil using a slotted spoon and set them aside to drain on kitchen paper. Lightly season the fried onion with a sprinkle of salt. Set aside and leave the oil in the pan for frying the venison.

Once the venison has been marinating for 1 hour, reheat the wok and leftover onion oil over a high heat. When hot, add the marinated venison and fry for 3 minutes, turning frequently, until coloured all over (you may need to do this in batches, so as not to overwhelm the pan). Add the patyo, reduce the heat to low and simmer gently for 30 minutes, with a lid slightly ajar, until the venison is tender and cooked through – low and slow is the key here.

Preheat the oven 190°C/170°C fan. Transfer the venison and sauce to an ovenproof serving platter, spreading it over the bottom. Pile the cooked rice over the top of the sauce, taking care not to squash the rice – gently push it across the sauce. Lay the crispy onions over the top in a layer, then scatter over the cashews. Cover the dish tightly with foil or a tight-fitting lid. Bake for 1 hour, until the rice is hot and steaming.

While the rice is baking, roll the kebab mixture into bite-sized balls. Tip the semolina into a large bowl and toss the balls through it to coat. Heat 200ml oil in a large frying pan over a medium heat. When hot, add the kebabs and fry for 5–6 minutes, turning frequently, until cooked through.

Assemble the final dish. Place the kebabs around the edge of the platter and scatter the barberries all over the top. Finish with a final flourish of coriander. Serve piping hot to your very impressed house guests.

SWEET THINGS

AND

ICE CREAMS

ORANGE AND LIME CURD

The perfect dollop for on top of your ice cream, or something sweet and sour within your knickerbocker glory (see page 303).

MAKES ABOUT 400ML, ENOUGH TO FILL 1 JAR

zest and juice of 1 orange
zest and juice of 1 lime
zest and juice of 1 lemon
230g caster sugar
150g salted butter
4 large eggs

Place all the ingredients in a metal bowl set over a saucepan of simmering water, taking care not let the bottom of the bowl touch the water. Gently whisk all the ingredients until they come together, then continue to lightly whisk for a further 5 minutes, or until the curd thickens enough to coat the back of a spoon.

Remove the bowl from the heat and pour the mixture through a sieve into a clean bowl, pushing it through using a spoon to collect the seeds and zest in the sieve. Discard the contents of the sieve and transfer the curd to a clean, sterilised jar. Store in the fridge for up to 1 week.

STRAWBERRY JAM

I think it is important to have one good jam under your belt – it's so useful for so many things other than your breakfast toast... think: a dollop on rice pudding (see page 288) or ravo (see page 283), a layer between sponge cakes, a base for a tart. You can use this recipe to make jams with other fruits and berries. I use the same ratios for raspberries, blackberries and rhubarb, or a mixture of these fruits.

MAKES ABOUT 500G, ENOUGH TO FILL 1 JAM JAR

300g strawberries, hulled and chopped
300g caster sugar or vanilla sugar (see page 277)
zest and juice of ½ lemon

Tip the strawberries and sugar into a large, sturdy-bottomed pot and place over a low heat. Melt the sugar and bring the liquid to the simmer – keep checking the temperature of the mixture. When it reaches 106°C on a sugar thermometer, turn off the heat and stir in the lemon juice.

While the jam is still hot, pour it into a clean, sterilised jam jar as far up to the top as you can and seal straight away. You can store the jam, unopened, in a cool cupboard for 1 year. Once opened, keep for 2 weeks in the fridge.

The rule is, jam tomorrow
and jam yesterday,
but never jam today.
-- Lewis Carroll

GREAT WAYS TO EAT JAGGERY

In Indian cookery, jaggery is used to bring sweetness. As Parsi cooking is a balance between sweet and sour, jaggery (also known as gor or gur) features in many of our recipes.

Many Indian villages are famous for their jaggery production. It's made by boiling down the juice of sugar cane or date palm over many hours in huge open vats over giant fire pits. Once the liquid turns to a thick, amber caramel, it is poured into moulds to cool and set. The result is a soft, dark brick with a complex flavour rather like a rich toffee, and a soft-fudge texture. It is a wonderful treat to eat chunks of jaggery either on its own, or with dates or nuts, or with chunks of fresh coconut.

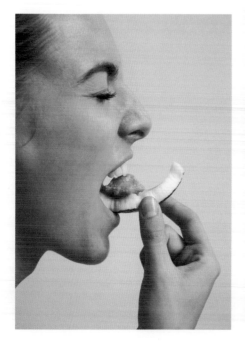

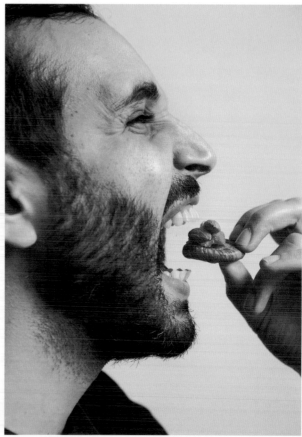

KOPRA NE TAL NI CHIKKI
COCONUT AND SESAME SEED THINS

 A quintessential Indian sweet that stores and travels very well, largely unaffected by the heat of the day, chikki is similar to a nut brittle or praline, typically made using jaggery and nuts, seeds, dried fruits and even puffed rice, and often spiked with saffron and cardamom. Chikki was a common treat for me as a kid during the long train journeys on the Kutch Express from Mumbai to Kandla – hawkers would sell boxes of it through the train windows as the train crawled through the villages.

For a great chikki, first and foremost have everything ready and to hand: caramelised sugar sets hard in no time at all and you won't have time to find the rolling pin or cut the greaseproof paper after the liquefying stage. Choose a pot with a heavy base (rather than a thin, tinny one), as this will conduct the heat at a slower and more even pace, making for an excellent caramel.

I strongly recommend the use of a thermometer to keep track of the temperature of the jaggery as it heats up. If the jaggery doesn't reach a specific temperature, you won't get that 'SNAP' that defines a great chikki.

MAKES 1 LARGE SHEET, ROUGHLY 10 X 20CM

120g jaggery, grated or
   well chopped
40g creamed coconut,
   grated or well chopped
20g unsweetened
   desiccated coconut
20g black or white
   sesame seeds
seeds of 3 cardamom
   pods, lightly crushed in
   a pestle and mortar, or
   chopped

Pour 100ml of water into a sturdy-bottomed pot and add the jaggery. Place it over a medium heat and stir with a spatula until the jaggery has dissolved. Increase the heat slightly until the syrup begins to bubble vigorously and eventually caramelise – use your thermometer and keep going until the syrup reaches 125°C.

Immediately turn down the heat to its lowest setting and add the creamed coconut, stirring to combine. Add the desiccated coconut and sesame seeds and fold and mix everything together, working fast, as the sugar begins to cool and firm up.

With urgency, tip the mixture on to a large piece of greaseproof paper, flatten it down with your spatula and place another large sheet of greaseproof paper over the top. You are now working against the clock to roll the mixture flat, using a rolling pin, between the two sheets of greaseproof, as thin as you possibly can before it sets hard. When I say thin, I do mean thin – only a few millimetres. (Any thicker and you will have to have a solid set of chompers to crack through the chikki!)

Once rolled, allow the chikki to completely cool down for 20 minutes before removing the top layer of greaseproof paper and succumbing to the bittersweet crunch. If you don't finish every bite in one go, then break it up into pieces and store it in an airtight container for up to 2 weeks.

KAJU NE KESAR NI CHIKKI
CASHEW NUT AND SAFFRON THINS

**MAKES 1 LARGE SHEET,
ROUGHLY 10 X 20CM**

150g jaggery, grated or
    well chopped
150g cashews
a healthy pinch of saffron
3 cardamom pods, lightly
    crushed in a pestle and
    mortar, or chopped

 *This popular version of chikki is made with some rather
indulgent ingredients. Make sure you have everything ready
before you start – you're working against the clock!*

Pour 100ml water into a sturdy-bottomed pot and add the jaggery.
Place over a medium heat and stir with a spatula until the jaggery has
dissolved. Increase the heat slightly until the syrup begins to bubble
vigorously and eventually caramelise – use your thermometer and keep
going until the syrup reaches 125°C.

Immediately turn down the heat to its lowest setting and add the
cashew nuts, saffron and cardamom, mixing everything together until
the cashew nuts are coated in the molten jaggery.

With urgency, tip the mixture on to a large piece of greaseproof
paper, flatten it down with your spatula and place another large sheet
of greaseproof paper over the top. You are now working against the
clock to roll the mixture, using a rolling pin, between the two sheets of
greaseproof, as thin as the pieces of cashew nut permit.

Once rolled, allow the chikki to completely cool down for 20 minutes
before removing the top layer of greaseproof paper and enjoying. If you
don't finish every bite in one go, then break it up into pieces and store it
in an airtight container for up to 2 weeks.

He who would eat the
kernel must crack the shell.
    -- Plautus

KOPRA PAK
COCONUT FUDGE

 Jaggery is not essential for this recipe, but it definitely gives that authentic, made-in-India flavour. Make the effort to get hold of a coconut you can crack and grate yourself. You can use desiccated coconut instead, but the final texture is not as moist and unctuous. If you and your family can resist the temptation to eat it all, this coconut fudge is a joyous way to end a dinner party and will be an absolute treat for your guests. You'll need a cake tin or baking tray that measures roughly 20 x 20cm.

Place all the ingredients except the almonds in a sturdy-bottomed pot over a medium–high heat and cook for 10 minutes, lowering the heat every 3 minutes and stirring continuously so that the sugar doesn't burn on the bottom of the pot. As the fudge cooks, the moisture will evaporate and the mixture will turn a golden brown with the slightest shiny appearance as it thickens up. To make sure your fudge sets properly, keep cooking the mixture, dragging a spoon across the bottom of the pan, creating a defined valley.

Lightly rub the inside of your cake tin or baking tray with butter. Carefully pour the coconut mixture into the tin or tray and give it a few short, sharp taps on the work surface to level it out. Take care at this stage as the mixture is very hot – this is not the time to dip in your finger for a taste!

While the mixture is still hot, sprinkle the almonds over the top and give them a very gentle press so they set into the fudge.

Allow the fudge to cool and firm up for 12 hours at room temperature, then cut it into 10 squares before serving. It will keep in an airtight container at room temperature for up to 2 weeks.

MAKES 10 BITE-SIZED SQUARES

110g grated coconut (roughly ½ coconut) or 200g unsweetened desiccated coconut
120ml whole milk
150g caster sugar
75g jaggery, grated (or a further 75g caster sugar)
1 teaspoon ghee or butter, plus extra for greasing
1 tablespoon rose water
1 teaspoon vanilla extract
seeds of 3 cardamom pods, crushed in a pestle and mortar
a pinch of salt
10 whole skin-on almonds, chopped

> Food is comforting at all times, even if one's heart is broken.
>
> -- Mary Burchell

BOOZY CARAMEL CUSTARD

SERVES 4

200g caster sugar
150ml Madeira wine
5 large eggs yolks
200g crème fraîche or
    thick double cream
a pinch of salt

FOR THE GLAZE
150g caster sugar
50g softened butter, cut
    into small cubes
½ teaspoon vanilla extract
1 tablespoon Madeira wine

 Parsis have a fondness for baked custards of all kinds – this one is a little on the boozy side. A small-sized flan dish (about 14cm in diameter) is a nice touch, but failing that a not-too-shallow ovenproof bowl will do.

Pour 100ml of water into a sturdy-bottomed pot and add the sugar. Place over a medium heat and stir. As the sugar dissolves in the water, it will bubble and steam until the water has evaporated and the sugar begins to turn a light golden colour and eventually dark brown – if you have a sugar thermometer, this happens at 170°C. Once you have a dark caramel, you're ready (be brave with how dark you go as this will add depth to the custard – it could take about 10 minutes). Note that it is possible to take a caramel too far and the burnt sugar will be too bitter to use.

Carefully pour the Madeira into the caramel and stir them together. Take care as this step creates lots of steam. Increase the heat to high and cook for 3 minutes, allowing the mixture to reduce to a syrup. Remove from the heat and leave to cool for 5 minutes.

Preheat the oven to 140°C/120°C fan.

While the syrup is cooling, in a separate bowl, whisk together the egg yolks, crème fraîche or double cream and salt. Slowly pour in the caramel mixture and gently whisk to combine. Pour the mixture into the baking dish and bake for about 50 minutes, until set. Remove from the oven while you make the glaze (you should make the glaze only once the custard has finished baking).

Tip the sugar into a sturdy-bottomed pot and place it over a medium heat. Allow it to heat as before – until you get to the same dark caramel stage. Remove it from the heat and whisk in the butter, followed by the vanilla and Madeira.

Pour the glaze over the baked custard and swirl the custard dish to distribute the glaze evenly. Allow the baked custard to sit for 20 minutes before serving, or place it in the fridge until ready to serve.

LAGAAN NU CUSTAR
BAKED CUSTARD WITH DATE AND TAMARIND

Carrying on in the tradition of dishes eaten during a wedding dinner, lagaan nu custar (the 'd' is purposely missed out because of Parsi quirkiness), as the name suggests, is a custard fit for a wedding. It doesn't have the delicacy of a crème brûlée or the subtlety of a crème caramel – rather it is a bold, flavourful, unashamedly eggy delight.

I like to smear a few spoons of date and tamarind preserve on the bottom of my baking dish before adding the custard – it gives the 'ooh' factor when you reach the bottom of your plate. You can also get your oohs from quince and rose paste (see page 62) or any nice jam or marmalade.

The addition of the mawa (a milk curd) makes for a richer custard with a fudge-like flavour. Alternatively, if you don't have time to make the mawa, you can use a penda, a common Indian, mawa-based sweet. Neither is essential, but they provide a lovely touch that makes the dish that little bit more in line with how granny would have made it. And, if you really want to make it extra-special, add a pinch of saffron to the hot mixture before you pour it into your dish – fit for a Parsi wedding!

SERVES 6

You'll need a 22cm-diameter flan dish.

500ml whole milk
200ml condensed milk
150ml double cream
30g caster sugar
25g mawa (see page 83) or 1 penda (optional)
seeds of ½ vanilla pod or ½ teaspoon vanilla extract
1 teaspoon rose water
1 teaspoon kerwa water
seeds of 4 cardamom pods, crushed in a pestle and mortar
4 large eggs
50g flaked almonds
2 tablespoons golden raisins (optional)
3 tablespoons date and tamarind preserve (see page 54)
nutmeg, for grating

Preheat the oven to 180°C/160°C fan.

Pour the whole milk, condensed milk, double cream and sugar into a sturdy-bottomed pot and place it over a low heat. Bring the mixture to a simmer, stirring to ensure the milk does not scorch on the bottom of the pot. Don't let the mixture boil. Crumble in the mawa or penda, whisking it into the milk until dissolved.

Add the vanilla, rose water, kerwa water and cardamom. (If you're using the ½ vanilla pod, put the scraped-out pod in your sugar bowl to make a wonderful vanilla sugar.) Remove the pot from the heat and, one at a time, whisk in each egg. Stir in half of the almonds and all of the raisins.

Spread the date and tamarind preserve (or your chosen spread) all over the base and sides of your flan dish, smearing it into every corner (imagine you are spreading jam generously onto toast). Pour the hot custard into the baking dish slowly and from a low height so as not to disturb the date and tamarind preserve on the bottom.

Scatter the remaining almonds evenly over the top and lightly dust the surface with rasps of nutmeg. Bake the custard for 30 minutes, or until it has a jelly-like wobble all the way to the middle. Remove it from the oven and leave it to rest for 15 minutes before serving. (It's ideal warm, but you could leave it to cool and chill it for up to 3 days, and enjoy it for pudding any time.)

SHRIKHAND
SWEETENED YOGHURT AND SAFFRON

SERVES 4

500g full-fat homemade natural yoghurt (see page 74) or store-bought Greek yoghurt
a big pinch of saffron
1 tablespoon boiling water from a kettle
115g icing sugar
1 teaspoon rose water
½ teaspoon vanilla extract
seeds of 4 cardamom pods, crushed in a pestle and mortar
1 tablespoon chopped pistachios
1 tablespoon chopped almonds
runny honey, for drizzling

 Although not traditionally Parsi, shrikhand is up there on my list of favourite desserts – the flavours of cardamom and saffron paired with the smooth, rich texture of the sweetened, strained yoghurt is decadent and memorable, yet reassuringly healthy (or at least healthier than most desserts). Shrikhand is one of those desserts that once you have tried it, you will wonder how you ever lived without it. I have this for breakfast with chopped fruits, nuts and honey. You'll need a large piece of muslin cloth to hang your yoghurt for superior thickness.

Place the muslin cloth in a bowl and pour in the yoghurt. Bring together the corners of the muslin and tie them in a knot.

Use the muslin to hang the yoghurt bundle over the tap to allow the whey to drain off directly into the sink (there are other ways to do this, but this is my favourite) – this will take 2 hours.

In a cup or small bowl, stir the saffron into the boiling water. Leave to infuse for 1–2 minutes.

Tip the drained yoghurt into a bowl along with the icing sugar, infused saffron water, rose water, vanilla extract, cardamom, and half each of the pistachios and almonds, making sure there are no lumps of sugar hiding in the yoghurt and all the flavours are mixed in.

Place the shrikhand into a serving dish and scatter the remaining nuts over the top. Finish with a drizzle of runny honey. Serve just as it is – or as a fool (see below).

SERVES 6

6 nankhatai biscuits (see page 320)
6 tablespoons orange and lime curd (see page 265)
a selection of chopped fruit (bananas, strawberries, raspberries and blueberries all work well)
1 recipe quantity of shrikhand (see above)
6 teaspoons mixed chopped almonds and pistachios
pomegranate molasses or runny honey, for drizzling

SHRIKHAND FOOL

Shrikhand is a delight all on its own, but I love to make this wonderful summertime dessert with it, too. You will need six bowls or sundae glasses, chilled in the freezer, if possible.

Break the nankhatai into the bottom of each serving glass. Top each portion with 1 tablespoon of curd, followed by a few good spoonfuls of chopped fruit. Spoon generous amounts of shrikhand over the top and decorate with chopped almonds and pistachios and a drizzle of pomegranate molasses or honey.

Left: Dadar Athoran Institute, Mumbai
Right: Mithaiwala, Khavda

SEV

SERVES 8

200g vermicelli
3 tablespoons ghee
3 cardamom pods,
  cracked
a generous pinch of
  saffron
4 tablespoons caster sugar
a few drops of rose water
a pinch of salt

FOR THE VAGHAAR
4 tablespoons ghee
4 tablespoons flaked
  almonds
4 tablespoons raisins

 Every birthday, Navroz, New Year, or family gathering would be an occasion to cook this Parsi dish of sweetened vermicelli noodles topped with crunchy almonds and golden raisins. Although its origins are a mystery to me, it is a quintessential part of any Parsi celebration and is prepared by Parsis the world over, as vermicelli noodles are very easy to get hold of.

On the occasions that I would be staying over at my grandma's house for a family gathering or birthday, I would wake up to the rich and comforting smell of vermicelli roasting in butter as my granny prepared her delicious sev; sometimes I wouldn't even get out of bed until I could smell it!

Gently crush the vermicelli into small pieces while they are still inside the packet so that they do not shoot off left, right and centre.

Place the ghee in a saucepan large enough to fit the vermicelli and melt it over a medium heat. Add the cardamom and saffron and heat for 30 seconds, until fragrant. Add the vermicelli and stir for a few minutes until the strands start to toast and become fragrant.

Increase the heat and add 250ml of water, immediately placing the lid on the pan to keep the raging steam inside. It's that initial kick of steam that will cook the vermicelli through so keep that lid on tight. After 1 minute, lower the heat and remove the lid. Gently stir to break up any clumps, freeing the strands from themselves and evaporating the excess moisture at the same time. Your heat should be low enough that it does not turn the strands to mush but high enough to cook the vermicelli dry.

Add the sugar, the few drops of rose water and the small pinch of salt and stir through. The vermicelli is ready when it is soft to the bite and somewhat loose from itself. It should be fragrant and nutty with a comforting sweetness.

This dish is not complete without its crunchy, chewy topping, a scattering of fried almonds and plumped-up raisins worthy of decorating the finest celebratory desserts. To make the 'vaghaar', heat the ghee in a small heavy-bottomed pan. Once melted, place over a medium heat and add the almonds. Keep stirring until they start to fry and turn golden brown. At this point, quickly add the raisins and keep stirring. The raisins will start to swell with pride as the juices inside them heat up. As soon as they do, turn off the heat and quickly strain the almonds and raisins through a sieve to avoid the nuts over-browning in the hot ghee. You can keep hold of that tasty ghee for making the next batch of sev, if you like.

Plate your cooked sev as desired – a large platter always goes down well for a family get-together. Generously sprinkle the toasted almonds and raisins all over and serve.

RAVO
SEMOLINA PUDDING

 Parsi ravo is a celebratory dish of semolina cooked in milk until silky smooth, spiked with cardamom, saffron and rose water, and finished off with a decoration of fried slivered almonds, and raisins. It would be a joy to wake up on my birthday to the smell of my mum roasting the semolina in ghee and toasting off the almonds for the decoration. So, banish those thoughts of the grey and stodgy school-dinner semolina pudding and rejoice in this gem from the Parsi culinary repertoire.

Find a sturdy-bottomed pot that is large enough to fit all the ingredients in with a bit more space for some vigorous stirring.

Place the pot over a medium heat and add the ghee and cardamom. Melt the ghee, then stir in the semolina, creating a texture similar to wet sand. Keep moving the semolina back and forth, toasting it until it slowly changes colour from a pale cream to a light autumn brown.

Add the saffron, sugar and salt, stirring these through. Start adding your milk, little by little, first adding enough to form a thick and smooth paste before adding any more. Vigorous and sustained beating and stirring with a wooden spoon is the key at this stage. You're aiming for a lump-free smooth texture with a porridge-like consistency. You may need to add a touch more milk to bring it to a smooth texture. (If you do end up with a lumpy semolina pudding, all is not lost – a stick blender or food processor will work wonders in blitzing out those lumps.) Finally, stir through the dash of rose water.

Serve with spoonfuls of fried almond and raisin vaghaar (I also like to add a lick of the hot ghee used for frying) and a rasp of freshly grated nutmeg.

SERVES 8

5 tablespoons ghee
4 cardamom pods, cracked
300g fine semolina
a pinch of saffron
200g caster sugar
a pinch of salt
1 litre whole milk, plus extra if needed
a dash of rose water
nutmeg, for grating
vaghaar (see opposite), to serve

See overleaf for images.

BAKED PANEER AND BOOZY APRICOTS

 Soaked in brandy, these apricots are for the grown-ups! For a more family-friendly version, replace the boozy apricots with fresh raspberries and blueberries, or a few healthy spoonfuls of bitter orange marmalade.

Preheat the oven to 200°C/180°C fan.

Beat the paneer, eggs, lemon and orange zest and juice, sugar, vanilla and a few tablespoons of brandy from the soaked apricots together in a bowl until evenly mixed.

Place the soaked apricots in a layer over the base of a 12cm baking dish. Pour over the paneer mixture.

Bake for 20 minutes, then lower the oven temperature to 160°C/140°C fan and bake for a further 25 minutes, until the top is golden and slightly burnt in patches, and the paneer has set firm. Allow the baked paneer to cool for 10 minutes, then finish with a rasp of nutmeg over the top before serving.

SERVES 4

250g unpressed paneer
   (see page 75)
2 large eggs
zest and juice of ½ lemon
zest and juice of ½ orange
60g caster sugar
1 teaspoon vanilla extract
10 dried apricots,
   soaked overnight in
   125ml brandy
nutmeg, for grating

After a good dinner, one can forgive anybody, even one's own relations.

—— Oscar Wilde

KHEER
RICE PUDDING

SERVES 6

200g pudding rice
500ml whole milk
50g creamed coconut
1 tablespoon unsweetened
   desiccated coconut
1 bay leaf
300ml double cream
3 large eggs yolks
75g caster sugar
50g jaggery, well chopped
3 drops of vanilla extract
nutmeg, for grating
strawberry jam, to serve

 There are few things in life that offer as much comfort as a bowl of warm rice pudding. My rendition brings the classic Parsi flavours of coconut and jaggery together for this bowl of deliciousness.

Tip the rice, milk, creamed coconut, desiccated coconut and bay leaf into a medium saucepan over a low–medium heat and bring the liquid to the simmer. Simmer for 25 minutes, stirring every few minutes, until the rice is tender with only the smallest amount of chalkiness to the bite. Add the cream and cook for a further 12 minutes, adding a few more splashes of milk if the rice starts to over-reduce and stick to the bottom of the pan, until the rice is cooked through and completely soft to the bite. Remove from the heat and fold in the egg yolks, sugar, jaggery and vanilla extract until fully combined.

To serve, spoon the rice pudding into bowls, rasp the nutmeg over the top with a fine grater and finish with healthy dollops of strawberry jam.

MANGO POACHED IN JAGGERY AND SAFFRON

 If faced with a glut of mangoes that you can't finish before they overripen, this is a great way to preserve them. Your choice of mango is very important, as it will be the star of the show – seek out the pleasures of Kesar, Badami or, of course, Alphonso mangoes. Choose one that is ripe yet firm – too soft and you run the risk of it turning to mush in the hot syrup. You want the pieces to keep their integrity. You might say that this dish is gilding the lily. I would say it's gilding it twice over. If mangoes are not in season, you can try making this with ripe pineapple, peaches or apricots.

How you choose to eat your poached mango should be whatever feels natural to you – hot, cold, on top of puddings or ice creams or just then and there from the pan. I love to eat it with a dollop of shrikhand (see page 278) or yoghurt and a scattering of chopped nuts. My dad would enjoy it with his morning porridge.

ALLOW FOR ONE MANGO PER PERSON

1 ripe mango
100g jaggery (see page 266)
2cm cinnamon stick
2 cardamom pods, cracked
a small pinch of saffron

With a sharp knife, slice the cheeks of the mango away from the stone. Lay the pieces of mango, skin side down, on a chopping board and slowly and steadily slide your knife between the skin and the flesh. Discard the skin (or, if you are like me and love every piece of mango, then the skin is a real treat to eat on its own).

Pour 100ml of water into a sturdy-bottomed pot and add the jaggery, cinnamon and cardamom. Place the pot over a high heat. Mash the jaggery into the water until it has completely dissolved and let the mixture boil for 2 minutes to a syrup. Lower the heat to medium and add the mango pieces. Hold the pan firmly by the handle and swirl it to coat the mango pieces in sticky, sweet syrup. Keep doing this for 5 minutes, allowing the syrup to reduce and form a lacquer over the mango.

Remove the pan from the heat and sprinkle in the saffron, again swirling the pan to evenly distribute the flavour.

The great news is that you can pour the mango pieces into a sterilised jar and cover them with the syrup (it's fine to leave in the spices for flavour), then store them in the fridge for up to 12 weeks (although I challenge anyone to show enough restraint to not eat them in one go).

Keep hold of your mango stones – drop them into your curries as they simmer to add a subtle sweetness and fruity flavour to them.

MANGO BUTTERMILK PUDDING

SERVES 4

1 bronze gelatine leaf
160ml double cream
100g caster sugar
1 strip of lemon zest (use a vegetable peeler)
200ml buttermilk
60g mango pulp, either from a tin or puréed fresh
2 drops of vanilla extract or the seeds scraped from ¼ vanilla pod
fresh berries or slices of Kesar or Alphonso mango, to decorate (optional)

 I will leave you in the capable hands of Terry for this pudding – a chef and a recipe from the far-flung reaches of the northern hemisphere. Buttermilk is a wonderful ingredient – its creaminess and acidity give the pudding a soft texture and tangy flavour. At a pinch, you could use a thick-set yoghurt if you can't get hold of buttermilk. If you use fresh mango rather than mango pulp from a tin, make sure you use a very sweet, ripe mango, otherwise the flavour won't come through.

Soak the gelatine leaf in cold water for 5 minutes. Once the leaf has softened, remove it from the water and allow any excess to drip off. Place the leaf in a saucepan with 80ml of the cream, and the sugar and lemon peel.

Place the pan over a low heat, and warm, stirring continuously, until both the sugar and the gelatine leaf have completely dissolved and the cream is hot enough that the first wisps of steam are visible. Once you are at this stage, turn the heat off and allow the cream to cool for 5 minutes. Remove the lemon zest.

While the cream is cooling, whip the remaining 80ml of cream with the vanilla extract or seeds in a large mixing bowl until it forms soft peaks and the texture is soft and airy (too much whipping, even by a few beats of the whisk, can stiffen the cream too far, which will make it harder to fold all the parts together without lumps appearing). Set aside.

Pour the warm cream and gelatine mixture into a large mixing bowl, ensuring none of it remains in the pan. Add the buttermilk and mango and stir it all together to combine.

A spoonful at a time, fold the mango and buttermilk mixture into the whipped cream until fully incorporated and uniform.

Where you go with your mixture from here is up to you. You can set it in one big mould or a few smaller ones, to turn out to serve. Or spoon it into glasses or small dishes as individual servings to eat just as it comes, with a spoon. (Although there is something quite pleasing about a wobbly pudding on a plate.)

Not every dessert needs a decoration, but if you want to add flourish, fresh berries or slices of Kesar or Alphonso mango go well.

Sweets to the sweet.
–– Shakespeare

ORANGE BLOSSOM JELLY

 Jellies are a familiar dish in Parsi cuisine, dating back to Persia when the gelatine was boiled from sheep's trotters. The resulting liquid was then sweetened with sugar and typically flavoured with orange juice before being set. I love the unique fragrance and subtle, bittersweet flavour that orange blossom brings to this jelly – very present, but not overpowering, allowing the flavours of the fruits to sing.

Food heightens moods – this is a cooling jelly, ideal for calming the body and mind during the warmer summer months.

SERVES 4

4 bronze gelatine leaves
4 teaspoons orange
    blossom water
juice of 4 oranges
4 tablespoons caster sugar

To serve
500g mixed fruits
    (strawberries,
    raspberries, mulberries,
    peaches, nectarines are
    all stellar options)
a drizzle of pomegranate
    molasses
200ml double cream
1 teaspoon caster sugar

Soak the gelatine leaves in a bowl of cold water, completely submerging them for 5 minutes to soften.

Meanwhile, pour 500ml of water into a jug and add the orange blossom water, orange juice and sugar. Stir to dissolve, then taste the water and add more sugar if desired.

Squeeze out the excess water from the gelatine and place the leaves in a small saucepan. Add one quarter of the orange-blossom-flavoured liquid, then place over a low heat. Stir for about 2 minutes, until the gelatine has completely dissolved, then pour the mixture into the jug with the remaining orange-blossom-flavoured liquid. Stir together very well, though try not to whip up a foam on the surface.

Pour the mixture equally into 4 individual serving bowls, or one large one, and refrigerate for about 8 hours, until set. (Cover the jelly if you have any strong-smelling foods in the fridge, as you don't want to interfere with the delicate flavours.)

To serve, toss together the fruits with a light drizzle of pomegranate molasses. In a separate bowl, whip the cream and sugar together until it forms stiff peaks. Either turn the individual jellies on to serving plates and top with equal amounts of the fruit and sweetened whipped cream, or top the bowl of jelly with dollops of each and serve in large scoops.

DAL NI PORI
TRADITIONAL SWEET LENTIL CAKE

MAKES 3

FOR THE FILLING

200g toor dal

100g caster sugar

10 glacé cherries, quartered

25g blanched almonds, chopped small

2 teaspoons rose water

1 teaspoon kerwa water

½ teaspoon vanilla extract

¼ teaspoon ground nutmeg

3 cardamom pods, seeds crushed to a powder

¼ teaspoon ground mace

zest of ½ orange

a pinch of saffron, ground to a powder and added to a tablespoon of warm milk

FOR THE MAAN

60g ghee or butter, softened

60g rice flour (or use cornflour), plus extra for dusting

FOR THE DOUGH

300g plain flour

a pinch of salt (if using unsalted butter)

1 teaspoon rose water

60g ghee or butter, plus extra, softened, for brushing

 A filling of sweetened lentils mashed with rose water, nuts, spices and dried fruits, encased in flaky pastry and baked until golden, dal ni pori is synonymous with Parsi sweet treats, yet it is such a rarity to find someone who can make it. When I was growing up, there was no one making these cakes in London, so every time we knew someone was coming over from India, we would ask them to section off a portion of their suitcase to bring the treats back for us. All exotic food excited me when I was young, but nothing excited me more than knowing someone was returning to London with a suitcase packed with dal ni pori.

This recipe has been my Everest – a mountain to conquer. I never quite understood what was in the filling or how to make the pastry. Old recipes were so vaguely written and with such assumption of knowledge that, decades down the line, the technique was a mystery to most. Mumbai provided one clue in a small community kitchen in the heart of Dadar Parsi colony, where 'aunties' would spend the day making all sorts of Parsi delicacies to sell, including dal ni pori. Through a small gap in the window to the kitchen, I watched these old Parsi ladies twisting and rolling handmade layered dough and wrapping it around moulded balls of sweetened lentil filling. Through that gap in the window, the mystery was solved.

Maan is a mixture of soft butter and rice flour that is spread between the layers of pastry to help them puff and flake, similar to how a puff pastry is laminated with soft butter.

Preheat the oven to 200°C/180°C fan – although, if you have a particularly strong oven aim for 20°C lower.

Make the filling. Wash the toor dal thoroughly, then cover with water and soak for 20 minutes. Drain them through a sieve.

Tip the lentils into a medium, sturdy-bottomed pot and cover with 800ml of water. Place over a medium heat and bring to the simmer. Reduce the heat to medium–low and simmer the lentils for 45 minutes (skim any scum that forms on the surface), until the lentils have turned soft and mushy. You will need to stir every now and then at the start, but stir continuously for the last 15 minutes. Once the lentils have cooked down to a thick mash, stir in the sugar. You want to get as much steam out of the mash as possible, so carry on stirring on a medium–low heat, allowing the mixture to bubble away for another 10 minutes.

Tip the mashed lentils out of the pan into a bowl. Leave uncovered to cool for 25 minutes, then mix in the remaining filling ingredients. Divide the

Continued overleaf...

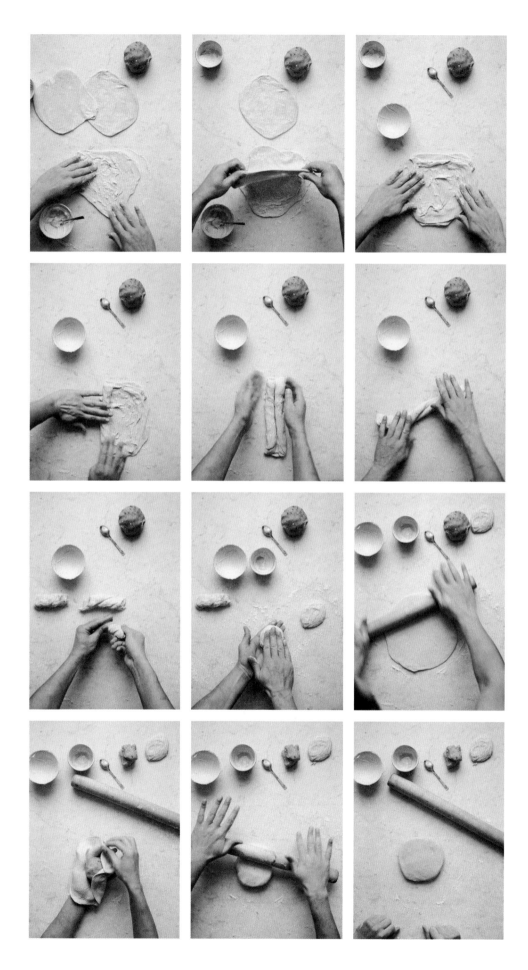

mixture into thirds (about 200g each) and, once cool enough to handle, form each third into a neat ball, like a dough. Set aside while you make the maan.

In a small bowl, beat together the ghee or butter with the flour for 1 minute, until light and soft. Set aside.

Make the dough. Either in a large bowl or on a clean work surface, mix the flour, salt and rose water together. Add the ghee or butter, rubbing it into the flour mixture until it resembles coarse breadcrumbs. A little at a time, add about 150ml of water until you have a soft, slightly tacky dough. Don't overwork the dough by kneading it more than it needs – stop once it has come together. Divide the dough into thirds and form each into a ball.

On a lightly floured work surface, use a rolling pin to roll each ball of dough into a disc about 25cm in diameter. Spread the soft maan equally over each disc, as if generously spreading jam over toast. Sprinkle a light dusting of rice flour over each disc, then stack each disc on top of the other, like a layered cake.

Pick up the left side of the stacked discs and roll it in towards the centre. Do the same with the right side, to meet the left in the middle, so that the dough now resembles a scroll. Pick up one end in each hand and twist in opposite directions, to create a large twist of dough. Cut the twist into three equal pieces.

One by one, tighten the twist in each piece, then push it down into itself on your work surface. The twist is now flattened into itself – this is the technique that forms the flaky layers in the pastry.

Using a rolling pin, roll out each squashed twist to a disc about 6.5cm in diameter and place a ball of filling in the centre of each disc. Place one disc, with the ball in the centre, into the palm of one hand and bring the dough up over the side of the ball, twisting and forming until you can pinch the dough closed to encase the filling. Fix any tears as you go. Put the ball on the work surface and flatten it with your hand to form a patty. Repeat for the other discs and filling.

Brush a baking tray with ghee or butter and place the poris on the tray. Bake for 45–60 minutes, removing the tray and turning the poris every 15 minutes to brush the top with ghee or butter, until evenly golden brown on both sides. Remove from the oven and allow to cool on a rack for 30 minutes before eating them warm, at their peak of deliciousness.

MAWA NI BOI

**MAKES 1 LARGE FISH
OR MANY SMALL FISH**

2 recipe quantities of
    unsweetened mawa
    (see page 83)
100g ground almonds
150g icing sugar
½ teaspoon rose water
seeds of 5 cardamom
    pods, crushed in a pestle
    and mortar
vegetable oil, for brushing
3–4 sheets of silver leaf
    (optional)
nuts and dried fruit,
    to decorate

Two-and-a-half thousand years ago in Pasargadae, the then capital of the Achaemenid Empire, there stood a bas relief of Cyrus the Great, wearing a crown adorned with three fish. In Zoroastrian religion, fish are a symbol of good luck, protection and prosperity and will always feature in some way during auspicious Parsi occasions and celebrations – whether that's as chalk patterns on the floor, eating fish as part of a meal, or enjoying sweets moulded into the shape of fish, such as these mawa ni boi.

Made from milk that has gently simmered for many hours until reduced to a rich paste (see page 83), the mawa is sweetened with sugar and enriched with ground almonds. The sweetened milk solids are moulded into the shape of a fish and garnished with silver leaf, nuts and dried fruits. The large, moulded sweet is usually the centrepiece of special occasions, left for everyone to admire until the end of the meal, when it's broken up and shared out.

You will do well to have a fish-shaped mould to make your mawa ni boi – a classic jelly mould will do; or you can free-form your fish shape by hand.

Place the mawa in a large saucepan over a low heat. Heat the mawa for about 5 minutes, until soft and warm to the touch. Transfer the mawa to a bowl and add the ground almonds, icing sugar, rose water and ground cardamom seeds. Knead everything together with your hands until all the ingredients are evenly mixed through and you have a dough-like consistency.

Brush the inside of your mould very lightly with some vegetable oil, then line it with cling film (this will help the mawa come away neatly from the mould).

Once the mawa has cooled slightly, but is still warm enough to be soft and malleable, push it in to the mould, making sure to fill all the nooks and crannies so that you get every last detail of the mould pressed into the mawa.

Transfer the mould to the fridge for 3–4 hours, until the mawa is solid. Remove the mould from the fridge and turn out the mawa by gently pulling on the corners of the cling film to release it.

Invert the mawa ni boi so that it is presentation side up and place it on a large serving plate. Remove the cling film. With the gentlest of touches, use tweezers to lay the silver leaf across the top of the fish – keep a steady hand and hold your breath as even the smallest movement of air will blow the thin leaf away. Sprinkle almonds, walnuts, golden raisins, dates and dried apricots around the fish to decorate.

KNICKERBOCKER GLORY

My favourite childhood birthdays would be the ones where my mum and dad would take my sister and me to our local Pizza Hut. From the minute we sat down, my mind was on one thing: dessert. Specifically, the knickerbocker glory and I'd be damned if I was going to share it!

I started serving these at work out of a sense of nostalgia for those childhood birthdays. It was a joy to watch the chefs build them with the same amount of excitement with which the guests would receive them. When the knickerbockers were taken out into the restaurant, I would always ask the servers to do a lap of honour with them so they would pass as many guests as possible before they landed at their designated table – heads turned, eyes widened and a restaurant full of minds set on what desserts they would be ordering later.

Go to the effort of finding an elegant sundae glass and chill it in the freezer before you build your knickerbocker.

Build the glory from the bottom up – first the strawberry jam, then the curd, then the nankhatai or other crushed biscuit, then the gluttonous scoops of glorious ice cream. If you still have space at the top of your glass, nestle in the crème fraîche or whipped cream, then finish with a scattering of toasted almonds or pistachio nuts. And, finally, what knickerbocker would be complete without a cherry on top?

Food should never look better than it tastes. This looks stunning and tastes sublime.

INDULGENT ENOUGH FOR TWO TO SHARE (THOUGH I RECOMMEND KEEPING IT TO YOURSELF)

1 teaspoon strawberry jam (see page 265 for homemade)

1 tablespoon orange and lime curd (see page 265)

1 nankhatai (see page 320), crushed (or use any shortbread or other sweet biscuit)

a small handful of raspberries or strawberries, puréed with a pinch of caster sugar

2 scoops of raspberry and rose or mango ice cream (see pages 312 and 311)

1 tablespoon crème fraîche or whipped cream (optional)

1 tablespoon flaked almonds or chopped pistachios, toasted, for sprinkling

1 perfect cherry, ideally with the stalk attached, to finish

The end is important in all things.
-- Yamamoto Tsunetomo

CRAWFORD MARKET

Next, a word on the often-fraught task of buying mangoes at Mumbai's Crawford Market. It is all too easy to get ripped off, get undersold on quality, or even get sold mangoes that are not the variety you think they are.

First, never dive straight in (that's amateur, you are going pro!). Circle the market scouting the stalls from a distance with no obvious intention to buy. Look for the busier stalls, ones where there is lots of hustling going on with mangoes and money changing hands frequently. Keep an eye on what notes are being handed back and forth and how many mangoes are being bagged up – they are usually sold in 6, 8 or 12s. Just from this, you can figure out a rough going rate.

Once you have chosen your stall, approach with confidence and indifference: you don't want the mango wala to know how desperate you are for the sublime flesh. Look, touch, smell, but never squeeze; squeezing bruises the fruit and the mango wala will not take kindly to this.

If you were vigilant enough to see some exchanges going on, you may have a good idea of the going rate for the mangoes. With this knowledge to hand, first ask how much – Kitane? If the answer to this question is in the ball park of what you were expecting, then bingo! BUY, BUY, BUY! If, on the other hand, you are given a number that seems to be plucked out of the air and extremely exaggerated, then it's time to HAGGLE, HAGGLE, HAGGLE! Don't be coy. Haggling is the norm in all but a few market situations. Go low and expect the seller to laugh and come back up high. Let the seller know you mean business and will not back down from the right price and, all being well, you will find a happy place to meet in the middle. If you do not meet on the right price, then it's time to walk away and find another business partner – though nine times out of ten, you will be beckoned back with a more reasonable offer.

Something to note: never walk away from Crawford Market empty handed. This is a lose-lose situation. Part of the experience is in the hustle and the haggling. You will be better off with mangoes in hand and your mango wala will be better off with Rupees in their pocket.

From April onwards, India becomes a mango-lover's paradise, as Crawford Market bustles with lorries laden with Kesar, Badami and Alphonso mangoes brought in from all corners of the subcontinent. Huge wicker baskets overflow with pale yellow orbs, carried into the large indoor market atop sellers' heads. Inside the market, workers sitting on beds of straw pack barely ripe mangoes into colourful boxes to be exported across the globe, each mango inspected to ensure that by the time it arrives at its destination it will have ripened to perfection.

By the time the mangoes have reached London, the price has gone up considerably – Alphonso mangoes especially are sold at a premium. That (and the fact that they were available all year round) meant that tins of Alphonso mango purée were a great alternative in our house when I was growing up. They became a store-cupboard staple, pulled out for dinner parties or special occasions, and at other times indulged in straight from the tin. Tins of Alphonso and Kesar pulp are both readily available at Asian stores, and both are sweet, fragrant and delicious.

FALOODA

MAKES 1 TALL ICE-CREAM GLASS

200ml whole milk (or single cream, if you're feeling luxurious)

1 tablespoon condensed milk (or 1 tablespoon caster sugar to keep things simple)

5 saffron strands

1 teaspoon rose water

2 teaspoons basil seeds, soaked in water for 5 minutes until they swell

3 teaspoons vermicelli, soaked in boiling water with 1 teaspoon sugar for 10 minutes

3 ice cubes

about 2 scoops of mango ice cream (see page 311)

½ teaspoon each of chopped almonds and pistachios, for the topping

a drizzle of rose-flavoured syrup, to finish

 Once you have chosen and bargained for your dozen or so ripe mangoes and you just cannot wait to taste their flesh, you can risk life and limb crossing the chaotic Lokmanya Tilak road directly in front of Crawford Market (see page 304) and arrive at the doors of Badshah Cold Drinks.

Standing tall for more than 100 years, it serves some of the finest falooda in Mumbai. A refreshing dessert of sweetened rose-flavoured milk, swirled with soft strands of vermicelli and crunchy basil seeds that float like frog spawn in the tall glass, top this with a handsome scoop of the most seasonal fruit ice cream and serve with a spoon and straw. It is quite simply the perfect remedy for any weary traveller exhausted from the chaos of Crawford Market.

Falooda is less of a recipe and more of an instruction on how to bring together some magnificent ingredients.

Pour the milk or cream into a chilled tall glass and add the condensed milk or sugar, saffron, and rose water. Vigorously stir until all the ingredients are mixed together and the sugar (if using) has dissolved.

Add 1 tablespoon of the hydrated basil seeds and 2 tablespoons of the drained vermicelli. Stir everything together and throw in the ice cubes.

Top the glass with the ice cream (use as much that can fit into the glass without spilling the milk). Scatter the chopped nuts over the top and finish with a healthy drizzle of rose syrup.

Enjoy with a long spoon, dipping down to the bottom of the glass to bring up the basil seeds and vermicelli. My favourite part of falooda is that you have to eat the ice cream before you can get to the milk. A happy challenge.

KERI NU ICE CREAM
MANGO ICE CREAM

 Although this recipe uses mango purée, the purée of blackberries, raspberries, strawberries, apricots, peaches or papaya, or any mixture of these fruits works brilliantly, too. The only equipment you need is a whisk and a bowl.

Measure 5 tablespoons of the purée into a small saucepan and add the lemon juice and sugar. Place over a low heat and leave the sugar to completely dissolve so that you have a mango syrup. Pour this into a bowl with the remaining mango purée and mix it through thoroughly.

In a separate bowl, whip the cream with the rose water and kerwa water (if using), until it almost doubled in volume and it forms stiff peaks. Fold the mango purée through the whipped cream, being as gentle as possible, until no streaks remain.

Pour the mixture into a freezer-proof container (30 x 20cm and at least 4cm deep, greased with oil and lined with cling film, if you're making the ice-cream sandwiches on page 315), cover with a lid and freeze for at least 4 hours to set. (If you intend to make the ice-cream sandwiches, you can slice the frozen ice cream and freeze it in slices to be sandwich-ready as soon as you need it, if you like.)

Serve as it is or with rose-flavoured syrup and a sprinkling of chopped pistachios.

MAKES JUST OVER 800ML

300g mango purée, preferably Alphonso or Kesar
juice of ½ lemon
175g caster sugar
250ml double cream
1 tablespoon rose water
½ tablespoon kerwa water (optional, but good for a typical Indian flavour)

RASPBERRY GULAB ICE CREAM
RASPBERRY AND ROSE ICE CREAM

**MAKES JUST OVER
1 LITRE**

600g raspberries
juice of 1 small lemon
350g caster sugar
500ml double cream
2 tablespoons rose water
1 tablespoon kerwa water
(optional)

Ice cream doesn't get any easier than this. With minimal effort, you can have delicious homemade ice cream in hours without the need for any fancy equipment – just a whisk and a bowl. The addition of rose water and kerwa water gives the ice cream that authentic Indian flavour. You could almost imagine yourself sitting on Mumbai's Marine Drive with a K Rustom's ice-cream sandwich (see page 315) dripping down your arm.

I have written this recipe for raspberries, but you can use any fruit purée you want – some fruits that work well are apricots, blackberries, mango pulp, strawberries, peaches, or any combination of these.

Blitz the raspberries to a purée in a food processor (a thorough crushing with a whisk will also suffice).

Measure 5 tablespoons of the purée into a small saucepan and add the lemon juice and sugar. Place over a low heat and allow the sugar to completely dissolve so that you have a raspberry syrup. Pour this into a bowl with the remaining raspberry purée and mix it through.

In a separate bowl, whip the cream with the rose water and kerwa water (if using) until it almost doubled in volume and it forms stiff peaks. Fold the raspberry purée through the whipped cream, being as gentle as possible, until no streaks remain.

Pour the mixture into a freezer-proof container (30 x 20cm and at least 4cm deep, greased with oil and lined with cling film, if you're making the ice-cream sandwiches on page 315), cover with a lid and freeze for at least 4 hours to set. (If you intend to make the ice-cream sandwiches, you can slice the frozen ice cream and freeze it in slices to be sandwich-ready, if you like.)

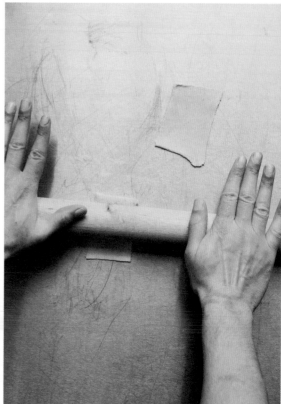

PISTACHIO ICE CREAM SANDWICH – A NOD TO K RUSTOM'S

Inspired by the fun ice-cream sandwiches my family and I used to eat at K Rustom's ice-cream shop in Churchgate, Mumbai, which is now an institution, here is a version I created for a Parsi dinner I held in Soho, London.

SERVES 6

1 loaf of medium-sliced white bread (the cheaper, the better)
icing sugar, for dusting
melted ghee or butter, for brushing
1 recipe quantity of mango or raspberry and rose ice cream (see page 311 and 312), cut into 2cm-thick slices
200g pistachios, finely chopped, or colourful sprinkles

Preheat the oven to 200°C/180°C fan. Line two equal-sized flat baking sheets with baking paper.

Sparingly cut the crusts off the bread, until you're left with white rectangles. Take 1 slice of bread and, using a rolling pin, roll it flat using lots of pressure to squash it down, giving a few firm rolls in each direction. Do this to all the slices. Cut the slices into rectangles each measuring roughly 6.5 x 4cm.

Lay the slices out on a tray and brush them liberally with melted ghee or butter on both sides – no corner must be left unbrushed. Using a sieve or shaker, liberally and evenly dust each side of the bread with icing sugar.

Place the slices of bread on one of the lined baking sheets. Invert the lined second sheet to sandwich the bread pieces between the two lined baking sheets, pinning the slices flat.

Place the stack in the oven for 15 minutes, then check to see whether the slices of bread are golden brown and smelling like biscuits. If they're not ready yet, keep baking for up to about another 10 minutes – the precise baking time depends on the efficiency of your oven. Once you're happy with your bread slices, remove the tray from the oven and transfer the wafers to a wire rack to cool.

Once the wafers have cooled, remove the ice cream from the freezer, invert it on to a chopping board and carefully peeling away the cling film. Cut the ice cream into rectangles, roughly the same size as your caramelised bread slices. Sandwich the ice-cream slices between the wafers. Without wasting a moment of time, tip the pistachios or sprinkles into a bowl and dip in the 4 edges of the sandwich. Enjoy with childlike abandon.

BISCUITS

AND

CAKES

NANKHATAI
CARDAMOM SHORTBREAD

MAKES 16

100g ghee or unsalted
    butter
100g icing sugar (or caster
    sugar finely ground in a
    pestle and mortar)
zest of ½ lemon
1 teaspoon full-fat natural
    yoghurt
80g chickpea flour
40g plain flour
40g fine semolina
¼ teaspoon baking
    powder
⅛ teaspoon cream
    of tartar
a pinch of fine salt
seeds of 8 cardamom
    pods, crushed in a pestle
    and mortar
16 shelled pistachios, or
    8 almonds/cashews,
    cut in half

 These sweet, soft and crumbly biscuits, lightly spiked with cardamom, are somewhat reminiscent of shortbread. Traditionally, they don't contain lemon zest, but I find it imparts uplifting qualities. Go out of your way to make or find ghee for this recipe, as it really enhances that irresistible, biscuity flavour.

Preheat the oven to 150°C/130°C fan. Line a baking tray with baking paper.

In a food processor or a stand mixer fitted with the paddle attachment, cream together the ghee or butter, icing sugar, lemon zest and yoghurt until pale and fluffy. This stage can be done by hand with a mixing bowl, wooden spoon and some elbow grease. Add the remaining ingredients and gently combine everything with your fingertips, until they form delicate crumbs – take care not to be heavy-handed at this stage as a lighter touch will give a more delicate biscuit.

Divide the mixture into 16 equal pieces (about 20g each) and form each piece into a ball in the palm of your hand. Gently press so that it's ever so slightly flatter than a ball, then place it on the lined baking tray, spacing the biscuits a few centimetres apart.

Push either a pistachio or a halved almond/cashew into the centre of each biscuit and bake for 30 minutes, until very pale golden (like shortbread). Serve with an ice-cold glass of milk.

There is crack in everything, that's how
the light gets in.

              -- Leonard Cohen

SHREWSBURY BISCUITS

 This recipe has been adapted from Dinoo Bastavala's submission to The Time and Talents Club *cookbook of 1934–1962. It is a wonderful example of a no-fuss classic biscuit loved by Parsis.*

MAKES ABOUT 12

110g unsalted butter, softened
110g caster sugar, plus extra for sprinkling
a pinch of salt
1 large egg, lightly beaten
225g plain flour, plus extra for dusting
½ teaspoon baking powder

Beat together the butter, sugar and salt in the bowl of a stand mixer fitted with the paddle attachment until completely combined, pale in colour and fluffy in texture and look.

Add the beaten egg to the bowl and beat again until fully incorporated. Combine the flour and baking powder in a separate bowl. Then remove the bowl from the stand mixer and fold in the flour mixture, a few tablespoons at a time, keeping your folds gentle to keep that soft, fluffy structure intact. Your biscuit mix will be too soft to work with at this stage, so place the bowl in the fridge for 30 minutes to rest and firm up.

Preheat the oven to 180°C/160°C fan. Line a baking tray with baking paper.

Lightly dust your work surface with flour and tip out the chilled dough. Then, either, using a rolling pin, roll it out until 5mm thick and use a 2.5cm round cutter to stamp out as many biscuits as you can, re-rolling the trimmings as necessary. Or (my preference), using your hands, gently roll the dough into a log about 2.5cm in diameter. Use a small, sharp knife to efficiently cut along the log creating 5mm discs without any waste. (The log method also enables you to bake fewer biscuits at a time – simply cut as many as you need, then wrap the remainder of the log, freeze it and bring it out, defrost and cut some more delicious biscuits another time.)

Place your dough rounds on the lined baking tray, spacing them 1cm apart. Bake for 30–35 minutes or until light golden brown. Remove from the oven and sprinkle a pinch of sugar over each biscuit for added crunchy sweetness. Leave to cool on the tray.

Enjoy with hot tea, family and friends (if there are any biscuits left over, keep them in an airtight container for up to 1 week).

They say if it ain't broke, don't fix it, but I have never been one to leave things be. Imagine the results of ¼ teaspoon ground cinnamon or cardamom mixed in with the flour, or a few spoonfuls of flour substituted with ground almonds. What would the results be from a drop of vanilla extract or orange blossom water through the mixture? How about some chopped raisins or almonds stirred through? With such a simple recipe it's quite easy to have some fun – with guaranteed delicious results.

CHAAPAT
TEA TIME PANCAKES

MAKES ABOUT 14

120g plain flour
250ml whole milk
1 large egg
2 tablespoons caster sugar
a pinch of salt
seeds of 4 cardamom
    pods, crushed in a pestle
    and mortar
8 rasps of nutmeg
¼ teaspoon vanilla extract
½ teaspoon rose water
50g ghee or unsalted
    butter, melted
a few tablespoons of
    vegetable oil, for frying
about 2½ tablespoons
    finely chopped almonds
    (or charoli seeds
    if available)

Chaapat are pancakes, similar to French crêpes – the only difference being that at that point where you grip the handle and steady your nerves to flip over a crêpe, you instead sprinkle chopped nuts over the surface and gently fold the chaapat over on itself, encasing the crunchy nuts in a soft and unctuous pancake.

These pancakes are traditionally made with a seed called charoli, which has the crunchy texture of a nut. Charoli is not easy to come by outside of India, so I have substituted with almonds, which are similar in flavour and texture.

During her childhood, my mother spent the summer months in Deolali, a small hill station just outside Mumbai with a large Indian army base. Every evening the chaapat wala would come by the houses with his cart, selling freshly made chaapat to the kids and adults alike.

With a whisk or blender, mix together all of the ingredients except the ghee or butter, almonds and oil, in a large bowl until completely smooth. Whisk in the ghee or butter. Leave the batter to rest at room temperature for 30 minutes.

Heat 1 teaspoon of oil in a heavy skillet or non-stick frying pan over a medium heat. Once hot, use kitchen paper to wipe the oil around the pan, and reduce the heat to low.

Place 3 tablespoons of batter in the pan, instantly swirling it around to create an even thickness (you're not looking to make a wafer-thin crêpe, but a slightly thicker pancake). Once the batter has spread out, sprinkle ½ teaspoon of chopped almonds over the top. Cook the pancake for 1–2 minutes, until the underside is light brown and the top of the chaapat has set and is no longer wet. Gently fold the chaapat over on itself to create a half-moon shape, remove it from the pan and repeat the process until you have finished the batter (about 14 chaapats in total). Every now and then apply a scant layer of oil to the pan. Keep the cooked chaapats warm by placing a tea towel over the top of them – as you layer the chaapats up, they will keep their warmth as they huddle up under the cloth.

BUN MASKA
BUN AND BUTTER

 If you ever happen to be wandering down the dusty back streets of the Fort area in Mumbai, you may well stumble past Yazdani Bakery, which opened over half a century ago in what, during World War II, was a Japanese bank. The building and interior remain unchanged – I doubt there is anything thought through about the décor, but it works in its own unique way. Pictures of Irani boxers hang on the walls, a vintage Seikosha regulator clock keeps time close by – and it has been this way for decades.

The seating arrangement is informal and convivial. Fixed wooden benches and tables serve as a perch and you'll usually end up sharing the table with Mumbai's working class – from bankers and clerks to labourers and cleaners, all are welcome for a quick chai break before scurrying back to their daily duties. The cakes are fine, the biscuits, too – but it's the freshly baked buns, served with churned soft white butter that gets me every time. That, and the unforgivingly sweet tea. Don't be fooled by this bakery's unassuming, almost dilapidated appearance. Here you will find some of the freshest bun maska and chai in town.

Bun maska is synonymous with Parsi cafés around India – either fresh or crusty, buttered or plain, it's always eaten with hot chai for dipping. This is my version, sweetened with a smattering of dried fruit. Maska is the fresh cream that we beat to a soft, pale state of delicate, spreadable goodness. An electric mixer is very useful for this recipe, but by no means essential.

MAKES 10–12

FOR THE MASKA
125ml thick double cream
a small pinch of salt

FOR THE BUNS
Part one
450g plain flour
35g caster sugar
15g fresh yeast or 8g
   dried active yeast
1 tablespoon mixed spice
zest of 1 orange

Part two
215ml whole milk
1 egg yolk (20g)

Part three
1 teaspoon salt
65g unsalted butter,
   softened

Part four
4g mixed peel
100g glacé cherries,
   chopped
150g raisins

FOR THE WASH
1 egg, beaten with 100ml
   whole milk

First, make the maska. Pour the cream into a large bowl and, using a hand-held electric whisk, whisk the cream until it holds stiff peaks. Then keep whisking until you notice the texture go from stiff to crumbly with slightly yellow curds. Keep whisking until you a start to see milky water separate from the yellow crumbly curds. This milky liquid is buttermilk and you can use it for other recipes throughout this book.

Transfer the crumbly yellow curds to a sieve and rinse them under cold water to wash off any remaining buttermilk. Sprinkle the salt over the curds, then tip them into a cloth or muslin and wrap them tightly, tying the cloth into a ball and squeezing out any remaining moisture. Set the curds in a bowl and let them sit in the fridge for an hour before unwrapping and enjoying with your freshly baked buns.

While the curds are refrigerating, make the buns. Combine all the ingredients for Part One in a large mixing bowl until full incorporated.

Combine all the ingredients for Part Two with 85ml of water in a large bowl, or in an electric stand mixer fitted with the dough hook.

Continued overleaf...

Bit by bit, add Part One to Part Two and lightly knead it together until the mixtures comes together to form a sticky dough. Set aside in the bowl to rest for 30 minutes.

Add Part Three and mix for 5 minutes, then rest for a further 5 minutes. Finally, mix in Part Four until all the fruits are fully dispersed.

Divide the dough into 120g pieces (you should get 10–12 of them). Roll each piece into a ball and place on the lined baking tray, well spaced out. Set aside the shaped balls for about 1½ hours in a warm part of your kitchen, until they are well risen and have almost doubled in size.

Preheat the oven to 200°C (this is the conventional temperature – it's better not to use the fan oven, if possible). Line two baking trays with baking paper.

Delicately brush the top of each bun with the wash, then bake in the oven for about 30 minutes; the buns should be well risen and golden brown on the top. Once baked, allow the buns to cool on a wire rack before diving in with the maska.

I could suggest so many ways to eat these buns – toasted, buttered, with jam, with clotted cream… and always with a cup of chai.

KHARI BISCUITS
SAVOURY BISCUITS

 These ethereal, buttery, puff-pastry biscuits are sold in Parsi bakeries and cafés all over Mumbai. They are a favourite of my granny, who always kept a jar of them in the cupboard for when the grandkids would come over. We would dip them into our tea and eat them – although I would often dunk for a moment too long and lose my biscuits to the cup. They make a perfect light breakfast, midday snack, teatime treat or sneaky night time nibble... you get the picture – they are awesome.

MAKES 16

250g plain flour
2 teaspoons fine salt
475g unsalted butter, 125g chilled and cut into small cubes, 350g softened
2 teaspoons distilled malt vinegar
225ml ice-cold water
1 teaspoon cumin seeds

Tip the flour, salt and chilled cubes of butter into a bowl. Using your fingertips, press the butter into flakes and incorporate it into the flour until the mixture resembles fine breadcrumbs. Add the vinegar and ice-cold water and slowly knead it into the flour mixture until it forms a dough.

Knead the dough in the bowl for 15 minutes, until it forms a smooth ball without any rough cracks. Cover the bowl with cling film and leave it to rest for 1 hour.

Tip out the rested dough on to a well-floured work surface. Using a rolling pin, roll the dough into a rectangle measuring roughly 20 x 10cm. Turn the rectangle so that the short end is closest to you. Spread the softened butter evenly over the bottom two thirds of the rectangle, leaving a 1cm border around the edge.

Fold the top (uncoated) third of the rectangle down over the middle third, and the bottom (coated) third up over the first fold, as if you were folding a business letter. You should be left with a rectangle of dough with a butter filling. Wrap the dough in cling film and refrigerate for 30 minutes, to rest.

Repeat the rolling, folding and chilling twice more, each time rolling the dough into a 20 x 10cm rectangle and folding it like a business letter (but without adding more butter). Then make a final roll and fold (four rolls and folds in total). This time, instead of chilling the rectangle after folding, fold each short end of the rectangle inwards to meet in the middle and then fold in half, as if you were closing a book. (The process of rolling and folding will create layer upon layer throughout the dough – each separated by a thin layer of butter. This creates the puff as the biscuits bake.)

Preheat the oven to 200°C/180°C fan. Line two baking trays with baking paper.

Continued overleaf...

To make the khari biscuits, roll the dough into a rectangle roughly 12 x 6cm and 1cm thick. Using a sharp knife, cut the rectangle in half down the length (a dull knife will squash the layers together and the biscuits will struggle to puff up), then cut each strip into 8 finger slices.

Place each finger on a lined baking tray, spacing the fingers at least 1cm apart. Sprinkle a few cumin seeds over each biscuit.

Bake the biscuits for 30 minutes, then reduce the heat to 160°C/140°C fan and bake them for a further 20 minutes, until they are puffed up and dried out. Remove from the oven and leave to cool before enjoying with a cup of chai.

If you don't eat all the biscuits immediately, they will keep crisp in an airtight container for up to 3 days.

Twixt the optimist and pessimist
The difference is droll:
The optimist sees the doughnut
But the pessimist sees the hole.
                        -- McLandburgh Wilson

BHAKRA
CARDAMOM DOUGHNUTS

Parsis would say that bhakras are biscuits. I, on the other hand, refer to them as doughnuts. Soft, lightly fermented dough spiked with cardamom and nutmeg is deep-fried until light, fluffy and golden. This favourite snack is best eaten hot from the fryer.

Traditionally bhakra dough is fermented using toddy, the sap from the palm tree, which is full of natural yeasts. A fascinating ingredient, toddy is 'tapped' from the palms in the early morning and consumed almost immediately as a refreshing drink. Within a few hours, the toddy begins to ferment, and by evening it has transformed into a potent palm wine. When there's no toddy available, natural yoghurt takes its place with similar results.

Part of Zoroastrian prayer rituals is the offering of foods to be blessed during ceremonies of thanksgiving. Worshippers lay fruits, nuts, pastries and sweets on silver platters next to the priests as the priests recite prayers from the Avesta (the Zoroastrian holy scripture). Once the prayers are over, the food is divided among the worshippers to be taken home and shared amongst the family. Eating these blessed foods has a spiritual importance and was my first introduction to bhakra.

MAKES ABOUT 30

125g caster sugar
40g ghee or unsalted butter
1 egg
125g full-fat live natural yoghurt
½ teaspoon rose water
¼ teaspoon vanilla extract
125g fine semolina
150g plain flour, plus extra for dusting
⅛ teaspoon baking powder
½ teaspoon grated nutmeg
seeds of 3 cardamom pods, ground to a coarse powder in a pestle and mortar
a good pinch of salt
500ml vegetable oil, for frying
icing sugar, to serve (optional)

In a bowl with a wooden spoon, or in a stand mixer fitted with the paddle attachment, beat together the sugar and ghee or butter until smooth. Add the egg, yoghurt, rose water and vanilla and beat again to combine. Fold in the semolina, flour, baking powder, nutmeg, cardamom and salt until you have a soft paste. Set aside the mixture to rest somewhere warm (but not hot) for 2 hours – this gives the natural yoghurt time to slightly ferment in the dough.

Turn out the dough on to a well-floured work surface and scatter more flour over the top. The dough will be very soft and slightly sticky, so make sure the flour gives a good, even coating. Using a rolling pin, roll out the dough to a rough square about 1cm thick. Use a small, sharp knife to cut the dough into 3cm squares (you can use a 3cm diameter round biscuit cutter if you prefer, but I find a knife more efficient and it saves ending up with wasted trimmings from between circles).

Pour the oil into a large, deep saucepan and heat it until it reaches 170°C on a cooking thermometer (or until a small amount of dough sizzles, floats to the surface and turns golden within 60 seconds). Add the cut pieces of dough to the hot oil a few at a time and use a long-handled slotted spoon to keep them moving, turn them to cook on both sides until golden brown all over and cooked through (about 3 minutes per batch). Set aside the cooked bhakras to drain on kitchen paper while you cook the remaining batches.

To serve, move the bhakras to a serving plate and, for extra sweetness, dust with icing sugar. They keep in an airtight container for a few days.

FENNEL AND POPPY SEED LOAF

 Good-quality cakes are a mainstay of the Parsi cafés and a must during tea time. Transport yourself into the hustle and bustle of Mumbai's finest Parsi bakeries with this loaf – hot out of the oven, alongside a cup of masala chai. The loaf is wonderfully easy to make and its moistness, combined with the zesty flavours and scintillating pop of seeds, make it utterly delicious. The use of buttermilk adds a lovely tang to the cake, but if you do not have any, using yoghurt will give similar results.

MAKES 1 LARGE (900G) LOAF

150g unsalted butter, softened, plus extra for greasing (or grease with oil)

130g caster sugar

20g demerara sugar

a pinch of salt

3 large eggs

1 teaspoon fennel seeds, lightly crushed in a pestle and mortar

2 tablespoons poppy seeds

zest of 1 lemon (or any other zest – orange or grapefruit also works well)

170g self-raising flour, plus extra for dusting

80ml buttermilk or full-fat natural yoghurt

Preheat the oven to 200°C/180°C fan. Prepare your loaf tin by first brushing it with a thin coating of butter or vegetable oil and dusting it with flour. Then give it a good tap upside down on the counter to get rid of any excess flour – make sure the inside is perfectly floured with no patches (patches will cause the cake to stick to the tin when it's time to turn it out).

In a large bowl with a wooden spoon, or using a stand mixer fitted with the paddle attachment, beat together the butter, sugars and salt until smooth, light and fluffy. Beat in the eggs one by one until fully incorporated.

Add the crushed fennel seeds, the poppy seeds and the lemon zest and beat in. Fold in the flour until fully incorporated and you have a thick, even mixture. Finally, stir in the buttermilk or yoghurt until fully incorporated.

Pour the mixture into the prepared loaf tin (it should come no more than three-quarters of the way up the sides). Give the tin a few short, sharp taps on the counter to get rid of any air pockets and to even out the mixture. Bake for 45 minutes. Turn the cake halfway through for an even bake. It is done when it is golden on top and a knife inserted into the centre comes out clean. Remove the cake from the oven and give the tin another short, sharp tap on the counter – this will burst all the small, spongey bubbles in the cake, allowing the steam to escape to ensure your cake will not sink into itself as it cools. When cool enough to handle, turn out the loaf and enjoy warm in slices with a cup of masala chai (see page 345).

If you don't finish the cake in one sitting, it will happily keep in an airtight container on the kitchen counter for 2–3 days.

One cake eaten in peace
is worth two in trouble.
–– Proverb

MAWA CAKE

**MAKES 1 LARGE (900G)
LOAF OR 12 CUPCAKES**

150g unsalted butter,
    softened, plus extra
    for greasing
100g mawa (see page 83)
150g caster sugar
a large pinch of salt
seeds of 6 cardamom
    pods, crushed in a pestle
    and mortar
3 large eggs
190g self-raising flour, plus
    extra for dusting
90ml buttermilk or full-fat
    natural yoghurt
2 tablespoons finely
    chopped almonds

*There are many stories of how the mawa cake became one of
Bombay's most beloved sponge cakes and a highlight of most
Irani and Parsi cafés and bakeries. The cake is usually sold in
individual portions, similar to a cupcake, and I've given the
alternative instructions for these at the bottom of the method.
I enjoy making mawa this way if I know the individual cakes
will be eaten straight away. At home, though, I bake the cake
as one loaf, as I find it keeps for much longer.*

Preheat the oven to 200°C/180°C fan. Grease the loaf tin with a little
butter and dust it with flour, then tap it upside down on the counter to
release the excess flour – make sure the inside is perfectly floured with
no patches (patches will case the cake to stick to the tin when it's time to
turn it out).

In a large bowl with a wooden spoon, or in a stand mixer fitted with the
paddle attachment, beat the butter, mawa, sugar, salt and cardamom
together until smooth, light and fluffy. One by one, beat in the eggs, until
fully incorporated.

Fold in the flour until fully incorporated, then beat in the buttermilk or
yoghurt, until you have a smooth batter.

Pour the mixture into the prepared loaf tin (it should come no more than
three-quarters of the way up the sides). Give the tin a few short, sharp
taps on the counter to get rid of any air pockets and to even out the
batter. Sprinkle the almonds over the top. Place the cake in the oven and
bake for 45 minutes, or until golden on top and a knife inserted into the
centre of the cake comes out clean.

Remove the cake from the oven and give it another short, sharp tap on
the counter – this will burst all the small, spongey bubbles in the cake,
allowing the steam to escape to ensure your cake will not sink into itself
as it cools. When cool enough to handle, turn out the loaf and enjoy warm
or cold in slices with a cup of hot masala chai (see page 345). If you don't
eat it all straight away, this will keep in an airtight container for 5 days.

As an alternative you can bake these as individual cupcakes as shown
here – simply three-quarters fill each cupcake case and sprinkle each
one with almonds. Bake them for 25 minutes, until a cocktail stick comes
out clean.

DRINKS

NIMBU PANI
FRESH LIME SODA

MAKES 1 GLASS

1 teaspoon sugar
¼ teaspoon kala namak
    (black salt)
juice of 1 lime
ice
1 bottle of chilled
    soda water

On my first few trips to India as a youngster my mum was always dubious about the drinking water and packaged bottle water, knowing that one wrong sip could spell disaster for the rest of the trip. Bottled sodas are very popular in India, many of the brands are iconic, and are quite trustworthy.

Fresh lime soda is a drink that is usually made either salty or sweet, and most street corners in Mumbai will have someone standing under a big umbrella next to stacks of soda bottles and a basket of limes selling this drink. My uncle Percy introduced me to the half-and-half mix, both sweet and salty, refreshing and delicious. Many a time on our trips I would feign dehydration just to have my mum buy me one of these.

In a tall glass, mix the sugar, black salt and lime juice until dissolved. Add the ice and pour over the chilled soda water. Sit back and enjoy.

Small beginnings end in
great successes.
-- Proverb

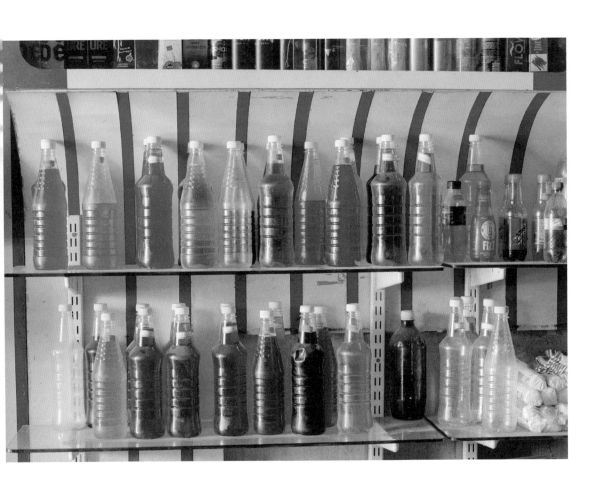

MASALA CHAI

Tea: the backbone of India. At every street corner, alleyway, market place, train station or shop you will find hot, sugary, spicy tea. Like rats in New York, you are never more than a few feet away from a fresh cup of tea in India. A lot of the time, the tea is brewed in large pots where it is continuously boiled and stirred until strong, sweetened with sugar, sometimes far too much, and served up in small paper cups to be slurped up and tossed away. Tea is a great way to pass the time in India; a reason to catch up with others or just have a few moments to one's self.

SERVES 4

4 teaspoons loose-leaf black tea
1cm of fresh ginger
2 tea cups of water
2 tea cups of whole milk
4 teaspoons any white sugar (optional)
1 teaspoon chai masala (see page 49)

Lightly crush the ginger under a heavy bowl or rolling pin. Place all the ingredients, except the black tea, in a large, sturdy-bottomed pot and place it over a high heat. Heat, stirring every now and then, until the mixture begins to boil. Add the tea, then lower the heat to medium and allow the tea to come to a gentle boil. Then lower the heat to low. Don't forget to keep stirring – an unattended pot will happily bubble over.

Allow the tea to simmer gently for 3 minutes before turning the heat off. Let the tea stand for a minute, then pass it through a strainer into a large jug or other vessel. To get a lovely froth on your tea, pass it from one vessel to another, 'stretching' it and allowing it to froth and cool as it flows. This is not an essential technique but it is very fun! Your tea is now ready to pour and enjoy.

CHAAS

SERVES 1

3 tablespoons full-fat
   natural yoghurt
300ml ice-cold water, or
   (better still) whey (see
   page 75)
4 grinds of black pepper
a good pinch of salt
a small pinch of ground
   cumin
a few ice cubes, to serve

 I have always loved gulping down cold glasses of salty, savoury and slightly sour chaas while waiting for the midday sun's intensity to abate. I use a stick blender and a tall jug to blend my chaas, but if you do not have one, a whisk is just as good.

Place all the ingredients in a tall jug or a mixing bowl and blend or beat enough that a layer of froth forms on top.

Drop the ice cubes into a tall glass and pour the chaas over. Finish with a crack of black pepper and a pinch of cumin. Keep the jug of chaas in the fridge for topping up.

MANGO LASSI

 Who doesn't love mango lassi? This is my favourite way to use up mangoes that are otherwise too overripe or soft to eat.

Cut and scrape all the flesh off the mango and discard the stone and skin. Place this with the banana, buttermilk, honey and ice cubes in a blender and blitz for 30–60 seconds, until smooth.

Pour into a tall, chilled glass and enjoy as a filling drink.

SERVES 2

2 very ripe mangoes or alternatively use 300g mango purée
1 very ripe banana, peeled and chopped
600ml buttermilk
30g runny honey
5 ice cubes

DOODH NA PUFF
MILK PUFF

SERVES 2

500ml whole milk
1 teaspoon caster sugar
nutmeg, for grating
a pinch of ground
    cardamom

This is such a quirky drink that it is no surprise to me that it exists only within the Parsi culinary world. Typically a wintertime treat, doodh na puff – or milk puff – is made from boiled whole milk that has been left out in the cold night air to cool so that, in the morning, the dew has collected on the surface. The milk would then be hand-whisked until it frothed up, the froth then scooped out and placed in a glass. The process continued until the glass was brimming with white fluffy clouds. Finished with a rasp of nutmeg and a pinch of cardamom powder, the 'puff' was then eaten with a spoon as a morning treat.

At the Parsi hotels in Udwada, you order your doodh na puff the night before. Then local village women make them early in the morning, dropping them off outside your door for when you wake up. Quite a fun way to start the day.

Pour the milk into a sturdy-bottomed pot and place it over a low–medium heat. Bring the milk to the boil and turn off the heat. Add the sugar and stir to dissolve (stirring also helps the milk to cool and is important for preventing a skin forming on the surface). Once the milk is cool, place the mixture in the fridge for at least 8 hours, or ideally overnight.

When you're ready to serve, pour the sweetened milk into a large bowl or other vessel. Using a whisk (electric or otherwise), begin to beat the milk vigorously back and forth, aiming to make as much froth as possible. When a big cloud of froth forms, use a spoon to gently scoop it up and place it into your glass. Keep frothing until you have harvested enough froth to fill your glass.

Once you have a full glass of 'puff', dust the top with a rasp of nutmeg and a pinch of cardamom. Enjoy by the spoonful.

PARSI TIPPLES

 I am not a big drinker myself, though I do happen to know a few, so I shall hand you over to my good friend and bon vivant Joni who is quite the dab hand at mixing cocktails.

PINK ELEPHANT

To make a Pink Elephant, place all the ingredients in a cocktail shaker and shake for 30 seconds. Then fill to the top with ice and shake again for 10 seconds as vigorously as you can. Strain into a chilled martini glass, garnish with a single rose petal and serve.

SODABOTTLEOPENERWALA

To make a Sodabottleopenerwala, add the whisky, orgeat syrup, lemon juice and absinthe to a cocktail shaker and shake vigorously for 10 seconds. Strain into a highball glass filled with ice, top up with soda water and enjoy!

SERVES 1

FOR A PINK ELEPHANT
50ml Plymouth gin
25ml Cointreau
25ml freshly squeezed
  lemon juice
5ml rose water
3 dashes of Peychaud's
  bitters
1 medium egg white
1 rose petal, to garnish

FOR A SODABOTTLE-
  OPENERWALA
50ml infused Johnnie
  Walker Black Label
  whiskey
25ml orgeat syrup
25ml freshly squeezed
  lemon juice
2 dashes of absinthe
soda water, to top up

EPILOGUE

My grandad on my mother's side was an architect by profession. He designed many of the municipal buildings in the city he finally settled in with his family, including the schools and libraries of Gandhidam in Kutch. Gandhidam once was a dusty desert landscape. My mum remembers it being so bare she could see the school far in the distance from the house.

Time marched on and the city developed and built up. From the open landscape I remember visiting as a six-year-old to a bustling city full of life, diversity and the ensuing noise and chaos that comes from this.

When my grandfather passed away at the grand age of 99, my uncle found some of his old notebooks. One had some pages headed 'Gratitude'. In it there were many sentences, each beginning with 'Thank you for...'

The last page was a thank you to his wife, my grandmother, and the last sentence on this page I found very stirring and a lovely way to end this book.

'We know not from where we came, and we will not know where we will be going, but one thing is certain, that wherever we will be going will depend on the quality of the life lived on this earth, during this birth.'

On that note, be happy and eat well...

Happiness unto him who
brings happiness unto others,
Peace unto him who brings
peace unto others.
-- Zarathustra

INDEX

THANK YOUS

This book has only been possible with the help and encouragement of many, many people.

Thanks to Tim Bates and Tessa David at PFD for being so encouraging and enthusiastic about my work and the project. To the amazing team at Absolute: Jon Croft, Emily North, Joel Arcanjo and Marie O'Shepherd. You all made this a such a wonderful and immensely enjoyable and fulfilling experience, thank you!

Thank you to Sam and Paris for a most enjoyable photoshoot; your patience, skills and can-do attitude made this book what it is.

Thank you to Oli and Fi, for lighting the spark many years ago; your amazing energy made me realise this book could actually be. Thank you, Oli, for such an wonderful experience in India. Your professionalism and 'Jugaad' has made for many incredible photographs throughout this book. What a joy and a privilege it was to shoot with you.

To the ever-inspiring Trevor and Fergus, thank you for being so supportive in this project and for being brilliant people to work for. Long may you run.

Thank you Homi and Leah for your gorgeous foreword. I am so pleased you have been a part of this. How fortuitous it was to meet that lunchtime at Bread and Wine.

To my family in India, Adil Uncle, Dinaz Aunty and Percy Uncle, thank you for opening your homes up to us with such warm hospitality.

Anoz and Goolrukh, thank you for taking us all over Kutch in the 45°C heat. From the markets to the saltworks, you showed us a unique side of India, which we would not have seen otherwise. Anoz, thank you for your impeccable organising of much of our trip. You helped make lots possible in a short period of time. Thank you Percy Uncle for being our Bombay fixer – we thoroughly enjoyed bouncing around the city with you, as you showed us the best places to eat.

Finally, to Otto, for being the best friend ever and to Neil and Bob for their words of wisdom over the years.

ABOUT THE AUTHOR

Farokh Talati has been working as a chef since he was 16 years old, travelling around the world for work and exploring different cuisines, before eventually becoming the Head Chef at St. John Bread and Wine.

Born to Parsi parents who emigrated to the UK before he was born, Farokh also runs a Parsi supper club, introducing the food of his heritage to Londoners and visitors alike. This is his first book.

BLOOMSBURY ABSOLUTE

Bloomsbury Publishing Plc

50 Bedford Square, London, WC1B 3DP, UK

29 Earlsfort Terrace, Dublin 2, Ireland

First published in Great Britain 2022

A catalogue record for this book is available from the British Library. Library of Congress Cataloguing-in-Publication data has been applied for.

HB: 9781472988690

ePub: 9781472988706

ePDF: 9781472988713

2 4 6 8 10 9 7 5 3 1

Printed and bound in China by C&C Offset Printing Co. Ltd

To find out more about our authors and books visit www.bloomsbury.com and sign up for our newsletters.

Publisher
Jon Croft

Commissioning Editor
Meg Boas

Project Editors
Emily North
Joel Arcanjo

Art Direction and Design
Marie O'Shepherd

Production
Laura Brodie

Recipe Photography
Sam A. Harris

India Photography
Oliver Chanarin

Food Styling
Farokh Talati

Prop Stylist
Lauren Miller

Home Economy
Adam O'Shepherd

Copyeditor
Jude Barratt

Proofreader
Sally Somers

Indexer
Vanessa Bird

FRESH
Apple Pie

BREADS

7 MULTI GRAIN
WHOLE WHEAT
BROWN BREAD
OLIVE AND HERB
CINNAMON BUN
RAISIN BUNS

HOT
BRUN
&
BUN
MASKA
and
TEA